THE CLASS OF 1861

THE CLASS OF 1861

Custer, Ames, and Their Classmates after West Point

Ralph Kirshner

With a Foreword by George A. Plimpton

SOUTHERN ILLINOIS UNIVERSITY PRESS

CARBONDALE AND EDWARDSVILLE

02 01 00 99 4 3 2 1

Library of Congress Cataloging-in-Publication Data
Kirshner, Ralph, 1946–
The Class of 1861 : Custer, Ames, and their classmates
after West Point / Ralph Kirshner ; foreword by
George A. Plimpton.
    p.   cm.
Includes bibliographical references (p.   ) and index.
1. United States Military Academy. Class of 1861—
History. 2. United States Military Academy. Class of
1861—Biography. 3. United States. Army—Officers—
Biography. 4. United States—History—Civil War,
1861–1865. 5. Custer, George Armstrong, 1839–1876. 6.
Ames, Adelbert, 1835–1933. I. Title.
U410.N1 1861
355'.0092'273—dc21   98-51309
[b]   CIP
ISBN 0-8093-2066-5 (cloth : alk. paper)

To Blanche Ames
daughter of General Adelbert Ames, class of May 1861,
for setting an example for anyone upset at an author.
When President John F. Kennedy would not make corrections
about her father, General Ames, in his *Profiles in Courage*—
she wrote her own book.

Contents

Illustrations

Members of the May 1861 Class in Order of Class Standing

Following page 12

1. Henry Algernon du Pont
2. Charles E. Cross
3. Orville Elias Babcock
4. Henry Walter Kingsbury
5. Adelbert Ames
6. Llewellyn Griffith Hoxton
7. Adelbert Rinaldo Buffington
8. Emory Upton
9. Nathaniel Rives Chambliss
10. Edmund Kirby
11. John Isaac Rodgers
12. Samuel Nicoll Benjamin
13. John Adair
14. John Whitney Barlow
15. Charles Edward Hazlett
16. Charles E. Patterson
17. Hugh Judson Kilpatrick
18. Franklin Harwood
19. George Warren Dresser
20. Charles McKnight Leoser
21. Henry Cornelius Hasbrouck
22. William Anthony Elderkin
23. Francis Asbury Davies
24. Charles Carroll Campbell
25. Malbone Francis Watson
26. John Benson Williams
27. Guy Vernon Henry
28. Jacob Henry Smyser
29. Jacob Beekman Rawles
30. Erskine Gittings
31. Jacob Ford Kent
32. Eugene Beauharnais Beaumont
33. Leonard Martin
34. John Scroggs Poland
35. Robert Langdon Eastman
36. Henry Beach Noble
37. Leroy Lansing Janes
38. Campbell Dallas Emory
39. James F. McQuesten
40. George Oscar Sokalski

Members of the June 1861 Class in Order of Class Standing

Foreword

Some years ago I went to a large dinner at the White House, a social evening, and after dinner a few of us were taken on an informal tour by the president. At one point, I believe in the Oval Office, President Kennedy motioned to me and said, "George, I'd like to talk to you about your grandmother."

I was, as you can imagine, somewhat startled by this request. It turned out the problem had to do with my grandmother's father—a Civil War "boy" general named Adelbert Ames . . . the commander of the 20th Maine, wounded at the Battle of Bull Run, veteran of Antietam, Fredericksburg, Chancellorsville, Gettysburg, Cold Harbor—just the sort of man whom President Kennedy would have thought the highest of. The trouble came when, at the age of thirty-three, Adelbert Ames was appointed governor of Mississippi. There he ran afoul of Lucius Quintus Cincinnatus Lamar, the Mississippian who went to Congress and gave the famous eulogy of Charles Sumner, the Radical Republican, earning him a place in the history of reconciliation and a chapter in John F. Kennedy's *Profiles in Courage*. In that chapter, Mississippi is described as follows: "No state suffered more from carpet-bag rule than Mississippi. Adelbert Ames, first senator and then governor, was a native of Maine, a son-in-law of the notorious 'Butcher of New Orleans,' Benjamin F. Butler. His administration was sustained and nourished by Federal bayonets." On and on.

When my grandmother ran across this affront, not only to her father but to her grandfather, she began writing letters to the then Senator Kennedy explaining that during the Reconstruction there were obviously men of integrity and distinction and honor who had served the government in the

South and that Adelbert Ames was one of such men. She wished that Senator Kennedy would change the offending chapter about her father (she was willing to forgo Benjamin F. Butler) and put his portrait in a more proper perspective. She wrote a lot of these letters. The senator wrote her back that there was a revisionist swing in consideration of the Reconstruction and it was likely there was a lot to be said for her views—but he was stuck with his position and that was that. Besides, he went on to say, it was very unlikely that there would be subsequent editions of *Profiles in Courage*. The deed had been done, right or wrong.

Then, of course, the senator went on to become the president of the United States and there were a number of subsequent editions of his book, and in a lot of languages, too, including Urdu, and in each of these editions were those offending passages about Ames's administration being "nourished by Federal bayonets." This induced, of course, further letters to the White House from my grandmother. It was this that the president wished to speak to me about.

He took me aside and asked if there were any way this steady flow of letters could be stopped . . . could I persuade my grandmother to cease and desist . . . it was cutting into the work of government.

I said that the only way was to remove or change the paragraphs in *Profiles in Courage*—that, after all, my grandmother was a Massachusetts woman, and as the president well knew, being a Massachusetts man himself, that was a species especially resilient and uncompromising.

I didn't say that, but I wanted to.

What I said, of course, was that I quite understood the president's position and that I would see what I could do.

The president nodded, and then he did the most remarkable thing. He asked me, "How much do you know about your great-grandfather Ames?"

Well, I said that I knew some of the family stories about him, that I actually could remember, as a boy of seven or eight, looking into the pale eyes of this elderly man—he died at ninety-eight—sitting in a rocking chair with a shawl over his knees and realizing, even then, that I was looking into eyes that had seen Pickett's charge at Gettysburg . . . and the president said, "Well, do you know what your great-grandfather's favorite epithet was?" I looked surprised and said no. The president said, "Well, when your great-grandfather commanded the 20th Maine he was a stickler for his men *looking* like soldiers. When reviewing his troops, if he saw anyone slouching in ranks, or whose posture was atrocious, he would stand in front of this miserable soul and shout out at the top of his lungs, 'For God's sake, draw up your bowels!'" The president gave this quite a "reading" as they say in the theatrical business. He drew himself up and delivered the line very much as Adelbert Ames must have delivered it out on those New England parade grounds. It caused no end of quick consternation in the Oval Office. The two or three people in there looked around with startled looks and I suppose they wondered, My God, what is Plimpton up to now?

But I think I must have been the most startled person there—to think that a president of the United States knew more about my great-grandfather, a relatively obscure Civil War hero, than I did . . . and I remember observing to myself how fortunate it was that the country was being served by an intellect to which such astonishingly obscure details could be drawn to mind with such ease. As a matter of fact, I ran across verification of what President Kennedy had shouted at me. It's in John J. Pullen's book, *The 20th Maine* . . . with the line tucked away in there just as President Kennedy delivered it.

You may want to know what my grandmother went on to do. When it was apparent that *Profiles in Courage* was not going to be dismantled and put together again to suit her views, she did what any sensible Massachusetts woman would do: she sat down and wrote her *own* book.

                                                    George A. Plimpton

Preface

The Class of 1861 is, in a way, a book of collective autobiography. Two classes graduated from the United States Military Academy at West Point in 1861 because of Lincoln's urgent need for lieutenants. This book covers all members of Adelbert Ames's May class and George A. Custer's June class—including Southerners who left before graduation to join the Confederacy. I use Custer's fame to introduce the other 1861 graduates, some of whom, like Custer, became "boy generals" in the Civil War that was just beginning. For the most part, they tell their story in their own words. This book is their view of themselves; naturally, it is very favorable. Others, of course, would have a very different view of them, as many of these figures are controversial. But *The Class of 1861* tries to maintain an autobiographical tone, with each sketch told from its subject's point of view.

In part one, class members give not only accounts of battles but analysis of the war. Much of the analysis is by Emory Upton, "the class genius," and his friend Henry A. du Pont, whose estate is now Winterthur Garden. Also heard from is mathematics professor and West Point librarian Lieutenant Oliver Otis Howard, after whom Howard University is named. The chapters in part two deal with their lives after the war. Excerpts from a variety of writings make it possible to hear a subject's voice, as in Adelbert Ames's "Journal While Abroad," written before he became governor of Mississippi.

The first time a cadet is mentioned, his class (May or June) and class standing will be included in parentheses. Appendix A, "Roll Call," gives brief biographical sketches of all the cadets and lists them in order of class standing. That is also the order of their photographs in the gallery, which includes nongraduates John Pelham and the Southerners who became generals.

Acknowledgments

Pauline Ames Plimpton generously shared her reminiscences, reflections, and enthusiasm about her grandfather Adelbert Ames. She was the first of three people I talked with who knew members of the class of 1861. Her son, George Plimpton, also knew General Ames, and I am grateful to him for letting me use his reflections on the general (given at the Kennedy Library and published in *The New York Review of Books*, December 18, 1980) as a foreword to this book. I also want to thank Mrs. Plimpton's secretary, Mary Johnson.

Mary Hains, granddaughter of General Peter C. Hains and great-granddaughter of Admiral Thornton Jenkins, who had been Admiral Farragut's chief of staff, described growing up in her grandfather's house in Washington, where guests often included Admiral George Dewey and General George Goethals. I am particularly indebted to Mary Hains for information about her grandfather's active duty career in World War I.

Edwin C. Bearss, chief historian emeritus of the National Park Service, read my manuscript and, as on his battlefield tours, kept me from taking the wrong path. I would like to thank my former colleagues at the New York Public Library, especially Brigid Cahalan, Robert E. Powers, Lucy Kung, Elizabeth Diefendorf, Rita Bott, Sandy Bye, and Jessie Lee Johnson. At the United States Military Academy Library at West Point, I want to thank Associate Director Suzanne M. Christoff, Gladys Calvetti, Marie Capps, Kenneth Rapp, Elaine Eatroff McConnell, Susan Lintelmann, Sheila Biles, Debby McKeon-Pogue, Judy Sibley, and Alan C. Aimone. Mary Elizabeth Sergent—who has been working on John Pelham and his classmates for over half a century—graciously shared information by telephone as well as in her books.

For their kindness and encouragement, I am extremely grateful to the

Ulysses S. Grant Association's Executive Director John Y. Simon, Robert K. Krick, Gary W. Gallagher (whose annual Civil War Conference I often attended) and Gabor S. Boritt (whose Civil War Institute I also attended). Krick's *Lee's Colonels: A Biographical Register of the Field Officers of the Army of Northern Virginia* was the indispensable source for West Pointers who fought for the Confederacy, since General George W. Cullum rarely gave them more than a line—"Joined in the Rebellion against the United States"—in his *Biographical Register*. I am also grateful to Harry W. Pfanz for his letter noting which items in Colonel John J. Garnett's *Gettysburg* have not appeared elsewhere and to Robert E. L. Krick for sharing his knowledge of Confederate staff officers.

I want to thank the curator and executive director of the Gilder Lehrman Collection, Paul Romaine, and his assistant, Sandra M. Trenholm, for their help and enthusiasm. At the Pierpont Morgan Library, I want to thank Dr. Charles E. Pierce Jr. and Marilyn Palmieri. At the Hagley Museum and Library, I am grateful to Dr. Michael Nash, Marjorie McNinch, and Lynn Catanese for their gracious help with and expert knowledge of the Henry Algernon du Pont Papers.

I want to express my appreciation to the following individuals and institutions: Sophia Smith Collection, Smith College: Cheryl Redman and Amy Hague; Special Collections Department, University of Virginia Library: Michael Plunkett and Christina M. Deane; Bowdoin College Library: Sherrie Bergman and Susan Ravdin; U.S. Army Military History Institute: Dr. Richard J. Sommers, Pam Cheney, Michael J. Winey, and David Keough; Library of Congress; National Archives: David H. Wallace; Huntington Library: Karen E. Kearns and Alan Jutzi; Virginia Historical Society: E. Lee Shepard; Alabama Department of Archives and History: Debbie Pendleton and Victor Nielsen; Perkins Library, Duke University; Davis and Wilson Libraries, University of North Carolina, Chapel Hill: Carol Tobin, William S. Powell, Alice Cotten, John E. White, Cindy Adams, and Jill Shires; Victoria Doyle-Jones (granddaughter of Hamlin Garland) and Special Collections, University of Southern California: John Ahouse; Newberry Library, Chicago: Diana Haskell and Julie Cobb; Second/II Corps Civil War Books, Petersburg, Virginia: Merlin E. Sumner (for permission to quote from his Orville E. Babcock diaries); for computer and other help: Dave Suwala, Ann Frey, John J. Delaney, Timothy J. DeWerff, John Herbert, Joyce Hitchings, Eli Rubenstein, Suzanne Cloutier, Jack Salzman, and Muriel Gray; Civil War Round Table of New York: Sue Slack, Pierce Byrne, Harold Holzer, Hans Trefousse, and, especially, George Craig.

At Southern Illinois University Press, I want to thank John F. "Rick" Stetter (the director), John K. Wilson (the extremely helpful project editor, as well as assistant managing editor), Karl Kageff (the acquisitions editor who also did a great deal of work on this book), Dan Seiters (publicity manager), Lisa Bayer (marketing manager), Jonathan Haupt (marketing assistant), Carol A. Burns (managing editor), Kathleen Kageff, Barb Beaird (design and production manager), Mary Rohrer (who designed the jacket), Teresa White (production editor), Mona Ross (rights and permission), and Gipsey Hicks.

I am grateful to Wayne Sarf (Little Big Horn Associates, Peggy Vogtsberger (John Pelham Historical Association), Michelle Rogers (Bartow History Center), Eric Mink (Fredricksburg and Spotsylvania National Military Park), Brian A. Sullivan (Harvard University Archives), Kevin Carpenter, Rob Gelles, Anne Weitzer, Stephen Laird, Keith S. Bohannon, Calvin Kytle, and Nancy Boucher.

I want to thank William H. du Pont, who is writing a biography of Colonel du Pont, the subject of a fascinating chapter in his granddaughter Ruth Lord's *Henry F. du Pont and Winterthur*.

At the Royal Military College of Canada in Kingston, Ontario, I want to thank the officers, cadets, and professors, especially Joel Sokolsky, for their reception in 1997 to my talk on the class of 1861. My friends from McGill, Vincent and Pam Osteria, told me to use their house in Maryland as my headquarters while doing research in the Washington area. Marc Boucher, my classmate in graduate school at the University of Maine, translated Henry A. du Pont's preface to *Mémoires de Du Pont de Nemours*. My McGill classmate Penny Elias-Winship helped with this book from England. Alice Arvan has helped enormously. To my parents, Harold and Tamar, grandparents, and sister, Judith, I owe more than I can say. All errors, of course, of any kind, are mine alone.

PART ONE

War Years

Introduction:
Buglers' Assembly

George Armstrong Custer (#34, June) was last in his class, or, as he put it, "only thirty-four graduated, and of these thirty-three graduated above me."[1] In his unfinished "War Memoirs"—on which he was still working while riding to Little Bighorn—Custer says, "The first official notification received by me of my appointment to the Military Academy bore the signature of Jefferson Davis, then Secretary of War in the cabinet of President James Buchanan."[2] Jefferson Davis, who graduated twenty-third in West Point's class of 1828, actually served as secretary of war (1853–1857) in the administration of President Franklin Pierce. Davis extended the time cadets spent at the Academy from four years to five, a change that remained until 1861, when Abraham Lincoln's need for lieutenants resulted in two classes graduating from the Military Academy in May and June of the same year, as well as a return to the four-year curriculum. The five-year course at West Point was one of Jefferson Davis's ideas that did not work out.

Custer and Adelbert Ames (#5, May) exemplify different paths taken by Lincoln's lieutenants. Between the Civil War and his appointment as governor of Mississippi, Ames spent a year in Europe, where he wrote his "Journal While Abroad" and met Napoleon III, William Cullen Bryant, Sir Edward Bulwer-Lytton, and Hiram Powers, who gave Ames a tour of his studio in Florence. In London, Ames heard Charles Dickens read, noting in his diary on March 26, 1867, "One of the two pieces was Pickwick's trial and, more especially, Sergeant Buzfuz's address to the jury. . . . I remember a classmate speaking this same speech."[3]

The head of the class of May, Henry Algernon du Pont, won the Medal of Honor. After the war, he served in the family business, E. I. du Pont de Nemours & Co., and in the United States Senate (1906–1917). In the 1920s, at Winterthur, his home in Delaware, Henry A. du Pont wrote several books, including *Rear-Admiral Samuel Francis Du Pont, A Biography* of his uncle. His son, Henry Francis, developed Winterthur Garden.

As a cadet, Henry A. du Pont told his aunt on January 17, 1857, "I am quite busy as usual, this monotonous life, with every minute, as it were, having something which must be done in it, makes the time pass very quickly and before we know of it, warm weather will be upon us, bringing a copious crop of dress parades, guard mountings and drills."[4]

Du Pont explained to his mother on October 3, 1858, why he was not a better student: "not being very strong the drills & riding make me so tired and sleepy at night that I am not able to study to much advantage."[5] Yet, he was first in his class and lived until the last day of 1926.

Du Pont's father, also named Henry and also a graduate of West Point, learned in a letter dated October 29, 1859, "Col. P. St. George Cook[e] has been here for the last week experimenting on us in various movements of the new cavalry tactics which he is preparing."[6] Although a Virginian, Philip St. George Cooke would fight for the Union, unlike his famous son-in-law, Jeb Stuart, who would be killed by Custer's cavalry.

Custer noted in his "War Memoirs: From West Point to the Battlefield" that the cavalry was especially a young man's branch of service. "Of those who were cadets with me between the years of 1857 and 1861," Custer recalls, "there were quite a number who became more or less distinguished during the war." He names Ames, Emory Upton (#8, May), and Judson Kilpatrick (#17, May), of the class of May. "Among those joining the Confederate force who rose to distinction," according to Custer, "were Wheeler, Rosser, Young, Robertson and Kelley [sic]. . . . It is somewhat remarkable that these five general officers held commands in the cavalry. . . . I might add my own name—thus showing that the cavalry offered the most promising field for early promotion."[7] All except Wheeler graduated in 1861.

Some of the training they received has been described by Henry A. du Pont in a letter to his mother:

We have commenced riding & cutting heads without saddles & stirrups. . . . I do not know whether you understand what is meant by cutting heads, it consists in cutting or thrusting with sabres at balls of leather stuffed with straw & which are placed at various heights on posts, one or two being always placed on the ground so that you have to bend down to cut it as you gallop around the hall. We often have quite lively times down there especially when the bars are put up to jump, this being the signal for our numerous vicious & balky animals to display their accomplishments, refusing to go out when their turn comes, rearing plunging & kicking & throwing the ranks into the utmost confusion. However next year when we are first class-men we choose horses instead of having to take those which are left for us and of course have very good ones.[8]

The most influential soldier in the class of May is Emory Upton of upstate New York, "the class genius," who would write *The Military Policy of the United States.* George S. Patton's marked-up copy of Upton's book is in the U.S. Military Academy (USMA) Library at West Point.

Edmund Kirby (#10, May) received a deathbed promotion—from lieutenant to brigadier general—from Abraham Lincoln.

Judson Kilpatrick of New Jersey appeared in Herman Melville's poem "The March to the Sea." Kilpatrick is also mentioned in Gloria Vanderbilt's *Black Knight, White Knight*; he is her great-grandfather.

Henry Walter Kingsbury (#4, May) was killed by the troops of his brother-in-law, Confederate General David Rumph Jones.

One of the gray cavalry generals mentioned by Custer was Tom Rosser, one of his best friends in the class of May. Thomas Lafayette Rosser, born in Virginia and appointed from Texas, was huge. He spent six months in the guardhouse for beating up an upperclassman who hazed him. He also spent time in Benny Havens' tavern, drinking with Custer. Ex-cadet Edgar Allan Poe, class of 1834, reportedly called Benny Havens "the only congenial soul in the entire God-forsaken place."[9] Yet the second edition of *Poems by Edgar A. Poe* is dedicated "to the U.S. Corps of Cadets."

John Pelham of Alabama was Rosser's roommate and probably the most popular man in the class.

John Whitney Barlow (#14, May), born in New York and appointed from Wisconsin, would explore Yellowstone and play a small part in creating a large national park. In his "Personal Reminiscences of the War," Barlow describes some of his classmates: "There was Adelbert Ames, a modest boy from Maine, who became a Major General, a United States Senator, and a Governor of Mississippi; Kilpatrick, of cavalry fame; Babcock [#3, May], the favorite aid and private secretary of Gen. Grant." Barlow adds, "and upon the Southern side was Rosser, who distinguished himself as a dashing cavalry leader, and since the war, has met success and fortune on our Northern railways."[10]

John Adair (#13, May), born in Kentucky and appointed from Oregon, was the only deserter in the class. He went to Canada.

Justin Dimick (#26, June) was a member of both the May and June classes. An example of why he did not graduate with his first set of classmates is given by one of the second, Joseph Farley (#21, June), who describes a moral science class in *West Point in the Early Sixties*. "Cadet Dimick," Farley recalls, "having entered the recitation-room with his section . . . proceeded . . . to use his text-book as a football, shouting as he did so, 'The virtues are what we are, the duties are what we do; what we are is more important than what we do. Therefore the virtues are more important than the duties.' All this with resultant smashing of a window pane at the moment when the instructor entered." Farley adds, "the order, 'Go to your quarters in arrest, Mr. Dimick,' was anticipated, the usual reproof for pranks of this kind."[11]

Patrick O'Rorke (#1, June), an immigrant stonecutter from County Cavan, Ireland, was head of the class of June, of which Custer was the foot.

Alonzo Cushing (#12, June)—older brother of William Cushing, who blew up the *Albemarle* and received the Thanks of Congress—appears in Stephen Vincent Benét's *John Brown's Body*, where he "held his guts in his hand."[12]

Alfred Mordecai (#9, June) was the son of the distinguished ordnance officer of the same name.

Frank Reynolds (#33, June)—who graduated behind everyone in the June class except Custer—joined the Khedive's army after the war and lived in a run-down palace in Alexandria, Egypt.

Peter Conover Hains (#19, June)—who fired the signal gun at Bull Run and served as an engineer at the siege of Vicksburg—was the only member of the class of 1861 to serve on active duty in World War I.

John J. Garnett of the June class, after serving in the Confederate artillery, became an editor and publisher in New York, where he edited a biographical sketch of Ulysses S. Grant and published the official program of the opening of Grant's Tomb.

Grant says in his *Memoirs*, "There is a fine library connected with the Academy."[13] If people reveal themselves in their amusements, West Point's library circulation records and Delinquency Register can be useful. In the 1850s, the Military Academy (unencumbered by the privacy laws of the next century) kept a record of who checked out each book.

On April 10, 1858, Henry A. du Pont took out *Motley's Dutch Republic*; Tom Rosser, Prescott's *Philip II*; Custer, Cooper's *Novels*; Emory Upton, Creasy's *15 Decisive Battles*; and Adelbert Ames, *Aristotle's Rhetoric*. On the same day, John Lea checked out *Knickerbocker*; and John Kelly, Simms's *Charlemont*. Two weeks later on April 24, 1858, Alonzo Cushing borrowed *Harper's Magazine*; Alfred Mordecai, Hazlitt's *Life of Napoleon*; and Justin Dimick, *Lady Lee's Widowhood*.[14]

According to the Register of Cadet Delinquencies, John Whitney Barlow received four demerits for "introducing strangers into the Library" (July 27, 1859). Orville Babcock got five demerits for "visiting in division not his own & jumping out from window" (April 3, 1857). The popular John Pelham got demerits for "making unnecessary noise in tent" (August 18, 1856), "talking in the fencing Acad[em]y" (December 13, 1856), and "idle talking in Draw[in]g Acad[em]y" (April 14, 1860). Adelbert Ames got demerits for spending too much time reading and drawing—"Not returning book to Library at proper time" (October 7, 1857) and "Leaving section & entering Draw[in]g Acad[em]y without permission" (January 13, 1860). Custer got five demerits for being "off cadet limits in rear of confectionery shop" (August 11, 1858).[15]

West Point's tranquillity was broken by news of John Brown's raid on the United States arsenal at Harpers Ferry. Brown was hanged on December 2, 1859, and the next day du Pont wrote to his mother, saying, "there has been a good deal of talk here about Jno. Brown, as every where else. A good many here seem to think the Union is going to be dissolved."[16] Custer's family were Democrats (which was one reason he got along so well with Southerners) and had a low opinion of abolitionists. Yet Custer later wrote, "it required more than ordinary moral and physical courage to boldly avow oneself an abolitionist. The name was considered one of opprobrium, and the cadet who had the courage to avow himself an abolitionist must be prepared to face the social frowns of the great majority of his comrades and at times to defend his opinions by his physical strength and metal."[17]

Emory Upton did so in a fight with Wade Hampton Gibbs of South Carolina. Morris Schaff, of the class of 1862, reports, "When he was being quizzed on his arrival as a new cadet, as to what he had studied, and where he had been to school, he openly and frankly declared that he had been at Oberlin and was an Abolitionist. . . . Upton's sincere declaration . . . at once made him a marked man." Oberlin College, an anti-slavery stronghold in Ohio, admitted women and blacks. Gibbs made a remark about Upton at Oberlin and the fight that resulted on a December night in 1859 was perhaps the most famous at West Point. Morris Schaff says, "It was the most thrilling event in my life as a cadet" and reports that "I do remember . . . that when the fight was over, I saw Upton's resolute face bleeding."[18]

Upton's intensity and seriousness may have been connected to his religious views, as he explained to Oliver Otis Howard, whose weekly prayer meeting he attended. "I had heard but little profanity before I came here," Upton wrote in 1860 in a letter from West Point, "and on my arrival I was shocked." Upton said he felt best "after the performance of any service or duty, which tends to draw off my mind from worldly things."[19]

If John Brown's raid heightened sectional antagonism, the next year's presidential campaign brought it to the breaking point. Custer says, "The Republicans of course espoused the cause championed by Lincoln and Hamlin and the extreme Democrats announced themselves as under the banner of Breckenridge [sic] and Lane. A son of the latter was a member of my class, and occupied an adjoining room."[20] John Lane of the June class was the son of Joseph Lane, senator from Oregon and running mate of John C. Breckinridge, the vice president of the United States who would lose to Lincoln in 1860 and become a Confederate general. Senator Lane, who believed in the right of secession, was one of the few Northerners acceptable to the South. Although Senator Lane would not take part in the Civil War, his son John served in the Army of Northern Virginia and another son, Lafayette, served in the Oregon state legislature at the same time. There was another senator's son in the class of June—William Hamilton Harris (#8, June). His father was Ira Harris of New York. His sister Clara would be a guest of the Lincolns in the presidential box at Ford's Theatre on April 14, 1865.

Some cadets, even at the beginning of 1860, saw that war would follow the election returns (even if some of their leaders did not). Emory Upton told a sister on January 20, 1860, "There will be no limit to the opportunities of doing good in the army. There will be wounded soldiers to minister to, and the dying to comfort."[21] The next month, in an often quoted and accurate observation, Upton said, "Our profession differs from all others. It is a profession of fate and a fatal profession. A long war would make many of us, and prove the grave of as many."[22]

On March 4, 1860, a year before Lincoln took office, Henry A. du Pont wrote to his mother about "clear beautiful weather today, so fine as to have a dress-inspection on the plain for the first time since last fall. I enjoyed it exceedingly & have come to the conclusion that nothing can come up to a soldier's life even a cadet-soldier's."[23] Of course, du Pont was not the only one to write about the beauty of the Hudson Valley. Charles Dickens said in 1842, "any ground more beautiful can hardly be." Dickens was also struck by the casualty rate—"but, whether it be from the rigid nature of the discipline, or the national impatience of restraint, or both causes combined, not more than half the number who begin their studies here, ever remain to finish them."[24]

The national impatience would be seen during the 1860–1861 secession winter of discontent and before that during the presidential campaign. Custer recalls, "The Breckenridge army of Southern Democrats did not hesitate to announce, as their seniors in and out of Congress had done, that in the event of Lincoln's election secession would be the only resource [sic] left to the South. So high did political feeling run among the cadets, or a portion of them," says Custer, "that Mr. Lincoln was hung in effigy one night to a limb of one of the shade trees growing in front of cadet barracks. The effigy was removed early in the morning—so early that few of the cadets or professors even knew of the occurrence."[25]

On November 6, 1860, Abraham Lincoln won 180 electoral votes (to 123 for the other candidates) and 39.8 percent of the popular vote in a four-way race. On December 21, 1860, Emory Upton told his sister, "To-day's papers inform us that South Carolina has seceded. . . . Let her go. She has been a pest, an eye-sore, an abomination ever since she entered the Union. Were it not that her example may become contagious, few would regret her course."[26] Custer reports in his "War Memoirs" that

Among the first of the cadets to leave West Point and hasten to enroll themselves under the banner of the seceding States, were two of my classmates, Kelley [sic] and Ball of Alabama. Kelley became prominent in the war, and was killed in battle. . . . They took their departure from the Academy on Saturday. I remember the date the more readily as I was engaged in—to adopt the cadet term—"walking an extra," which consisted in performing the tiresome duties of a sentinel during the unemployed hours of Saturday; hours usually given to recreation. On this occasion I was pacing back and forth on my post, which for the time being extended along the path leading from the cadets' chapel toward the academic building, when I saw a party of from fifteen to twenty cadets emerge from the open space between the mess hall and academic building, and direct their steps toward the steamboat landing below. That which particularly attracted my attention was the bearing aloft upon the shoulders of their comrades of my two classmates Ball and Kelley, as they were being carried in triumph from the doors of the Academy to the steamboat landing. Too far off to exchange verbal adieux, even if military discipline had permitted it, they caught sight of me as step by step I reluctantly paid the penalty of offended regulations, and raised their hats in token of farewell, to which, first casting my eyes about to see that no watchful superior was in view, I responded by bringing my musket to a "present."[27]

Pierce Manning Butler Young was another friend described by Custer:

> I remember a conversation held at the table at which I sat during the winter of '60–'61. I was seated next to Cadet P. M. B. Young, a gallant young fellow from Georgia, a classmate of mine, then and since the war an intimate and valued friend—a major-general in the Confederate forces during the war and a member of Congress from his native State at a later date. The approaching war was as usual the subject of conversation in which all participated, and in the freest and most friendly manner. . . . Finally, in a half jocular, half earnest manner, Young turned to me and delivered himself as follows: "Custer, my boy, we're going to have war. It's no use talking: I see it coming. All the Crittenden compromises that can be patched up won't avert it. Now let me prophesy what will happen to you and me. You will go home, and your abolition Governor will probably make you colonel of a cavalry regiment. I will go down to Georgia, and ask Governor Brown to give me a cavalry regiment. And who knows but we may move against each other during the war."

Custer adds, "Lightly as we both regarded this boyish prediction, it was destined to be fulfilled in a remarkable degree."[28]

According to West Point's librarian, Oliver Otis Howard, "Probably no other place existed where men grappled . . . more sensitively . . . with the troublesome problems of secession." The prospect of friends fighting each other existed, of course, at every level, including the highest. Howard further recalls, "All the preceding winter, for example, our worthy professor of ethics, J. W. French, D. D., who had been a lifelong friend of Jefferson Davis, worked day and night in anxious thought and correspondence with him with ever-decreasing hope that he might somehow stay the hands which threatened a fratricidal strife."[29]

Emory Upton informed his sister on January 12, 1861, "The South is gone, and the question is, Will the Government coerce her back? . . . Four States are now out of the Union . . . and, no doubt, there will be bloodshed before you receive this, since the Brooklyn (man-of-war) is on the way to Charleston, and is bound to reinforce that fort. . . . Members of my class continue to resign."[30] That fort was Sumter; yet there was no bloodshed before Upton's January letter was received. In February of 1861, there was the inauguration of Jefferson Davis as provisional president of the Confederate States of America. On March 4, 1861, Abraham Lincoln's inauguration as the sixteenth president of the United States went smoothly, with a battery of horse artillery from West Point present.

On March 27, 1861, Upton remarked to his sister, "If we have war (mark my words), Jeff Davis will be successful in one or two campaigns. He is energetic, and he is drawing all the talent he can from our army. He will enter the war with his forces well organized, and it can not be denied that Southern men will fight well; hence, what is to prevent his success for a time?"[31] Upton's prediction was unusual, since most people expected their side to win quickly.

P. G. T. Beauregard, who had been superintendent of West Point in January, was commander of the Confederate forces in Charleston in April. On orders from Jefferson Davis, Beauregard fired on Fort Sumter on April 12, creating a shock in the North similar to Pearl Harbor. Custer says, "It is doubtful if the people of the North were ever, or will ever be again, so united in thought and impulse as when the attack on Sumter was flashed upon them."[32] Joseph Farley says, "Our class ring (June, 1861) bore inscribed 'PER ANGUSTA AD AUGUSTA' [Through Trials to Triumph], and the design upon it was even more appropriate than the motto. Cut in sardonyx from black to white, the seal shows an arm with sword in hand, interposed between the guns of a fort and the flag they are firing on."[33]

O. O. Howard, who would later become head of the Freedmen's Bureau, left West Point to accept the colonelcy of the Third Maine Volunteer Regiment. His description of the reaction to his resignation captures the confusion of the time. Howard says in his *Autobiography*, "I tendered a resignation of my army commission. Washington officials of the War Department were still obstructing such leaves. . . . But the resignations of Southern seceding officers were promptly accepted. When my resignation was also accepted with a batch of others and published in the newspapers, many old acquaintances, curiously enough, thought I had joined the rebellion."[34]

Members of the May class of 1861 petitioned the secretary of war to let them graduate early. Henry du Pont received a letter dated April 20, 1861, from his uncle, Samuel Francis Du Pont, one of the nation's leading naval officers, urging him to sign the petition. Written to "My dear Nephew" from the Navy Yard in Philadelphia, S. F. Du Pont says, "But, my dear Henry, your country which has educated you is in danger. . . . Sign the paper you write about, and don't let a Du Pont be wanting in this hour of trial. . . . My own heart has never before . . . been so shocked . . . as at the Army and Navy defecting." Next there is a reference to Benedict Arnold, who tried to sell West Point to the British. S. F. Du Pont asked his nephew, "Can it be, Henry, that the fetid vapors of Arnold's treason are still hanging in the highlands, and have penetrated those noble buildings intended to engender noble thoughts? I must be brief for I have been up most of the night fitting out an expedition to help save what ships they can at Norfolk and to burn the rest. I told the officers to spare all the humble workmen, if they could, but to shoot down their recent comrades if found with arms in their hands."[35]

The father of Alfred Mordecai of the June class had been head of the class of 1823 and was one of the first Jews to have a career as an officer in the United States Army. He was also the author of *The Ordnance Manual for the Use of Officers of the United States Army* (1841), *Report of Experiments on Gunpowder* (1845), and *Artillery for the United States Land Service* (1849). In his *Autobiography*, Oliver Otis Howard mentions "the venerable Major Alfred Mordecai and his family. Mordecai loved the Union, but, being from North Carolina, he concluded that he would not fight in a Civil War."[36] On May 8, 1861, the elder Alfred Mordecai resigned, refusing "to forge arms to be used against his aged mother, brothers and sisters in the South."[37] His son in the class of June fought for the Union.

Another member of the June class, Joseph P. Farley, writing in 1910 in *Three Rivers: The James, The Potomac, The Hudson, A Retrospect of Peace and War*, dedicates his book *"In memory of my classmates*, those who wore the blue and those who wore the gray."[38]

Members of the May 1861 Class in Order of Class Standing

Unless otherwise noted, all photographs are from the Special Collections, USMA Library.

1.

Henry Algernon
du Pont

2.

Charles E.
Cross

3.

Orville Elias
Babcock

4.

Henry Walter
Kingsbury

5.

Adelbert
Ames

6.

Llewellyn Griffith
Hoxton

7.

Adelbert Rinaldo
Buffington

8.

Emory Upton

9.

Nathaniel Rives
Chambliss

10.

Edmund Kirby

11.

John Isaac
Rodgers

12.

13.

Samuel Nicoll
Benjamin

John Adair

14.

John Whitney
Barlow

15.

Charles Edward
Hazlett

16.

Charles E.
Patterson

17.

Hugh Judson
Kilpatrick

18.

Franklin Harwood

19.

George Warren
Dresser

20.

Charles McKnight
Leoser

21.

Henry Cornelius
Hasbrouck

22.

William Anthony
Elderkin

23.

Francis Asbury
Davies

24.

Charles Carroll
Campbell

25.

Malbone Francis
Watson

26.

John Benson
Williams

27.

Guy Vernon
Henry

28.

Jacob Henry
Smyser

29.

Jacob Beekman
Rawles

30.

Erskine Gittings

31.

Jacob Ford
Kent

32.

Eugene Beauharnais
Beaumont

33.

Leonard Martin

34.

John Scroggs
Poland

35.

Robert Langdon
Eastman

36.

Henry Beach
Noble

37.

Leroy Lansing
Janes

38.

Campbell Dallas
Emory

39.

James F.
McQuesten

40.

George Oscar
Sokalski

41.

Olin F. Rice

42.

Wright L. Rives

43.

Charles Henry
Gibson

44.

Mathias Winston
Henry

45.

Sheldon Sturgeon

John Pelham

*Left West Point before graduation
to join the Confederacy*

Thomas Lafayette Rosser

*Left West Point before graduation
to join the Confederacy*

*(Courtesy of the Massachusetts Commandery
Military Order of the Loyal Legion and the
US Army Military History Institute)*

Flames of Rebellion

The senior class of 1861 graduated on May 6. The head of the class, Henry Algernon du Pont, remarked to his aunt, "I do not know why the list of graduates has not been published this year. The papers did not seem to get hold of the fact of our graduation at all, as all ceremony, grand reviews, etc. were dispensed with."[1] But of course the newspapers had more dramatic events to cover.

Emory Upton described the spring of 1861, noting, "The flames of rebellion kindled at Fort Sumter, did not stop at the Potomac. April 19, they burst out in Baltimore, where for several days they checked the advance of the Union troops, cutting off all communication with the Government." After mentioning the Sixth Massachusetts, which lost two dead on the streets of Baltimore, Upton continues, "It was no longer a question of repossessing our forts. Railroads and telegraphs had been cut . . . the capital was in a state of siege, and for the third time in our history appeared doomed to fall into the hands of its enemies."[2]

Upton explains and justifies Lincoln's extraordinary measures to defend the government and capital: "the President, trusting to popular approval, assumed and exercised the war powers of Congress . . . the President raised armies, provided navies."[3]

Upton's first roommate, John Whitney Barlow, gives an account of their class trip to Washington in his "Personal Reminiscences of the War," which also gives a glimpse into the paranoia of May 1861. In New York City, the classmates, who were new lieutenants, bought swords, pistols, and uniforms. "Nearly all of us, probably about thirty," Barlow reports, "took the next evening's train . . . on reaching Philadelphia, about midnight, an incident somewhat dramatic occurred." In fact, they were all arrested. "We were," Barlow recalls, "all young, active, and strong. We were, moreover, generally provided with pistols and swords; though fortunately, in view of what happened, these weapons were either among our baggage, or so wrapped up as to render their sudden use impossible."[4]

The trouble began when the West Pointers were disembarking from a ferry. Barlow "was descending the plank when, just ahead of me, I saw one of my class-mates struggling with a stranger. My first thought was, we have fallen among traitors. I rushed to my friend's assistance, caught the other man by the collar and whirled him off into the darkness, from which a voice called out, 'Seize that man!' . . . his cry from the darkness to seize me . . . sounded more funny than anything I had ever heard."[5]

Barlow adds, "Before I could think twice, two policemen who looked as large as the goddess of liberty on our court house, had me in a grip of iron. I just then caught a glimpse of two long lines of the city police reaching up the street, which suddenly closed in on us, and we were all prisoners." Barlow and his classmates "were at once escorted to the central police station, where we learned that our arrest had been ordered by the Mayor, on information received from Jersey City to the effect that a number of rebels were purchasing arms for the Confederacy, and would pass through Philadelphia that night."[6]

After explaining their identity, the West Pointers were treated "with great courtesy" by the police. Barlow recalls, "While waiting for the dispersion of a mob which had gathered outside the police station, on a report that a capture of rebels had been made we, at the request of one of the officers, gave a number of policemen some experience in *squad drill*; and, by the methods we had learned as plebes, were able somewhat to gratify our revenge by putting our captors through some of the liveliest movements they had ever experienced."[7] When the May class finally reached Washington, they were presented to General-in-Chief Winfield Scott.

Henry A. du Pont told his father in a letter dated May 8, 1861, "I reached here about 2 o'clock. . . . The whole class is assigned to duty in this department of Washington."[8] Adelbert Ames told Oliver Otis Howard, "At present all of us are attached to volunteer companies. I have a Co. of the 12th N.Y. . . . We have entire control of them—commissioned officers and all."[9]

On May 10, du Pont wrote to his father, saying, "Dr. Grimshaw is here and wants me to go back to Delaware and serve with the regiment forming there. He says that if I will consent he can get me detached, and wants me to be major. He also talks a great deal about the secessionists in the state & of their designs and of the absolute necessity of forming the regiment to remain *there* & keep them in check. To all of this I told him that if the state is actually in

danger I was willing to do everything in my power, but that I could not consent to have any application made until I had consulted you. . . . Though this
duty would enable me to be at home a good deal yet I am very dubious about
the Doctors accounts of the state of things at home. I think them grossly
exaggerated."[10]

Du Pont's decision not to join the Delaware volunteers prevented him
from becoming a boy general. By remaining in the Regular Army—a decision he made after consulting with officers in the War Department who
thought they were being helpful—he eliminated the possibility of high rank.
After graduation, du Pont had gone into the Corps of Engineers (which was
the usual choice for the head of a class). The doctor from Delaware,
Arthur H. Grimshaw, had actually given du Pont very good career advice
(whatever the accuracy of his political analysis of the secessionists' strength
in that state). But instead of joining the volunteers, du Pont joined the Fifth
U.S. Artillery on May 14, 1861, as a first lieutenant. He did not become a
captain until 1864, promotion being notoriously slow in the Regular artillery.
He did not even see combat until that year, since he became regimental
adjutant, and although some of the Fifth's batteries were in the Army of the
Potomac, its headquarters were not. When du Pont finally got into battle, he
was superb in his very first fight and won the Medal of Honor a few months
later. Since he had courage and coolness on the battlefield, administrative
ability (demonstrated during the war and after), and excellent connections
in Delaware, it is hard to believe that du Pont would not have achieved high
rank if he had chosen to serve in the volunteer infantry instead of the Regular artillery.

Adelbert Ames revealed his own high opinion of volunteers in his letter
to Oliver Howard dated May 12, 1861. "The city," Ames wrote from Washington, "is considered perfectly safe. We have at least not less than thirty
thousand troops here. The volunteers are all intelligent looking men. In fact
I never saw finer looking men taken in a body than they are." A New England regiment especially impressed the young man from Maine. According
to Ames, "The Rhode Island regiment pleases every one. Their gentlemanly
bearing—for they are all gentlemen—the happy adaptation . . . to service—
their intelligence, for they are of the first society in the New England
states—strike the beholder at once and he feels he is not in the presence of
ordinary troops."[11]

On May 12, 1861, du Pont told his mother, "I have left Willards & am now
staying at a boarding house . . . which I find quieter & more pleasant than
the Hotel. . . . Hoxton [#6, May] is 2nd Lieut. of Ordnance he is rooming

with me here."[12] Llewellyn Hoxton, who came from a distinguished family in northern Virginia, had been du Pont's roommate at West Point. On the same day, Adelbert Ames told Oliver Otis Howard, "Of our class the first three went into the Eng.—None in the Topog'. Eng. and two in the ordnance. Nineteen in the artillery."[13]

Ames became a first lieutenant on May 14, when he left the Second U.S. Artillery for the Fifth. On May 24, the Federals moved across the Potomac to Alexandria. Ames told O. O. Howard, "During the excitement consequent upon the occupation of the Sacred Soil of Virginia in this vicinity I had command of a section of our battery at the Georgetown Aqueduct bridge for some two days and one night. We were ordered to be ready at any moment but were not called on. The remainder went across long bridge where they were about as useful as I was. We hope we may do better the next time (if necessary)."[14]

In a letter to his father in May, a grateful du Pont says, "thank you again for the pistol which is exactly the thing I wanted and which will be I think very useful to me. . . . Hoxton is ordered to the St. Louis Arsenal and leaves here very soon perhaps tomorrow. He is in a very distressed state of mind in consequence of certain letters he has recently received from his friends who are red-hot secessionists. . . . Have you any friends in St. Louis you could give Hoxton a letter of introduction to?"[15]

Llewellyn Hoxton would not need any letters of introduction to St. Louis. On May 25, 1861, du Pont told his aunt, "L. Hoxton has resigned and gone to Virginia."[16] He eventually became chief of artillery in William Hardee's Corps in the Army of Tennessee. In another letter to his aunt, du Pont says, "I have been very much pained at the conduct of some of my best and most intimate friends of other days, but friends of mine no longer now. Hoxton you know very well. . . . however the less said about the business the better."[17]

His classmate Upton did say something about it. An argument that troubled Upton was the embarrassing one that since the most famous leaders of the Rebellion against the United States were graduates of the United States Military Academy—Davis, Lee, Jackson, and Stuart, to name a few—West Point's loyalty to the federal government might be questionable. Many arguments have been made to refute this, but Upton focused on the large percentage of West Pointers from the South who remained loyal to the Union. Quoting George Washington Cullum, Upton boasted, "Can Harvard, Yale, Columbia, Union, Princeton, or any other college in the land show a higher record of patriotism and sacrifice? Assuredly not, for their Southern graduates espoused the rebel cause almost *en masse*."[18]

In his *Military Policy*, Upton gave a statistical analysis of West Point graduates and the ranks they reached, and his mentor gave him an editorial comment that became a footnote on the same page: "'This mathematical discussion, though valuable to graduates, will not strengthen with the world your real argument.—W.T.S.' Note by General Sherman."[19]

The self-confidence of Upton's classmate Ames can be seen in his correspondence with Oliver Otis Howard. Adelbert Ames's letter of May 27, 1861, when he had been out of West Point less than a month, makes it look as if Howard had asked him for advice. In any case, Ames seems to be giving some when he tells O. O. Howard, "Allow me to congratulate you on your good fortune—a Colonelcy or Assistant Professor—both so good that you appeared to wish to keep both. . . . Still it is a question to be decided by yourself for you only know yourself well enough to be a judge."[20]

The experience of the junior class of 1861, which graduated on June 24, was described by Peter Hains in "The First Gun at Bull Run," which appeared in *Cosmopolitan* (August 1911) for the fiftieth anniversary of the battle. "'A fine crop, a fine crop, Mr. Secretary!'" Hains says, "These were the words with which Abraham Lincoln greeted us that memorable 25th of June, 1861, the day after we had arrived at the capital from West Point. We were mustered in the old Wilder Building, opposite the War Department. The President had done us the honor to come over and shake hands with each individual of us . . . all young men or almost 'boys,' for I was not quite twenty-one."[21]

Hains, nineteenth in the class of June, was assigned to a battery of the Second U.S. Artillery. "At once," he recalls, "we were all put to drilling troops, raw troops. . . . We had had the best the world afforded in the way of training. We had graduated from West Point, and a man from that institution at that time was a very valuable possession to the government."[22] So valuable that Custer, who had begun his military career under arrest at West Point for failing to stop a fistfight between cadets—instead, Custer recalled, "I . . . called out loudly, '. . . let's have a fair fight'"—was released from the guardhouse and sent to the capital.[23]

Emory Upton, serving as an aide to General Daniel Tyler, told his sister on July 9, 1861, "I meet many of my old West Point instructors daily. Captain Baird (mathematics) is on our staff; Captain Vincent (chemistry) is on General Schenck's staff; Colonel McCook, of tactics, who had my company; Colonel Howard, Captain Williams, and many others. Professor Mahan was out to see us to-day. . . . It seems quite strange to associate with these men on terms of equality."[24] That was probably an additional source of motivation for members of the May and June classes of 1861.

Peter Hains says, "I was assigned to train a gun-crew over at what is now
known as Fort Myer, Virginia, just across the river from Washington. It was
a great gun—a thirty-pounder Parrot rifle, drawn by ten horses as green as
could be, horses from the farm that had not been trained even to pull
together. . . . Some two hundred men were attached to the gun. . . . The
piece weighed six thousand pounds."[25] He further reports,

> we . . . went into camp to await the disposition of the army, facing the
> stream called Bull Run. . . . There was never a moment's peace, day or night.
> The slightest noise after dark brought forth a rifle shot from any one of these
> men who happened to be nervous and overwatchful. Horses were shot,
> mules killed as they grazed. Nine men were shot in one day by the careless-
> ness, or rather the ignorance, of the men who had for the first time in their
> lives borne arms. I saw one man take his loaded musket and strike with the
> butt at some very enticing apples above his head in an orchard. Before I
> could yell at him he had shot himself through the thigh, the lock of the gun
> catching in the branches. It was very discouraging, but we were new, young,
> and, in youth there is never any pessimism in the face of great undertakings.[26]

Hains's first great undertaking was to fire the signal gun on July 21, 1861, to
start the battle of Bull Run between the Union army of General Irvin
McDowell (class of 1838) and the Confederates commanded by McDowell's
classmate P. G. T. Beauregard and Joseph E. Johnston (class of 1829). Custer
arrived in the early morning at McDowell's headquarters with dispatches
from General Winfield Scott. Custer recalls,

> I had the good fortune to discover in an officer at headquarters one of my
> recent West Point friends, Lieutenant Kingsbury, aide de camp to General
> McDowell. Near the log fire . . . were some servants busily engaged in
> removing the remains of breakfast. A word from Kingsbury, and they soon
> prepared for me a cup of coffee, a steak, and some Virginia corn bread. . . .
> Had I known, however, that I was not . . . to taste food during the next
> thirty hours, I should have appreciated the opportunity I then enjoyed even
> more highly. As I sat on the ground sipping my coffee, and heartily enjoy-
> ing my first breakfast in the field, Kingsbury (afterward Colonel Kingsbury,
> killed at the battle of Antietam) informed me of the general movement
> then begun by the army, and of the attack which was to be made on Beau-
> regard's forces that day. Three days before I had quitted school at West
> Point.[27]

Custer's classmate Peter Hains explains how he got his own historic role:

"Three shots at daylight will be the signal for the fight to begin,". . . and as my giant gun was the loudest speaker of the whole united armies it was chosen. . . . I would open the fight between the armies of the North and South. I unlimbered the gun and waited. It was loaded with a percussion shell and was trained upon a house across Bull Run at about a mile and a half range. The size of the house told me plainly that it was some general's headquarters, but of course at the time I had no definite knowledge just whose it was. It was sufficient that it stood out large and white, a target for my gun which I could hardly miss.

At a little after six o'clock on as peaceful-appearing a Sabbath morning as that countryside ever knew, the order came. I sighted the rifle carefully, and the men grinned their delight. Then I stood back. "Fire!"

Across the little stream, true to its destination, sped that first shot. I saw it strike fairly upon the side of the house, and the smoke and dust that followed told of its excellent work. General Alexander, of Beauregard's army, tells of the effects of that shot in his report, and he describes the consternation of the officers and men as a giant shell came crashing among them from somewhere far across the Run and away beyond any range they had deemed possible. I followed that shot with two others, and the signal had been given to McDowell's army that they were to begin hostilities. The first big battle of the Civil War had begun.[28]

In a letter to his sister, Emory Upton said,

You spoke of the Hon. Owen Lovejoy. Did I tell you about meeting him at Bull Run? . . . General Tyler's division crossed Bull Run about forty rods above Stone Bridge. I crossed with the Sixty-ninth New York and passed up the opposite bank through a ravine. We had marched but a few rods when we came upon a regiment of secessionists. We were about eight rods from them, and not knowing them to be secessionists we asked them. I was between them and the leading company, and of course rode around the company so that they might open fire. I had but got behind it when my horse was shot and mortally wounded. I dismounted, and remained until the enemy ran. . . . I then went forward to a small house where the wounded were being carried. I saw there an old horse and, as I was an aide-de-camp, I mounted him. I asked for his owner, and Mr. Lovejoy made his appearance. He was assisting in taking care of the wounded, and had exposed his life freely. I told him I was an aide and my horse had been shot, and asked for his. He gave him to me immediately. . . . I have a high respect for Mr. Lovejoy, because he fights for his principles and is a brave man.[29]

Another brave man at Bull Run was Adelbert Ames, who won the Medal of Honor in his first fight. Commanding a section of Griffin's battery, Ames received a severe thigh wound. Captain Charles Griffin reported, "Lieutenant Ames was wounded so as to be unable to ride a horse at almost the first fire; yet he sat by his command directing the fire, being helped on and off the caisson during the different changes of front or position, refusing to leave the field until he became too weak to sit up."[30]

Hains mentions Adelbert Ames's roommate, Edmund Kirby, whose coolness was noted in his first battle as in his last. Hains says,

> a section of . . . two guns commanded by Lieutenant Kirby, came rapidly up the road and was just abreast of me, when it stopped and began to unlimber with feverish haste. . . . I suddenly became aware that the cavalry a few yards distant was not Union cavalry. The leader was dressing the line preparing for some work, and then like a flash it dawned upon me that the work was to destroy us. . . . The men were not willing to do much. They were green troops, and I was only a strange boy. . . . "Fire, for God's sake, fire—that's Virginia cavalry!" I yelled, now furious.
>
> Above the murmur I heard the order come from Kirby, "Canister—double charges."
>
> "Oh, fire, fire, you infernal fools, fire!" I yelled again. . . . Men shouted to fire; men shouted not to fire. . . . A couple of saddles were emptied . . . above the uproar and confusion came Kirby's cool order, "Canister—double charges—load."[31]

Kirby's guns fired and Hains describes the effect on horses and riders:

> The end of the squadron took the whole weight of that metal into it. The horses reared upward and fell over upon their riders; some, frantic under awful wounds, dashed into their own ranks and rolled the line up. Men toppled out of their saddles, and their horses ran madly for shelter. The line slowed, hesitated, and stopped under the shock of the canister. . . . The cannoneers toiled furiously, and there came another discharge from Kirby's guns. Horses reared, men screamed and yelled with pain. . . . The squadron rolled up upon itself, the horses crowding, struggling, falling, and rolling about the field. The rest broke and then galloped off. Carried away with the heat and excitement of the fight, I ran after them on foot, firing my six-shooter until it clicked empty in my hand.[32]

Hains's article does not stress the decisive role of infantry in this (and almost every other) Civil War battle. But Custer explains how the battle suddenly changed in his "War Memoirs":

With the exception of a little tardiness in execution, something to be expected perhaps in raw troops, the plan of battle marked out by General McDowell was carried out with remarkable precision up till about half-past three P.M. The Confederate left wing had been gradually forced back from Bull Run. . . . But at this critical moment, with their enemies in front giving way in disorder and flight, a new and to the Federals an unexpected force appeared suddenly upon the scene. From a piece of timber almost directly in rear of McDowell's right a column of several thousand fresh troops of the enemy burst almost upon the backs of the half victorious Federals. I was standing with a friend and classmate at that moment on a high ridge near our advancing line. We were congratulating ourselves upon the glorious victory which already seemed to have been won, as the Confederates were everywhere giving way, when our attention was attracted by a long line of troops suddenly appearing behind us upon the edge of the timber already mentioned. It never occurred to either of us that the troops we then saw could be any but some of our reinforcements making their way to the front. Before doubts could arise we saw the Confederate flag floating over a portion of the line just emerging from the timber; the next moment the entire line levelled their muskets and poured a volley into the backs of our advancing regiments on the right. At the same time a battery which had also arrived unseen opened fire, and with the cry of "We're flanked! We're flanked!" passed from rank to rank, the Union lines, but a moment before so successful and triumphant, threw down their arms, were seized by a panic, and begun a most disordered flight.[33]

The retreat turned into a rout, and Jefferson Davis, now on the scene, wanted to follow the Federals to Washington. "Of course," Hains adds, "in the capital the wildest rumors were going about . . . all the panic of conversation had full sway."[34]

Since most accounts of Bull Run (including Custer's) emphasize the rout—often suggesting that a Confederate march on Washington would have captured the capital—it is remarkable that Hains expressed the opposite view. "During that long ride back," Hains wrote in 1911, "over thirty miles of roads that had now turned to mud and swamps—for it had rained hard during the night after the battle—we had plenty of time to ponder over the defeat. Officers discussed it with heat and many criticisms. But it was really not a very desperate rout for the Union Army. The Confederates could not have forced the defenses of Washington. Half the army had not been under fire, and there were plenty of good troops in the defenses and fortifications that could have made an attack absolutely fatal to the assailants. Johnston was wise enough not to attempt it."[35]

Hains also notes, "officers, including myself, who had graduated and received such praise from our President were soon hard at work doing the work for which they have since become well known. As I write this there are but three living besides myself."[36]

The head of the May class did not like the work he had to do after Bull Run, or Manassas, as he tells his mother in a letter from Harrisburg, Pennsylvania. "I have had lately," Henry du Pont said on August 5, 1861,

> a most disagreeable duty to perform. The Secretary of War who is here on a visit sent for me last Friday night and dictated an order to me which he signed directing me to a little town named Alexandria, in Huntingdon Co. of this state, and arrest an escaped prisoner of war who was in the late battle at Manassas but who managed to change his uniform for private citizen's attire in the confusion after the battle and get off. His wife & father in law reside in Alexandria. You can imagine how painful it was to seize him in the midst of his family circle and the despair of his wife and friends. . . . I had with me two officers and a recruit of our regiment, all well armed and dressed in citizen's clothes. . . . We captured him and after some show [of] resistance on his part and that of his father in law took him away without trouble. He was unarmed at the time as it happened and could not do much, though the father in law ran and provided himself with means of defense and I thought for a few seconds that I would have to shoot him. I want no more such duty to do though, I can assure you, where you have to witness the grief and tears of his wife & mother etc.[37]

Du Pont's letter shows why armies are not always reliable in civil wars.

But Upton and Hains had very different assessments of Bull Run. "The effect," said Upton, "of this disastrous battle, which gave the enemy all the advantages of the initiative, had he chosen to use it, was to paralyze military operations for more than six months."[38]

The discouragement in the North after Bull Run can be seen in one of Henry du Pont's letters to his aunt. "I must confess," du Pont says on August 24, 1861,

> that I do not see a very bright future before us. I was peculiarly struck at the degeneracy of the times on looking over the long list of Brigadier Generals in the paper of yesterday: when I saw the large proportion of petty politicians, newspaper editors . . . I was more than ever confirmed in my opinion of the hopeless corruption of those in power, that is to say of politicians. It is an opinion I have entertained for years that our present form of government is incapable of controlling the destinies of an immense people like our own . . . a problem which will be solved in the next half-century. As to the imme-

diate events of the day it is hard to form an opinion: I doubt if the next few months will be equalized by any great success on our part, though we may have some more reverses to chronicle. However I hope for the best.[39]

Emory Upton wrote to his sister on September 30, 1861, from Alexandria, Virginia, right after the Confederates had evacuated Munson's Hill:

The conduct of our troops was disgraceful beyond expression. They burned buildings, destroyed furniture, stole dishes, chairs, etc., killed chickens, pigs, calves, and everything they could eat. They would take nice sofa-chairs, which they had not the slightest use for, and ten minutes after throw them away. Talk about the barbarity of the rebels! I believe them to be Christians compared to our thieves. The houses entered yesterday belonged mostly to Union people, yet they were unmolested by the rebels. One of our volunteer majors walked up to a looking-glass, worth about twenty dollars, and deliberately put his foot through it. I wish I had witnessed it. He would have had the benefit of a court-martial.[40]

Upton's friend Oliver Otis Howard became a general of volunteers in September of 1861 and would receive a letter congratulating him on his promotion from a member of the June class. Alfred Mordecai expresses a conventional view; yet the ranks involved are unusual. "I know," Mordecai told Howard, "you do not care for the rank, but since you have determined to serve in the war it is pleasanter to be a Brig Genl than a Col."[41]

Mordecai's classmate Pierce Young, who would become a boy general of the Confederacy, was experiencing one of the unpleasant aspects of promotion. Young was already a major commanding the cavalry in Cobb's (Georgia) Legion, where some of the men in his command were twice his age and had distinguished careers. Benjamin Cudworth Yancey (class of 1838 at Yale Law School) had been United States minister to the Argentine Confederation. On one occasion, when Yancey did not like the way his commander talked to him, he sent Young a letter of complaint. On October 26, 1861, Young, who would become a U.S. diplomat after the war, sent Yancey a diplomatic and very unusual reply, which actually included an apology:

Your communication is before me. I shall regard it as purely private and not as official for it would be highly improper for me to reply to any official communication of a similar nature. . . . I suppose that I was applied for by Col Cobb and appointed by the President to the command of the battalion of Cavalry, under the supposition at that time that I was capable of the command and whilst in command of the battalion I shall exact that respect which is due to the commander of such a body and that respect is the same as though the commander's head were hoary with age. I rebuked no one and if my remarks were so construed it could not have been from my language but *must* have been entirely from my manner. It seems that I am unfortunate in this respect as this is not the first time my natural manner of speaking in a loud tone has been mistaken for temper. . . . I consider it useless and unnecessary to reply to any other points of your communication.[42]

From Centreville, Virginia, on November 16, 1861, Confederate General Joseph E. Johnston wrote about troop movements to Judah P. Benjamin, the acting secretary of war in Richmond, using Young's classmate John Lane as courier and adding at the end of his letter, "This will be delivered to you by Lieutenant Lane, son of the late United States Senator from Oregon."[43]

Adelbert Ames wrote to his parents in Maine from Washington on December 21, 1861:

My battery is progressing finely. . . . The Maine delegation treat me very kindly. Vice President Hamlin, his wife and daughter have come out to camp expressly to see me and repay my call. . . . I am going to a wedding on Christmas Eve, and to another on the 26th. Neither of them, however, is to be my own. . . . We have had any number of marriages here among young people of the Army. In fact, a perfect mania appears to have seized them . . . I except myself. Such a step in such a time as this impairs a young officer's usefulness and advancement, so it will be a long day before we shall entertain any ideas of the kind.[44]

Around Christmas of 1861, Lieutenant John Adair, class of May, left the First U.S. Cavalry for Canada. Adair was dismissed on December 29, 1861, as a deserter.

3

Courage and Ambition

In a war where even generals sometimes led from the front, "boy generals" (in their mid-twenties) could earn the confidence of their men by displaying bravery on a regular basis. It certainly helped make Custer a popular commander despite his heavy casualties. Emory Upton said, "officers must expose themselves freely if they would have their commands do their whole duty."[1] In his study of combat, Gerald Linderman notes, "Most officers, lacking the heroic presence of a Jackson or a Stuart and thus unable simply to issue orders, had no alternative but to prove themselves exemplars of courage."[2] As examples, it is not surprising that he mentions Custer and John Pelham, who conspicuously remained fearless and on horseback under the heaviest fire.

There may have even been some advantages to being a boy general in the Civil War, where physical courage was of much greater importance to commanders of brigades and divisions than in later wars. Some young people think they are immortal. More remarkable are soldiers who have been wounded several times, such as Thomas Rosser and Pierce Young, and are still, as Rosser put it, "always ready 'to go in.'"[3] Rosser was referring to John Pelham, but his remark could also have been said of himself or of friends such as Custer.

Theodore Lyman says in a letter from *Meade's Headquarters*, "but I can tell you that there are *not* many officers who of their own choice and impulse will dash in on formidable positions. They will go anywhere they are *ordered* and anywhere they believe it is their *duty* to go; but fighting for fun is rare; and," according to Colonel Lyman, "unless there is a little of this in a man's disposition he lacks an element. Such men as Sprigg Carroll, Hays (killed), Custer, and some others, attacked wherever they got a chance, and of their own accord. Very few officers would hold back when they get an order; but the ordeal is so awful, that it requires a peculiar disposition to 'go in gaily,' as old Kearny used to say."[4]

Perhaps that peculiar disposition is more prevalent among the young. One of John Pelham's closest friends on General Stuart's staff, William Willis Blackford, gives his assessment of youth and West Point in his *War Years with Jeb Stuart*: "As adjutant, I met all the officers of our army frequently, either when they were visiting Stuart, or when I accompanied him on visits to them. Then began the impression, which has ripened into conviction since, that the average West Point officer who had reached the age of forty in the discharge of the duties of the army officer, in time of peace, is worthless in war. Of course there are brilliant exceptions in both the Northern and Southern armies, but they are *exceptions*."[5]

Whatever the validity of Blackford's remarks, he goes on to include useful reflections on the advantages of youth in a commander. Blackford recalls, "The young men from West Point, who had to win their way and had not been fossilized by garrison or bureau life, as a rule did splendidly, those of thirty and under, say." But according to Blackford, "the 'old soldiers' are so intensely jealous of each other. . . . The country or their cause is nothing to them when opposed to their feelings, and it is so deeply seated that they really are not aware of its existence. . . . Then, when high in rank"—and this is the most important disadvantage of age in a commander—"some of them are so afraid of losing their reputation that they won't take the risks necessary in war, and avoid a battle they are not certain of winning, when the chances are still in their favor."[6]

Admiral Alfred Thayer Mahan, whose father taught at West Point, observes, "the average man wants to be much too sure of success before venturing to move."[7] According to Mahan, "only men of the temper of Farragut or Grant—men with a natural genius for war or enlightened by their knowledge of the past—can fully commit themselves to the hazard of a great adventure."[8]

Custer would say after he became a general,

> Often I think of the vast responsibility resting on me, of the many lives entrusted to my keeping, of the happiness of so many households depending on my discretion and judgment—and to think that I am just leaving my boyhood makes the responsibility appear greater. This is not due to egotism, self-conceit. I try to make no unjust pretensions. I assume nothing I know not to be true. It requires no extensive knowledge to inform me what is my duty to my country, my command. . . . "First be sure you're right, then go ahead!" I ask myself, "Is it right?" Satisfied that it is so, I let nothing swerve me from my purpose.[9]

Custer certainly had the self-confidence and drive of a superb battle leader. He was ready to push ahead at the critical moment (even if his critics would say at any moment). Philip Sheridan would note that "Custer is still pushing on" in a letter to Grant the night before the surrender at Appomattox. Like other generals writing about Custer, Sheridan often uses some form of the word "pushing" to describe what the most famous boy general is doing.[10] That kind of relentless confidence and drive is most likely to be found in young commanders. At least that is the view of Emory Upton, who mentions Custer at Gettysburg in an article called "Facts in Favor of Compulsory Retirement."[11]

Upton might have called the case of Admiral Farragut—who was over sixty and exceeded by no one in drive and daring—an exception. Blackford might have pointed out that Farragut did not go to West Point. In any case, Blackford has his own explanation for why the South lost: Jefferson Davis was a West Pointer and Abraham Lincoln was not. Contrasting the leadership styles of Lincoln and Davis, the former Confederate officer says, "our President insisted upon retaining direct personal control of every detail of every department, and placed only men in his Cabinet who were of abilities sufficiently moderate to consent to occupy the position under such restrictions. How differently Lincoln managed! But he, fortunately for his side, had not been educated at West Point."[12]

In a letter from West Point, Alfred Mordecai of the June class, now assistant professor of mathematics, told Oliver Otis Howard what it was like on February 11, 1862. "All here are as usual," Mordecai remarks, "only more quiet than formerly, not the place it used to be." The elder Alfred Mordecai, after resigning from the United States Army and refusing to take part in the war, was not sure what he should do. His son tells O. O. Howard, "I was in Philadelphia at Christmas . . . my father in poor spirits but well . . . the only source of worry is that father can find nothing that he will do or rather thinks he ought to do whilst remaining perfectly neutral."[13]

The elder Alfred Mordecai eventually became a mathematics teacher in Philadelphia. His son in the June class continued the family tradition in ordnance, becoming a brevet major in 1863 for the siege of Fort Wagner, South Carolina, and chief of ordnance in the Army of the James (May to September 1864), the Army of the Ohio (October to November 1864), and the Department of the Cumberland (November 1864 to June 1865).

Henry du Pont's problem was that he wanted to fight but was stuck at Camp Greble, near Harrisburg, Pennsylvania, as adjutant of the Fifth U.S. Artillery. "I am here," du Pont told his father on March 17, 1862, "still feeling very much disgusted . . . at not being able to see active service in these

stirring times. . . . I am thus kept here nolens volens [whether willing or not].
It is going to kill me professionally I fear. I don't see really that I can do anything now in this eleventh hour however and only can hope that something
will turn up." Du Pont was more optimistic about the regimental band. "The
leader," he informs his father, "is an excellent one, he was the first cornet
player of the West Point Band and we got him transferred to our regiment."[14]

According to Emory Upton, "The failure to subdue the Rebellion in 1861
has already been explained by our total want of military organization and
preparation. The failure to subdue it in 1862, with the amazing advantages
possessed by the Union, proceeded from a cause entirely different—the mis-
management of our armies. . . . The country at this early day," Upton recalls,
"was filled with a multitude of amateur strategists, who, after reading up a few
of Napoleon's campaigns, lost no opportunity of laying their plans before the
President, at the same time striving to commend themselves to his notice by
vilifying his military subordinates."[15]

Vilifying Federal generals (especially if they were Democrats) was institu-
tionalized by the radical Congressional Joint Committee on the Conduct of
the War by its endless investigations. "Had the investigations been confined
to transactions which had already occurred," Upton says, "no harm would have
ensued beyond the injury done to discipline by encouraging officers to criticize
their superiors with a view to securing promotion, or to the gratification of personal ill will. But a knowledge of past events by no means satisfied the committee. It pried into the present and sought to look into the future."[16]

Upton's tone changes when discussing the role of General Ulysses S.
Grant in the capture of Forts Henry (on the Tennessee River) and Donelson
(on the Cumberland) in February of 1862. According to Upton,

> Never was the value of professional training more conspicuously illustrated
> than in the conception and execution of the Fort Donelson campaign. . . .
> Judging, with the intuition of a great commander that the Confederates . . .
> failure to renew the battle denoted a demoralization as great as that among
> his own troops, the Union general instantly resolved to take the offensive.
> . . . The night of the 15th closed with the Union troops in possession of the
> key to Fort Donelson, and next morning the enemy surrendered. The strate-
> gical effect of this victory was the immediate evacuation by the Confeder-
> ates of Missouri, Kentucky, and nearly all of Tennessee.[17]

Exploiting the "unconditional surrender" of Donelson, Grant's Army of
the Tennessee advanced to Pittsburg Landing near Shiloh Church. Don Car-

los Buell was to follow with his Army of the Ohio. Upton observes, "The Confederates in the meantime were not idle. Recognizing Corinth, the intersection of the two great lines of the Memphis and Charleston and the Mobile and Ohio railroads, as the next objective point of the Union forces, General Albert Sidney Johnston summoned to its defense troops from Kentucky, Tennessee, Arkansas, and Florida, until by the end of March he found himself at the head of an effective force of 40,000 men."[18]

Upton explains what the Confederate commanders, A. S. Johnston and P. G. T. Beauregard, intended to do with their new force: "Determined, if possible, to destroy the Army of the Tennessee before the impending junction could be effected, General Johnston left Corinth April 3, and on the 6th assaulted the Union lines at Shiloh. After a furious battle, lasting nearly a day, the last desperate charge was repulsed just as the leading division of Buell's army succeeded in crossing the river . . . the combined armies took the offensive in the morning, and after a severe engagement drove the enemy in disorder from the field."[19]

The extent of the Confederate defeat was not fully appreciated, partly because of 13,000 Federal casualties. The Confederate dead, wounded, and missing exceeded 10,000 and included General Albert Sidney Johnston, who bled to death. Another Confederate casualty was Charles Patterson (#16, May), who had been in Custer's D company at West Point. After a month in the Fourth U.S. Infantry drilling volunteers in Washington, Patterson was dismissed on June 6, 1861, for tendering his resignation in the face of the enemy. After switching to the Confederate army, Patterson rose to lieutenant colonel of the Second Arkansas and died on April 8, 1862, from wounds received at Shiloh two days before.

Also at Shiloh was John Herbert Kelly, who resigned from West Point on December 29, 1860, and whose departure—on his classmates' shoulders— has already been described by Custer. After serving as a captain on General William J. Hardee's staff, Kelly became a major in the Fourteenth Arkansas in September of 1861, and at Shiloh commanded the Ninth Arkansas Battalion. His brigade commander, Brigadier General S. A. M. Wood, described Kelly at Water Oaks Pond after 11 A.M. on the second day at Shiloh: "We were met in front and to the right of Shiloh Church. The charge was most gallantly made, crossing a pond of water in some places waist-deep, and then entering an open field. Major Kelly here displayed the greatest gallantry . . . dashing through the pond, sat on horseback in the open ground and rallied his men in line as they advanced."[20]

Kelly ended his own report with his own enthusiasm: "The gallant bearing of the officers and men under my command could not be surpassed by veterans. . . . Our battle flag was completely riddled; not a string of it is left. With men like these, who will bear their flag so gallantly, brilliant triumph is certain."[21] In any case, promotion was certain for an officer whose men—regardless of their experience or lack of it—always seemed to fight like veterans (something that would be noted about Kelly in other battles as well). General Wood said in his report of April 15, 1862, "It is my duty to the country to recommend for promotion, for great gallantry shown on the field of Shiloh on Sunday and Monday, Maj. John H. Kelly."[22] The next month Kelly would be a colonel (of the Eighth Arkansas) and the next year a general.

Upton also gave an analysis of the navy and David Glasgow Farragut:

April 24, after a brilliant engagement, Rear-Admiral Farragut destroyed the Confederate fleet and ran by the batteries of Forts St. Phillip and Jackson. April 25, anchored off New Orleans; demanded and received its surrender, May 1. The troops, without loss, occupied the city. From New Orleans Farragut steamed up the river and successfully took possession of Baton Rouge and Natchez. June 28, having assembled his squadron, including the mortar fleet used in the reduction of the forts below New Orleans, he bombarded the batteries at Vicksburg, but being unable to reduce them, he repeated his previous exploit—ran past them and communicated with the gunboats which had come down from Cairo.[23]

Getting in a jab at the militia, Upton adds, "Thus, before the middle of the year 1862, the Navy, that branch of the public defense which has always been national in its organization and training, had the honor of carrying the flag of the Union throughout the length of the Mississippi." In a reference to the next year's Vicksburg campaign, Upton notes, "one more movement was necessary to open the Mississippi and sever the Confederacy."[24]

The Union also used its naval superiority in the east, beginning in March to move the Army of the Potomac by water to the James and York rivers on the Peninsula of Virginia in another attempt to take Richmond. Upton wrote to his sister that month to share some thoughts not every sister would want to hear. "General McDowell reviewed his corps yesterday. . . . As he was riding along he asked, 'Which is Upton's battery?' which shows I am known to him. Give me one chance, and I shall be contented; and, if I don't acquit myself with honor, you will never see me again."[25]

In April 1862, there was another siege of Yorktown (eighty-one years after Lord Cornwallis surrendered to General Washington). On May 5, 1862, at

Williamsburg, Custer, now an aide to General George B. McClellan, fought against friends. He tells his sister about meeting one of them, John "Gimlet" Lea, in a letter of May 15, 1862:

> A classmate of mine was captain of one of the rebel regiments, and was taken prisoner after being badly wounded in the leg. I took care of him, and fed him for two days. When we first saw each other he shed tears and threw his arms about my neck, and we talked of old times and asked each other hundreds of questions about classmates on opposing sides. I carried his meals to him, gave him stockings of which he stood in need, and some money. This he did not want to take, but I forced it on him. He burst into tears and said it was more than he could stand. He insisted on writing in my notebook that if ever I should be taken prisoner he wanted me treated as he had been. His last words to me were, "God bless you, old boy!" The bystanders looked with surprise when we were talking, and afterwards asked if the prisoner were my brother.[26]

Custer later served as best man at Lea's wedding.

After leaving Williamsburg, John Barlow remarks, "Operations on the Chickahominy followed, in which we shared the comforts and discomforts of that swampy region with the rest of the army."[27] Upton comments on the Union's success at Fair Oaks: "Again, profiting by the information of Confederate reports, that on the 1st of June their troops retreated from Fair Oakes in great confusion, it his been alleged that a heroic commander might have marched into Richmond. But why did not General Grant, on being joined by the fresh army of General Buell at Shiloh, pursue Beauregard's shattered army into Corinth? The answer is, that military commanders on the spot, know after a battle the condition of their own army, while, unlike the critic, they do not know that of the enemy."[28]

At Fair Oaks, also known as Seven Pines, General Joseph E. Johnston received two wounds. His replacement was Robert E. Lee, who quickly displayed aggressiveness and a willingness to take casualties. During the last week of June 1862, outnumbered Confederates drove the Federals away from Richmond in the Seven Days' Battles, which included Mechanicsville (June 26), Gaines' Mill (June 27), Savage's Station (June 29), White Oak Swamp (June 30), and Malvern Hill (July 1). According to Barlow, "It was a hard week, fighting by day and marching by night; the two armies often so mixed up that friend and foe frequently camped side by side in the darkness, enjoying unwittingly a few peaceful hours in each other's company."[29]

At Malvern Hill, the Union army was on top of a superb defensive position. Barlow said, "It was like other great battles; the roar of artillery and

musketry was incessant, the stream of ordnance wagons bringing up ammunition uninterrupted, and the ambulances and field hospitals were taxed to
their utmost." To Barlow, "it seemed as though great results must follow; but,
notwithstanding the fact that we had beaten the enemy at all points, had
repulsed again and again his most reckless and determined charges, we were
to retire from the field as we had been doing for the past week."[30] By way of
Harrison's Landing, the Union army left the Peninsula.

Henry du Pont told his mother, "I am not at all surprised at the events
which have recently transpired in front of Richmond. As long as we have a
lawyer-politician for 'General in-chief' we may expect nothing but reverses.
I think that the assumption of supreme command by the secretary of war—
a man entirely devoid of military knowledge, is the most stupendous piece of
assurance ever rendered in history." After that denunciation of Edwin Stanton, du Pont makes a suggestion: "I see but little hope for a speedy termina-
tion of the contest unless a radical change be made. We must have a single
military head, so that the efforts of our different armies can be combined and
great strategical plans for the whole campaign harmoniously followed."[31]

Why was McClellan, so obviously reluctant to fight, still commanding
troops in May and June of 1862? Emory Upton has an explanation, noting
that "when the President looked about for a successor, no soldier had yet
proved himself worthy. In the West, General Grant had won no fame as an
independent commander; his victory at Shiloh at this particular moment
being considered a defeat. Sherman, still laboring under the charge of insanity, had not risen above a division."[32]

Upton also analyzes the cumulative effect of reverses—including McClellan's retreat, and Confederate General Bragg's invasion of Kentucky—on the
mind of the North. According to Upton, "The withdrawal of the Army of
the Potomac from the James River to Washington and Alexandria, the
retreat of the Army of Virginia from the Rappahannock to the Potomac, the
invasion of Maryland, and the retreat of the Army of the Ohio to Louisville,
produced a depression in the public mind nearly as great as that which succeeded the battle of Bull Run."[33]

If one looked at more than the eastern theater, as Upton had, Lee's invasion of Maryland in 1862—rather than Pennsylvania the next year—could
be considered the high tide of the Confederacy. (If one believes in the pri-
macy of the west and the irrelevancy of Gettysburg, First Bull Run could
be considered the high tide.) Lee took greater risks in Maryland than at
Gettysburg—dividing his army, not just his cavalry as in the Gettysburg

campaign—but managed to retreat into Virginia after taking enormous casualties at Antietam Creek.

One of the casualties at Antietam on September 17, 1862—the bloodiest day of the war—was Colonel Henry Walter Kingsbury, fourth in the class of May. Henry's wife, Eva Taylor, had a sister married to Confederate General David Rumph Jones. Henry's sister Mary was the wife of Confederate General Simon Buckner, who transferred Mary's Chicago real estate to Henry for the duration of the war. The origin of the Kingsbury fortune was explained by the elder Alfred Mordecai, who had a son in the class of June. At the time of the Black Hawk War, Mordecai said, "The site of the City of Chicago was then known only as the Military Post of Fort Dearborn, & when Genl-Scott's army passed through, my classmate Julius Kingsbury laid the foundation of a subsequent large fortune by investing a few hundred dollars in the purchase of land which proved to be afterwards in the centre of the City."[34]

At Antietam, while commanding a volunteer infantry regiment, Henry Kingsbury was shot four times. The troops who killed him were his brother-in-law's, whose grief was described, in the style of the time, by General James Longstreet: "One of those peculiarly painful personal experiences which are innumerable in war, but seldom get into print (save in fiction), came under my observation in this battle. Colonel H. W. Kingsbury, who was killed while gallantly leading the Eleventh Connecticut Regiment at the ford near Burnside Bridge, was a brother-in-law of General D. R. Jones, who commanded the Confederates immediately opposing him. His taking-off was a severe blow to Jones, and one from which he never recovered . . . gradually but hopelessly sinking, in a few months passed over to the silent majority to join his fallen kinsman."[35]

Kingsbury's classmates remembered him too. When Judson Kilpatrick wrote a play about the war, *Allatoona: An Historical and Military Drama*, the only classmate he put in it (besides himself) was Kingsbury, who plays a cadet at West Point. Henry du Pont wrote to his mother about Kingsbury's death, saying, "I feel very sorry for his poor wife, whom I have known very well for a number of years."[36] Kingsbury's widow, Eva Taylor, did not want to honor her husband's agreement with his sister, and it took a law suit before the Buckners won their share of the Kingsbury estate.

Emory Upton, commanding an artillery brigade in the First Division of the Sixth Corps, in a letter to his sister written ten days after Antietam, announces,

The pleasant campaign of Maryland has closed with the expulsion of the rebel invaders. From the time we left Alexandria . . . till the close of the battle of Antietam, I never spent any hours more agreeably or enjoyed myself better. We lived well, marched through a lovely country, had beautiful weather, magnificent scenery, and above all two glorious battles. At the battle [on September 14] of Crampton's Gap, although not actively engaged, I was under fire. It was, however, at the battle of Antietam that I had full swing. The artillery is a pretty arm. . . . From 2 P.M. till dark we fed the rebels on shells, spherical case, and solid shot. They . . . entertained us in like manner. . . . The sharp-shooters were very busy all the time, and annoyed us very much. . . . The infantry fighting was terrible. I do not believe there has been harder fighting this century than that between Hooker and the rebels in the morning. I have heard of the "dead lying in heaps," but never saw it till at this battle. Whole ranks fell together.[37]

Earlier in the year, Henry du Pont had told his mother, "I stood up at a grand wedding in Brooklyn. . . . Parsons [#13, June] of the 4th Art. was married. . . . The groom and groomsmen were in uniform."[38] On October 8, 1862, at Perryville—during Braxton Bragg's invasion of Kentucky—the courage of Charles Parsons was admired by both sides. Perhaps no battery commander ever received more praise after losing his guns. One Federal report said, "The conduct of First Lieut. C. C. Parsons, Fourth Artillery, who commanded an eight-gun battery manned by volunteers, cannot be too highly praised. He fought his guns nobly and drove back the advancing enemy, and not until overpowered by numbers did his men give way. Even then Lieutenant Parsons, deserted though he was, remained bravely at his post and had to be removed by force."[39]

An account of Parsons at Perryville by a Confederate chaplain is even more unusual. According to Charles Todd Quintard,

> The battle began at break of day by an artillery duel, the Federal battery being commanded by Colonel Charles Carroll Parsons and the Confederates by Captain William W. Carnes. Colonel Parsons was a graduate of West Point and Captain Carnes was a graduate of the Naval Academy at Annapolis. I took position upon an eminence at no great distance, commanding a fine view of the engagement, and there I watched. . . . Captain Carnes managed his battery with the greatest skill, killing and wounding nearly all the officers, men and horses connected with Parsons' battery. Parsons fought with great bravery and coolness and continued fighting a single gun until the Confederate infantry advanced. The officer in command ordered Colonel Parsons to be shot down. As the muskets were leveled at him, he drew his sword and stood at "parade rest," ready to receive the fire.

The Confederate Colonel was so impressed with this display of calm courage that he ordered the guns lowered, saying: "No! you shall not shoot down such a brave man!" And Colonel Parsons was allowed to walk off the field.

In a reference to their postwar careers, Quintard adds, "Subsequently I captured Colonel Parsons for the ministry of the Church in the Diocese of Tennessee."[40]

In addition to displaying bravery on the battlefield, a young commander could win support from his men by looking out for them in camp. On December 7, 1862, Emory Upton wrote to his sister from Belle Plain, Virginia, noting,

> Day before yesterday our brigade marched to this point, the confluence of the Potomac River and Potomac Creek. When we arrived it was snowing and quite cold, and we had to encamp on the plain. There were no woods to break the wind, no wood to build fires, and the men were wet to the skin; the ground was covered with snow and water, and with but a thin shelter-tent over their heads, and nothing but the cold ground to lie on and one blanket for a covering, you can imagine how the poor soldiers fared that night. Yesterday it was clear and cold, and last night colder than any night last winter. The ice froze thick enough to bear a horse. Today I took the regiment from the plain to the woods—dense cedar and a high ridge—to protect them from the wind, and to-night they are very comfortable. . . . I like the regiment very much. The men know that they will be taken care of, and they are quite contented.[41]

At Fredericksburg, Virginia, on December 13, 1862, John Pelham distinguished himself again. He commanded the Confederate horse artillery, which Jeb Stuart had described in a January letter to his brother-in-law John R. Cooke, noting, "It is called the 'Stuart Horse Artillery' and is commanded by Captain John Pelham—a graduate of May last."[42]

Robert E. Lee described the opening of the battle of Fredericksburg and Pelham's part in it: "Shortly after 9 A.M. the partial rising of the mist disclosed a large force moving in line of battle against Jackson. Dense masses appeared in front of A. P. Hill, stretching far up the river in the direction of Fredericksburg. As they advanced, Major Pelham, of Stuart's Horse Artillery, who was stationed near the Port Royal road with one section, opened a rapid and well-directed enfilade fire, which arrested their progress. Four batteries immediately turned upon him, but he sustained their heavy fire with the unflinching courage that ever distinguished him."[43]

A famous account appears in the eccentric Heros von Borcke's *Memoirs of the Confederate War for Independence*. According to Borcke,

Pelham . . . begged Stuart to allow him to advance two of his light pieces to the fork of the road where the turnpike branches off to Fredericksburg, as from this point the masses of the enemy offered him an easy target. The permission being given, Pelham went off with his two guns at a gallop, amidst the loud cheering of the cannoneers, and in a few minutes his solid shot were ploughing at short range with fearful effect through the dense columns of the Federals. The boldness of the enterprise and the fatal accuracy of the firing seemed to paralyze for a time and then to stampede the whole of the extreme left of the Yankee army, and terror and confusion reigned there during some minutes: soon, however, several batteries moved into position, and uniting with several of those on the Stafford Heights, concentrated a tremendous fire upon our guns, one of which, a Blakely gun, was quickly disabled and compelled to withdraw. . . I was now sent by General Stuart to tell Pelham to retire if he thought the proper moment had arrived, but the young hero could not be moved. "Tell the General I can hold my ground," he said, and again and again pealed out the ringing report of his single gun, upon which at one time 32 pieces of the enemy's artillery were brought to bear in a sweeping cross-fire, which killed and wounded many of the men, so that at last Pelham had to assist himself in loading and aiming it. Three times the summons to retire was renewed; but not until the last round of ammunition had been discharged . . . did the gallant officer succumb to necessity in abandoning his position.[44]

While watching Pelham sustain heavy fire, Lee is reported to have said, "It is glorious to see such courage in one so young!"[45] Like Lord Nelson—whose "Nelson touch" was described by Joseph Conrad—Pelham had an effect on those above and below him. Novelist John Esten Cooke, a friend on Jeb Stuart's staff, celebrated Pelham. Another friend, W. W. Blackford, said that you could be with him for months and not know that he had been in a single fight. His roommate at West Point, Tom Rosser, called Pelham the mildest man he ever knew out of a fight and the fiercest in one.

Adelbert Ames, who became colonel of the Twentieth Maine on August 29, 1862, and had briefly been John Pelham's roommate, reflects on uses of courage for a young commander in a letter to his parents. "Up to the battle of Fredericksburg," according to Ames, "I have been somewhat disliked by my men and officers, but at that battle the feelings in the Regt. changed completely. I was the only Colonel in the brigade who went in front of his Regt. and led his men into the fight. All of my men who were killed and wounded (thirty-six) were in rear of me when struck. My men now have confidence in me."[46]

The Vicksburg Campaign

Peter Conover Hains, who fired the signal gun at Bull Run, was still alive when *The Military Engineer* published his article "The Vicksburg Campaign" in its issue of May–June 1921. At Vicksburg, he was the chief engineer of the Thirteenth Corps in the Union Army of the Tennessee. According to Hains,

> The annals of history do not disclose the story of a military campaign of greater interest than the campaign of Vicksburg fought by Gen. U. S. Grant in 1863, nor one that teaches better the lessons of grand tactics. Grant had already proved himself a great general on other fields, but the Vicksburg Campaign stands out in bold relief as the most daring and at the same time the most completely successful one in all the career of this remarkable man. . . . Grant was no stickler for the rules either of strategy or logistics as laid down in the books. It is probable that he never opened a book on those subjects after he left West Point. He followed the dictates of common sense, and he had more of that commodity in his make-up than most men. . . . the rules of strategy are based on common sense. One fundamental rule, is that it is wise to do that which your antagonist does not think you will do, and to avoid doing that which he thinks you will do. This rule of common sense was followed by Grant in the entire Vicksburg Campaign, as well as other of his campaigns, both before and after. It contributed in no small measure to his success."[1]

David D. Porter, U.S.N., commander of the gunboats, also contributed, running the Vicksburg batteries on the night of April 16, 1863, with eight gunboats and three unarmed steamboats, losing only one of the latter. Grand Gulf was thirty-three miles south of Vicksburg, and Hains reports, "General Grant and Admiral Porter held a conference on the question of landing, and it was decided to try to effect one on the water front of Grand Gulf itself."[2] Hains gives the result as well as his opinion of Grant:

At 8 A.M. on the 29th of April the gunboats went into action, and kept up a steady bombardment for five hours. . . . At the end of this time, no visible impression having been made on the batteries, the gunboats . . . withdrew out of range. After another conference between Porter and Grant, it was determined that it was not wise to resume the fight. . . . Herein Grant displayed that keen judgment for which he was so noted, for if an attempt had been made to land our troops on that shore front, we would surely have been repulsed. It was decided in an interview between Grant and Porter, after the engagement, that a landing must be found lower down the river. We now had a sufficient number of transports and barges to ferry the army over the river with some rapidity. But we had no time to waste, for we could not expect our enemy was going to make no further resistance to our landing.[3]

They could not expect it, but that is what they found when Grant had them land further south at Bruinsburg on April 30, 1863. Hains gives some observations of an army engineer:

To cross a river of moderate size in the face of an alert and enterprising foe, of about equal strength, is as a rule, no easy proposition. The difficulties are not lessened if the river is very deep, very wide, and with a 5-mile current. Ordinarily your adversary would be watching you from his side and would be prepared to give you an enemy's welcome . . . but when we landed there was not a Confederate picket or patrol in sight. No one but a poor old negro, who was anxious to lead us to a corral where he said there were a number of horses. As very few of us had horses, this was welcome news and we proceeded to benefit by that information.[4]

Supplying the army with food was not as difficult as Hains had expected. "When we landed," he says, "we had no idea of the piece of good luck that had fallen into our hands. The land was literally flowing with milk and honey. There was bacon and beef in abundance, corn meal and all the eatables that a hungry soldier, who had been floundering for six months in mud and swamps, could want. Not the least welcome of all things was good dry ground on which to sleep with no mosquitoes to keep us awake."[5]

"But where was the enemy?" Hains asks. He answers his question by observing, "Evidently the Confederate commander had been completely hoodwinked into the idea that Grant's main attack was to be on his right flank at Haynes Bluff, so he reinforced that flank and left the other to take care of itself."[6]

Hains adds, "It was a serious blunder when on April 29th, Pemberton mistook the demonstration against his right flank, made by Sherman, for a real attack and the real one on his left flank made by Grant for a feint."[7] Contributing to the indecision of Confederate commander John C. Pemberton, class of 1837, was Federal Colonel Benjamin Henry Grierson's magnificent diversionary raid (April 17 to May 2) through central Mississippi, which started in La Grange, Tennessee, and ended in Baton Rouge, Louisiana, spreading confusion along and beyond the route.

The article by Hains is both analysis and reminiscence from a staff officer who had a good vantage point for both. "One conspicuous blunder made by our adversaries was in failing to make any provision whatever for an attack from the south. The problem for the Confederate Army was to prevent the crossing of the Mississippi River by the Union forces in such numbers as would threaten the capture of Vicksburg or the destruction of the Confederate Army protecting it."[8]

Hains continues, "It is obvious that if the crossing of the river could be prevented the object of the Confederate Army of the Mississippi would be achieved. . . . The problem then was to prevent the crossing, and, failing that, to meet Grant's army in the field before it could be concentrated for attack. Pemberton made no effort to prevent our crossing the river, nor did he make any effort to attack us. He merely waited, apparently, to see what Grant would do. The waiting policy," Hains points out, "is well known to military men to be dangerous, and is only justified when *it is known* that one's forces are greatly inferior in numbers or morale to those of one's antagonists."[9]

It is obvious from Hains's account that one of the things Pemberton mishandled was his cavalry. Hains observes, "If ever a defensive campaign was fought where a force of cavalry would have had telling effect, it was the Vicksburg Campaign. When Grant crossed the Mississippi River, he did not have a single squadron of cavalry with him. Indeed, he had none to speak of at any time during the campaign." To highlight the contrast, Hains lists twenty Confederate cavalry units, remarking, "even though some may have been mere skeletons, it would seem that a respectable cavalry force could have been organized. An insignificant force of cavalry patrolling the shore from Vicksburg to Rodney could have kept Pemberton advised of the position of Grant's force, the number of transports, the position of Porter's fleet, and other items of information of value to a commanding general. A good brigade of cavalry under a competent officer could have delayed Grant at the landing until the whole of Bowen's Division could have been deployed along the bluff."[10]

Almost thirty years later, Hains recalled the marches and battles leading to the siege of Vicksburg in a paper read to the Loyal Legion in Washington.

"We crossed the Mississippi river, on April 30, 1863," Hains told an audience in 1891, "and pushed rapidly into the interior of the State of Mississippi. Within a period of eighteen days the Army of the Tennessee met and vanquished the foe on the fields of Port Gibson, Raymond, Jackson, Champion Hills, and Black River Bridge, so that, when we closed in on Vicksburg, that army felt itself equal to any emergency. It is not strange that our great commander should have participated in that feeling."[11]

Grant's decision to storm the Vicksburg defenses in May was defended by Hains in his article as well as in his speech. "As the Confederates were supposed to be very demoralized as well as disorganized," Hains reports in *The Military Engineer*,

> an attempt was made on the 19th to carry the defenses of Vicksburg by assault before the enemy had time to recover their morale. It failed. After the enemy got behind their line of works they seemed to recover their spirits and made a good defense. The 20th and 21st were spent in pushing our lines up close to their works and in getting our artillery in position. . . . On the morning of the 22nd after a severe bombardment of the enemy lasting two hours, from all the guns in position, about 200, aided by all the guns and mortars of Porter's fleet in the river, a fierce assault was made along the whole line, but this was also repulsed. The men who could not apparently fight in the open now fought like demons behind their fortifications. Some of our regiments succeeded in planting their colors on the parapets, but they could advance no further. That night after dark our troops were withdrawn to more secure positions and siege operations were ordered to begin at once. But we had no tools and had to wait for them to be sent from the North.

Hains remarks, "The siege lasted just 42 days," adding "only two over the number laid down in the books as allowable."[12]

Hains later asks, "Did Grant make any blunders?" He answers his own question, saying, "In the light of all the information now available, and which was not available at the time, it must be conceded that Grant made no blunders. Some mistakes of judgment he made, but they were few. It is believed his worst mistake was made when on May 22d he ordered an assault along the entire line in an effort to carry the enemy's works by storm. However, he had good reasons for it at the time. It was a case of assault or siege. If an assault succeeded a siege would be avoided. If it did not, a siege would follow as a matter of course."[13]

In Hains's view, "Grant made a mistake when, on May 22nd, he yielded his better judgment to the importunities of his subordinate, General McClernand, commanding the 13th Army Corps (in the center of the line of investment), who called for reinforcements to support an alleged capture of part of the enemy's works and requested that a diversion be made in his favor by a renewal of the attacks of Sherman and McPherson on their fronts."[14]

Hains was in an excellent position to comment on the controversial decisions of that day. As he notes,

> The writer was with General McClernand all day of May 22, being a member of his staff. He remembers that General McClernand received a piece of an envelope purporting to come from Colonel Stone of the 22d Iowa Infantry, who was at that time in the ditch of the redoubt, saying in substance that he held part of the fort and needed the support of reinforcements, or words to that effect. When we saw prisoners (about a dozen) come out of the end of the redoubt, General McClernand remarked in substance that we had possession, for there were Confederate prisoners coming into our lines. The writer remarked, in substance, "Yes, General, there are prisoners coming in sure, but we have not possession of the works," and in support of his statement, called attention to the fact that just at that moment one of our soldiers lying on the superior slope of the redoubt, rolled back in the ditch, killed by a Confederate soldier inside.[15]

Hains gives unusual importance to the exploits of one sergeant, Joseph Griffith, of Company I, Twenty-second Iowa Infantry, who captured a dozen Confederates and their lieutenant in one compartment and brought them all to General McClernand's headquarters. Hains recalls, "When Griffith related the manner of his capturing so many prisoners . . . the writer turned to the Confederate officer and asked him if he had surrendered with all those men to that boy (Griffith was only 19 years old at that time). He replied in an angry tone, 'What the hell could we do? My men had all discharged their guns and he had that rifle.'"[16]

Yet, in Hains's opinion,

> This exhibition of courage on the part of Sergeant Griffith proved to be a most unfortunate incident, for it seemed to convince General McClernand that we had actual possession of a part of the enemy's works, and it may have been the chief cause of his sending word to Grant to that effect. From a technical point of view, McClernand was within the bounds of truth when he stated that we had possession of "a part of the enemy's works." The ditch was unquestionably a part of the enemy's redoubt, and we had possession of it for several hours. . . . The ditch was, in fact, a trap. We could not advance, nor could we retreat. . . . Grant undoubtedly assumed, as he had a right to assume from the dispatches he received, that McClernand had possession of something of value. These dispatches to Grant (there were two

of the same tenor), which caused him to issue the unfortunate order to resume the attack on the other corps fronts, did not tend to heal the feeling of antagonism that existed between these two men.[17]

Hains was not the only 1861 graduate on McClernand's staff. Wright Rives (#42, May) was the son of influential editor John Cook Rives, a member of Andrew Jackson's "Kitchen Cabinet," who founded the *Congressional Globe* and, with Francis P. Blair Sr., the *Washington Globe*. The younger Rives had been serving unhappily on General McClernand's staff since April 14, 1862. In June of that year, Rives had complained to Andrew Johnson, his father's friend who would become president, that he had "nothing to do, and all what I have done so far could be done, by a child in two hours."[18]

Further explaining Grant's decision to try to storm Vicksburg, Hains observes, "The Army of the Tennessee was not prepared for a siege. It had no entrenching tools whatever and they could not be had in much less than ten days or two weeks from the North. There were no engineer troops in his army. Hot weather was coming on and with it would come much sickness. We were liable to be attacked in the rear by an army that it was known was being formed under Johnston for Pemberton's relief, and it was possible the relieving army might be larger than Grant could cope with in addition to that of Pemberton."[19]

Although Hains was an engineer, he does not neglect the importance of morale: "Moreover, the men themselves were averse to settling down to the hard labors of a siege until after a trial had been made to take the place by storm. The men felt after the successful assaults on the works at Jackson and Black River Bridge that they were well nigh invincible. These reasons, it is believed, were sufficient to justify the order."[20] At Black River, on May 17, Brigadier General Michael Kelly Lawler (who was born in County Kildare, Ireland) broke the Confederate line with a charge of his brigade, taking over eleven hundred prisoners.

Hains says,

> The siege of Vicksburg officially began on May 23rd, the day after the unsuccessful assault. In reality, it did not begin until about June 1st, as up to that time there were not tools to work with. The ground for the most part on the hills around Vicksburg was dry and hard. . . . Picks were essential as well as shovels, and it is believed there were not 100 picks in the whole army. In the early days of the siege, there were only two officers of Engineers serving in their professional capacity as engineers, Captain Fred Prime and the writer. Two others were in the Army of the Tennessee, Major General

McPherson, commanding the 17th Army Corps, and Lieutenant Colonel James H. Wilson, who was Grant's Inspector General. Captains Comstock, McAllister and J. M. Wilson arrived after the siege was half over.[21]

Under an illustration in his 1921 article, Hains includes this caption: "Map of the country between Millikens Bend, La., and Jackson, Miss., showing route followed by the Army of the Tennessee. Taken from Atlas accompanying official records. . . . Original map prepared under the direction of Lieutenant-Colonel J. H. Wilson, A.I.G., and First Lieutenant Engineers. Surveys by First Lieutenant P. C. Hains, U.S. Engineers."[22]

One can only imagine what Lieutenant Hains thought of fraternization between blue and gray from the following example of it that he includes:

> The unscientific way in which some of the siege work was carried on is illustrated in the establishment of the second parallel in front of the 13th Corps. Lawler's Brigade, composed chiefly of Iowa troops, occupied a part of the line just where a wide deep ravine existed in front of them. The crest of the near side of this ravine was occupied by our people and that of the farther side by the Confederates. The two sets of pickets being close enough to engage in conversation (they were not more than 50 feet apart) soon became sociable and made an agreement not to fire on each other without giving warning. The Confederate picket line was exactly on the ground that we wanted for a part of the second parallel. The writer notified General Lawler that he wished to occupy that ground and requested him to advance his pickets when the two lines took their places for the night.
>
> On the evening of June the 20th, the two guards deployed and started forward from their works at a double-quick on the sounding of retreat, each trying to get as far forward as possible. In this double advance the two picket lines met and then passed each other before they could be halted. It was a novel situation. Our pickets were inside the Confederate line and their pickets were inside of ours, but as neither side could fire on the other without giving warning, according to agreement, a parley was held and it was agreed that the two lines should be established as they stood, the Confederates taking the line occupied by our pickets and ours taking the place of the Confederates.

Hains adds, "Agreements not to fire on each other were put into effect in other parts of the line and often men and officers met between the lines and settled the issues of the war in the most amicable manner."[23]

Continuing his analysis of Confederate mistakes, Hains notes, "The idea that Vicksburg was designed to protect a field army, and the field army was to protect Vicksburg, are incompatible. These duties were not dependent upon each other. If there was a field army, its place was in the field, not around Vicksburg. The army of the Mississippi was a field army, or, at least, it was used as such, and yet it was a garrison army as well. As a field army it was too small. As a garrison army it was too large."[24]

To Hains,

Vicksburg, itself, was of no special value to the Confederacy except insofar as the guns mounted on the river front closed the river to navigation. How, then, were these guns to be protected? The answer to that question depends on the answer to the further question. By what would their destruction be threatened? Certainly not by a cavalry raid nor by the navy alone operating from the river. The menace could only come from a field army, and the menacing army must be met by an opposing field army. The batteries could not be protected by chaining the army to the guns, but by giving it mobility.

History abounds in records of armies that have taken refuge in fortresses where there was a large civil population. Such civil population is a great hindrance to the defense. It is an aggravated hindrance when supplies from the outside are in danger of being cut off. In that case the fortress generally falls a victim of starvation, if not to the superior force of the enemy.

Hains goes on to say,

It is easy to criticize, but not always easy to suggest a course that would forestall criticism. In this case, however, certain things were obvious at the time. For instance, a strongly entrenched camp should have been established from which a mobile army could operate on the front, flank or rear of an invading army from the south. The next thing in order was the creating of a field army out of whatever forces were in the Department of the Mississippi or could be brought there. For this purpose every place of minor importance should have been altogether abandoned. If not abandoned, they should have been temporarily occupied by detachments only. . . . The field army concentrated in an entrenched camp midway between Vicksburg and Jackson would have protected Vicksburg on one flank and Jackson on the other.[25]

When Pemberton surrendered, there were some surprises for the engineer of the Thirteenth Corps. "On July 4th the Confederates stacked their arms just outside their works and," says Hains, "we took possession of them. We found they had better rifles than we had, that they still had a small supply of ammunition, but they had nothing to eat. Soldiers cannot fight without something to eat, so they surrendered." Hains further recalls, "Pemberton was a fine looking soldier in steel gray uniform as he sat down at the table to sign the document of capitulation, but one looking at him at the time could not help pitying him. He was a broken man. He had staked everything on a policy of defense, which he doubtless realized too late was a mistake. He had now lost Vicksburg and his army as well."[26]

Hains was more surprised at what Grant had done:

> The magnitude of Grant's victory was amazing, even to ourselves. He totally destroyed an army almost as large as his own, captured . . . guns of all calibers, besides about 60,000 muskets, caused the surrender of Port Hudson with all its armament and about 6,000 more men, opened the Mississippi River to the navigation of the great northwest, broke the Confederacy into two pieces, destroyed almost absolutely all communication of the Confederacy with foreign nations, cut in two the lines of supply the Confederacy had established to Mexico, and carried dismay to the hearts of the southern people, many of whom saw in the fall of Vicksburg the downfall of the southern Confederacy. All these results were accomplished with a loss on the part of the Union forces of about 10,000 men.[27]

Hains then asks, "To what can the magnificent success of the campaign be attributed? Certainly not to overwhelming numbers in Grant's Army. The field army of the Tennessee was not greatly different from that of the Confederate Army of the Mississippi. To what then can we reasonably attribute the magnitude of the victory? First and foremost it was due to the fact not known to everybody at that time that the army of the Tennessee was commanded by one of the greatest generals in history, and had two of the best corps commanders that the Civil War produced."

Hains concludes, "To sum up in a few words, the success of the campaign was due, first, to Grant's ability as a general, second, to the valor of his army, and third, to the blunders of his adversary."[28] According to Hains in 1921, "With Lee's failure at Gettysburg at the same time, the war should have then ended, for it was evident to the people of the South, as well as the North that a further struggle to disrupt the union of states was hopeless." Hains ends by explaining why the garrison surrendered to Grant. "We now found," says Hains, "that our prisoners amounted to no less than 31,000 men, including the sick. The Confederates . . . had made a gallant defense, but there could be no fight in men who were starving. . . . Our Commanding General, with characteristic generosity, granted liberal terms to the enemy, which, while it saved their honor, destroyed their capacity for further mischief."[29]

Grant also had a high opinion of Hains. On June 16, 1865, Grant would endorse one of Hains's letters, saying, "Capt Haines is a most excellent officer and was by me recommended for the Colonelcy of a N. J. regiment more than a year since."[30]

When he wrote his memoirs, Grant recalled the Vicksburg Campaign in April 1863. "On the 17th," Grant says,

I visited New Carthage in person, and saw that the process of getting troops through in the way we were doing was so tedious that a better method must be devised. . . . Four bridges had to be built across bayous, two of them each over six hundred feet long, making about two thousand feet of bridging in all. The river falling made the current in these bayous very rapid, increasing the difficulty of building and permanently fastening these bridges; but the ingenuity of the "Yankee soldier" was equal to any emergency. The bridges were soon built of such material as could be found near by, and so substantial were they that not a single mishap occurred in crossing all the army with artillery, cavalry and wagon trains, except the loss of one siege gun (a thirty-two pounder). This, if my memory serves me correctly, broke through the only pontoon bridge we had in all our march across the peninsula. These bridges were all built by McClernand's command, under the supervision of Lieutenant Hains of the Engineer Corps.[31]

Gettysburg

In the east, 1863 would also see Confederate "capacity for further mischief" reduced, but at a heavy price. John B. Williams (#26, May), who had fought at Bull Run, Yorktown, and Malvern Hill, was dismissed on February 11, 1863, for what would later be called combat fatigue. Orville E. Babcock noted on February 13, 1863, "Wrote to Cross. Visited Wall St. Received present of a sword and belt. Very nice." The next day, Babcock, who was third in the class of May, remarked, "Met Kent [#31, May] on Broadway & concluded to go to West Point. . . . Met all of classmates at Dresser's room."[1]

George Warren Dresser (#19, May), who was also a graduate of Andover, was serving as assistant instructor of artillery tactics at West Point when Babcock visited. Dresser was a staff officer, later becoming inspector of the Fifth Army Corps (1864–1865). Adelbert Ames said, "Dresser . . . the second ranking officer in our class in the corps of cadets, served most honorably in the Civil War. His duty as a cadet officer threw him among the southerners. He . . . was respected by all."[2]

The first in the class to become famous, John Pelham, was killed in a cavalry charge in Virginia on March 17, 1863. There was grief throughout the South. Jeb Stuart issued a General Order of March 19—"The noble, the chivalric, the gallant Pelham is no more"—which gave Pelham a place in the Dictionary of Military and Naval Quotations.[3] Pelham's place—best man at Tom Rosser's wedding in May to Elizabeth ("Betty") Barbara Winston—went to another man from West Point's D Company, James Dearing, class of 1862. Rosser said of Pelham, "The army loved him."[4] Another classmate, Ford Kent, serving in the Union army, told his own sisters, "poor Pelham . . . was killed at Kelly's Ford, (Southern service,) he was a gallant fellow."[5]

In a letter of April 8, 1863, Jeb Stuart told his wife, "Poor Pelham's death has created a great sensation all over the country. He was noble in every sense of the word; I want Jimmie to be just like him." Stuart also talks to his wife about the child they are expecting, asking, "An important question—What shall it be named?. . . If a boy, I wish him to be called John Pelham Stuart. I have thought of it much—it is my choice. His record is complete and it is spotless. It is noble. His family was the very best. His character was pure, his disposition as sweet and innocent as our own little Flora's."[6]

At Chancellorsville, on the second day, May 3, 1863, Justin E. Dimick, commanding Battery H, First U.S. Artillery, was described by Captain Thomas Osborn, chief of artillery, Second Division, Third Corps:

> At 5 o'clock in the morning, the enemy attacked us in force, and, after a very severe fight by our men, the Federal line began to fall back. From the first moment I learned the position of the enemy, I played upon him with the artillery, the section in the road using very short fuse and canister as the enemy moved to and fro. In the movement of this section, securing and defending the front of our line from the persistent attacks of the enemy, notwithstanding its own exposed condition, and under a most galling fire from the rebel sharpshooters and line of battle, Lieutenant Dimick showed the skill and judgment of an accomplished artillery officer and the intrepid bravery of the truest soldier. After holding this position for upward of an hour, his men fighting bravely, but falling rapidly around him (his horse being shot under him), and our infantry crowding back until his flanks were exposed, I gave him the order to limber and fall back. In doing this his horses became entangled in the harness, and in freeing them he received a shot in the foot. This wound he hid from his men, but in a moment received one in the spine, and from the effects of it died in two days after. I would, if possible, here pay a slight tribute to his memory, but I cannot. He was an educated and accomplished officer, just budding into the full vigor of manhood. As a line officer he has shown fine abilities, and on the battle-field was unsurpassed for gallantry.[7]

He was twenty-three.

At Chancellorsville, Lieutenant Edmund Kirby, tenth in the class of May, commanded Battery I, First U.S. Artillery. The compiler of one biographical dictionary thought Kirby, who remained in the artillery, "had perhaps the most singular career of any officer who took part in the Civil War."[8] Charles Morgan, chief of artillery for the Second Corps, gives an account of Kirby on the second day: "The Fifth Maine Battery was in position near the Chancellor house . . . it was exposed to a most destructive fire, badly cut up. . . . Lieutenant Kirby was placed in command of it about 9 A.M. by General

Couch, and was dangerously wounded. . . . It is due to the brave and gallant Kirby that a permanent record be made of his conduct. His thigh was fractured by a ball from a spherical case shot, yet when it was proposed to move him from the field he exclaimed, 'No! take off that gun first.'"[9]

Kirby's leg was amputated, but he did not recover. Fanny Ricketts, wife of General James Ricketts, cared for Kirby while he was dying at twenty-three. His father, Colonel Edmund Kirby, an army paymaster, had died in 1849. Kirby's maternal grandfather was Major General Jacob Brown, commander of the United States Army (1815–1828). At West Point—in response to a request from Oliver Otis Howard for a letter about his religious life—Kirby mentioned that when he was a small boy, his mischief was overlooked by townspeople because of "the respect . . . for my parents."[10] That respect was shared by several generals who wanted Kirby's mother to get a decent pension. On May 28, 1863, Kirby received a deathbed promotion from lieutenant to brigadier general from Abraham Lincoln.

After Chancellorsville, Orville Babcock noted perceptively, "News of Hooker's defeat, not as bad as might be."[11] But the casualty list was enormous. Ford Kent, after talking about Dimick and Kirby (and Rosser, who he thinks was killed), tells his sisters on May 12, 1863, "Others, nonclassmates, but good friends, were also killed in this last terrible fight. I wish indeed I were well out of it, & if I can, I will be! I think of making an application for the Commissary Dept."[12]

Colonel Rosser, Fifth Virginia Cavalry, also wrote on the same day: "The army is quiet, and unless Gen. R. E. Lee advances, I think there will be no fighting for some time. Stuart commanded Gen. Jackson's Corps after J was wounded and seems to have shown great skill in the management of it. He read me a portion of a letter from Gen. R. E. Lee last night in which he was very highly complimented indeed—I think Stuart will be made Lt. Gen. of Cav'y very soon and in such an event I will expect to get the much talked of Brig."[13] On May 20, Rosser mentions a member of the class of June to Elizabeth Winston, who was to become his wife in eight days, saying, "I invited Col. Young to act as Groomsman yesterday which he seemed delighted at."[14]

The fatalities among Rosser and Kent's classmates did not stop during the two months between Chancellorsville and Gettysburg. Charles Cross (#2, May), died at Franklin's Crossing, Virginia, on June 5, 1863. Adelbert Ames said, "Cross, the best beloved of our class, was killed by a rebel bullet while throwing a bridge across the Rappahanock River."[15] Babcock wrote in his diary, "Heard of Cross's death. Too bad, too bad. No other news. The above enough."[16]

On June 8, Lee reviewed his cavalry near Culpeper, Virginia, and Rosser recalled, "when it was announced to the cavalry, just after the review, that it should move to the front and upon the enemy across the Rappahannock on the morrow, the joyous news was received with the wildest enthusiasm." They were going, Rosser said, "to try our luck in an aggressive war."[17] The next day at Brandy Station, they had the largest cavalry battle of the war, with Rosser noting, "the Federal cavalry was improving and fought better on this occasion than ever before."[18]

In a cavalry clash of June 17, Rosser would have a chance to fight classmate Judson Kilpatrick. According to the Report of Colonel Thomas L. Rosser, Fifth Virginia Cavalry, "I caused sabers to be drawn, and charged immediately . . . I drove the enemy upon his main body, which was in the town of Aldie."[19] Rosser later said, "Our losses were heavy. My regiment alone lost 58 men in killed, wounded and captured."[20] According to Rosser, the Union cavalry commander, General Pleasonton, "had recognized and rewarded the merits of some of his young and enterprising officers such as Kilpatrick and Custer."[21] Custer's reward—command of the Second Brigade in Kilpatrick's Third Cavalry Division—came on June 29, 1863, along with promotion to brigadier general of U.S. Volunteers. Custer was twenty-three.

The day before Custer's promotion, Henry du Pont, at Fort Hamilton, New York, told his mother, "Great events seem to be hastening. I am sorry to say that I cannot see, much as I desire it, any thing very satisfactory in store for us. I only trust that we may be spared any great disasters." In the same letter, du Pont discusses his qualifications for analyzing recent military events: "When I say my views . . . they are . . . merely some of the ideas which I have gained from the books I have studied at West Point, etc. As to other views and facts connected with the . . . campaigns I have certainly had superior advantages in knowing the truth from eye-witnesses and actual participants than those whose notions are derived from what they see in the newspapers."[22]

Du Pont was not the only member of his class who wanted to share his views on the war. Judson Kilpatrick's "Lee at Gettysburg" would appear in the May 1871 issue of *Our Magazine* in response to an article with the same title by Confederate General John D. Imboden in *Galaxy*. Robert E. Lee died the year before the piece by Kilpatrick was published, which states, "Since the death of the Confederate chief, General Lee, his friends have spared no pains to immortalize his name, and convince the world that he was a great general . . . yet I submit to General Imboden that it would have been better for his purpose . . . if he had written his recollections of some one of Lee's defensive battles or campaigns, in which alone he was great." Continuing his criticism of Lee, Kilpatrick states, "And his last grand offensive campaign, culminating in disaster and ruin to his army and the Confederacy at Gettysburg, even convinced him, if it did not his historians, that he could not plan and successfully carry out an offensive campaign."[23]

A member of the June class and the Army of Northern Virginia, Colonel Pierce Young, commanding Cobb's (Georgia) Legion in Wade Hampton's cavalry brigade, later emphasized the crucial role of the Federal commanding general. In characteristic remarks—which made both blue and gray look good—U.S. Congressman Young would speak in 1874 in support of a bill granting a pension to Mrs. Margaretta Meade, wife of Major General George G. Meade: "But no man who did not serve in the army in which I had the honor to serve during the desperate campaign of Gettysburgh can appreciate the vigor and ability with which he handled his army on that great occasion, and during that entire campaign. He took command of the Army of the Potomac when it was partially demoralized by many defeats, and by his energy, courage, and ability brought it to that state of efficiency which enabled it to achieve a victory to which you probably owe the safety of your capital and the perpetuation of your Union."[24]

A sympathetic account of Lee appears in *Gettysburg*, by John J. Garnett of the class of June, published in 1888 for the Cyclorama of the Battle of Gettysburg. Lieutenant Colonel Garnett commanded a Confederate artillery battalion in Henry Heth's division containing these batteries: the Donaldsonville (Louisiana) Artillery, commanded by Captain Victor Maurin, a businessman born in 1818 who was twice Garnett's age; the Huger (Virginia) Artillery, Captain Joseph D. Moore; the Lewis (Virginia) Artillery, Captain John W. Lewis; and the Norfolk Light Artillery Blues, Captain C. R. Grandy.

In Major General Richard H. Anderson's division, the Sumter (Georgia) Artillery battalion was commanded by Garnett's classmate Major John Lane. William Pendleton had noted in a letter of February 11, 1863, to Robert E. Lee, "Captain Lane is from Oregon, though accredited to Georgia."[25] Garnett says,

I recall that Gen. Lee . . . issued a strict order forbidding any of the troops . . . to indulge in any species of foraging or raiding on the private property of the people through whose possessions they should pass. . . . I recall an amusing incident . . . on the day before the great fight began. I saw a number of my men . . . in pursuit of several fine porkers, turkeys, and other fowl.

. . . Calling my Adjutant, I ordered him to have the men brought into the ranks at once and to compel them to quit their plundering. Hungry men do not take kindly to discipline, and my Adjutant succeeded poorly. . . . While these depredations were going on the venerable old Dunker who owned the mansion . . . calmly sat on the porch and watched his despoilment in the most philosophical manner. Anxious to make amends, so far as my own con-science was concerned, I leaped the fence with my horse and rode up to where the old Dunker was sitting. "At what do you value your loss?" I said. "It is of no account," he answered. "The Town Council has given you per-mission to take all you find, and if they don't pay me, Abe Lincoln will."[26]

Garnett gives the location of the Confederate picket line on June 30 and the possible extent of the Confederate advance when he says, "At 9:30. . . morning, Gen. Hill, with a portion of his corps, advanced on the Cham-bersburg turnpike as far as the crest of Seminary Hill, half a mile northwest of Gettysburg, throwing about two dozen pickets as far down as a house, on the outskirts of the village, owned at that time by a man named Shead."[27] On the first of July, Garnett recalls,

The corps (A. P. Hill's) with which my command was moving occupied positions along the turnpike from Chambersburg to Gettysburg. . . . Not expecting the battle to open so soon I had ordered my horses to be taken inside a large field of clover . . . giving orders, however, that they be kept in harness and under the charge of drivers, who must be ready to hitch up and move forward at a moment's notice. A short time had elapsed when I heard the roar of musketry at the front. It came to me with that peculiar sound not unlike the rumble of a train of cars approaching at a distance, and I realized that the battle of Gettysburg had begun. . . . Calling my bugler to my side, I told him to hold himself in readiness to sound "Boots and saddles," as I expected every moment an order from the front to get my batteries into position on our line of battle. . . . Looking up the turnpike some consider-able time after the engagement had begun I saw a courier dashing madly along past the bodies of troops that were moving forward. Coming up to where I sat on a rail fence he handed me an order from Gen. Hill to at once move my battalion to a position indicated and relieve Major Pegram's bat-talion of artillery which had been engaged since the action commenced. In less time than it takes to write it we were galloping down the road to the front.[28]

The battalion commander's account shows an unusual involvement in a tactical matter by the commanding general. "As I was moving to the front with my command," Garnett says,

I saw Gen. Lee with his staff at a point to the right of the Chambersburg turnpike, and just in the rear of Seminary Ridge. He sent an officer with an order to me to report to him at once in person. Riding up to where he stood I dismounted, and, having saluted him, asked his pleasure. Pointing away beyond Seminary Ridge, and calling my attention to what seemed to be a large body of troops, with wagons and ambulances, he handed me a field glass, and asked if my guns would reach them from the Seminary. I replied that they would, and he said: "They seem to be moving towards the Emmittsburg road, do they not?" and added, "Place your batteries on Seminary Ridge and either disperse them or develop the purpose of their movement." Having complied with this order and drawn the fire of several batteries on Cemetery Hill upon me, I discovered that the troops which Gen. Lee had alluded to were in full retreat, and the General, coming up about that time, had the satisfaction of seeing the plain intervening between the two ridges filled with the retreating Federals.[29]

Adelbert Ames, who had been appointed brigadier general of volunteers on May 20, 1863, was at Gettysburg on the first day with the First Division of the Eleventh Corps. "Early in the morning of July 1," Ames reports,

my brigade left Emmitsburg, Md., and immediately upon its arrival at Gettysburg, Pa., it was pushed through the town and took a position near the pike leading toward Harrisburg. My brigade was ordered to a number of different positions, and finally it formed in rear of some woods . . . some half a mile from town. From this position we were driven, the men of the First Brigade of this division running through lines of the regiments of my brigade (the Second), and thereby creating considerable confusion. . . . At this time General [Francis Channing] Barlow was wounded, and the command of the division devolved upon me. The whole division was falling back with little or no regularity, regimental organizations having become destroyed. An order was received . . . to occupy the outskirts of the town, but soon after the order came to fall back through it. In this movement many of our men were taken prisoners. The hill in rear of the town was occupied . . . and in this position the division remained during the two following days.[30]

Garnett reports in *Gettysburg* that

when the retiring Federals reached Cemetery Hill they were met by Gen. Hancock, who arrived just as they were coming up from the town, with orders from Gen. Meade to assume the command. . . . With that quick perception which he possessed in a remarkable degree, Hancock recognized the character of the position on Cemetery Hill as one for a defensive battle, and at once determined to retain possession of it. He judged, as he afterward told me in a conversation at Newport, that this would be a difficult task, for the disorganized and demoralized condition of the troops as they came up the hill, and the delay in the arrival of fresh troops, gave him but little hope of success, should the Confederates make another determined assault.[31]

According to Garnett, "the whole of the Confederate army felt much elated over the success of the first day's battle, but there were those who looked upon the failure to capture Cemetery Hill that day as fatal. I remember a conversation with the gallant Gen. Ramseur, afterward killed in the valley of Virginia, which took place near the seminary, and while the Union batteries on Cemetery Hill were shelling us, in which he said, 'Garnett, we must get that hill to-night or never!' He was right. I believed so at that moment, and the desperate attempts to take it by assault during the next two days proved his words to be prophetic."[32] Garnett, like so many others, blamed General Ewell for not taking the hill and for losing the battle.

Judson Kilpatrick blamed someone else. According to him, "Lee's original and irretrievable error was his failure to seize and hold the line of hills at Gettysburg, and more particularly Culp's Hill, the commanding point of our position. Once having lost this golden opportunity, and Reynolds and Buford having secured the position for our own army, his experience of the skill of our officers, and spirit of our troops, should have deterred him from attacking our lines, even with his superior numbers."[33] Kilpatrick is not exaggerating when he notes the excellent work by Union generals, specifically John Buford—who chose the ground for the Army of the Potomac and whose First Cavalry Division held it till the infantry arrived—and John Reynolds, former commandant of cadets who commanded Union troops at Gettysburg on the morning of July 1, until he was shot from his horse by a bullet in the back of the head.

On the second day, the importance of Little Round Top was appreciated by Lieutenant Charles Edward Hazlett (#15, May), now commanding Battery D, Fifth U.S. Artillery, and his commander, Augustus Martin. While talking on Little Round Top with General Gouverneur K. Warren, Hazlett said, "the sound of my guns will be encouraging to our troops and disheartening to the others, and my battery's of no use if this hill is lost."[34] Hazlett's battery had an incredible engineering task in getting its guns up Little Round Top, with cannoneers and infantrymen sometimes doing the work of horses. A great engineer, Warren's aide, Lieutenant Washington Roebling, who would go on to build the Brooklyn Bridge, said in an 1877 letter to Patrick O'Rorke's adjutant, Porter Farley: "The tugging of the horses and men to get those guns up the hill, I remember as if it were yesterday."[35]

There was little room at the top for cannon—and none for limbers and caissons—but they were served well under the most difficult conditions, with ammunition carried to the guns on the crest by hand. Hazlett's battery also made an impression on Roebling's chief, General Warren, who described Hazlett on Little Round Top: "There he sat on his horse on the summit of the hill, with whole-souled animation encouraging our men, and pointing with his sword toward the enemy amidst a storm of bullets—a figure of intense admiration to me, even in that desperate scene. . . . There stood the impersonation of valor and heroic beauty."[36]

Colonel Strong Vincent's Federal infantry brigade was protecting Little Round from the Confederate attack of Major General John Bell Hood and Brigadier General Evander Law. John J. Garnett says, "Law . . . was on the very point of gaining the much coveted summit, when again fresh troops under Warren and my old classmate at West Point, O'Rorke, were pushed forward to the crest. Here victory was snatched from the grasp of Law by the impetuous valor of the troops under O'Rorke, who, having received a volley from the Confederates, clubbed their muskets and, with a wild shout of desperation, rushed upon those who, but a moment before, were the victors, and drove them down the hill. In this action the brave and gallant Hood was severely wounded, Vincent was killed, and O'Rorke also fell a victim to his courage."[37]

O'Rorke's 140th New York was part of General Stephen Weed's brigade, which reinforced the defenders. Lieutenant Benjamin F. Rittenhouse, of Hazlett's battery, says he heard a corporal yell, "'General Weed is shot.' I ran to him where he was lying alone . . . he said 'I am cut in two . . . I want to see Hazlett.' He was called, and Weed, after giving him directions about the payment of two or three small debts he owed his brother officers, drew him closer to him to give, as I supposed, a confidential message, when a ball struck Hazlett in the head, and he never spoke again."[38]

Eugene Beaumont (#32, May) wrote to his wife on July 4, 1863, saying, "Alas my Margie we are again called to mourn another gallant friend & classmate. Poor Charley Hazlett was killed day before yesterday by a sharpshooter. I saw him after his death & cut a lock of his hair for his friends. Several other graduates have been killed & wounded but you do not know them."[39] Malbone F. Watson (#25, May) had commanded Battery I, Fifth U.S. Artillery, when it was overrun on July 2 by the Twenty-first Mississippi, and he was hit in the right leg, which was amputated.

On July 3, Custer's cavalry repulsed Jeb Stuart, who had Rosser with him, and the latter gives one reason why: "Stuart had been marching constantly almost day and night, on scant forage and little rest for man or horse, for eight days, within the enemy's lines, and while his conduct displayed a daring almost to recklessness, he accomplished little, save the wear and fatigue of long marches."[40]

The stature of those who played Custer on the stage or screen or who wrote about him says something about the Custer myth. Theodore Roosevelt, who did a charge of his own at San Juan Hill, has described Custer's charge at Gettysburg, which prevented Stuart from reaching the Union rear: "Custer, his yellow hair flowing, his face aflame with the eager joy of battle, was in the thick of the fight, rising in his stirrups as he called to his famous Michigan swordsmen: 'Come on, you Wolverines, come on!' All that the Union infantry, watching eagerly from their lines, could see, was a vast dust-cloud where flakes of light shimmered as the sun shone upon the swinging sabers. At last the Confederate horsemen were beaten back, and they did not come forward again."[41]

The famous fight on the third day was, of course, an infantry charge. John J. Garnett said of Pickett, "He realized, as he afterward told me, that a duty had been intrusted to him the grandest that ever fell to the lot of a commanding officer."[42] Before the gray infantry began their frontal attack, Confederate artillery opened a massive bombardment. Garnett, who took part in it, gives their location: "We had placed our guns on the hills near the Bonnaughton road, near the York road, near the Harrisburg road, and on Seminary Ridge along our whole line to a point above Round Top, the purpose being to subject the Federal Artillery on Cemetery Hill to a circle of cross fires and to enable us to dismount and destroy it."[43] The officer who led Pickett's Charge was an ex-cadet, Lewis Armistead, who had been thrown out of the class of 1837 for breaking a plate over Jubal Early's head. General Armistead got as far as the cannon of Lieutenant Alonzo Cushing, class of June, where he fell mortally wounded at what is often called the high tide of the Confederacy.

What happened to Alonzo Cushing was described by his commanding officer. General Alexander Webb—whose statue would review generations of students at the City College of New York where he was president—said in his report on twenty-two-year-old Cushing: "Lieut. A. H. Cushing, Fourth U.S. Artillery, fell, mortally wounded, at the fence by the side of his guns. Cool, brave, competent, he fought for an hour and a half after he had reported to me that he was wounded in both thighs."[44]

Colonel Norman J. Hall, class of 1859, commanding the Third Brigade, said, "Lieutenant Cushing, of Battery A, Fourth U.S. Artillery, challenged the admiration of all who saw him. Three of his limbers were blown up and changed with the caisson limbers under fire. Several wheels were shot off his guns and replaced, till at last, severely wounded himself, his officers all killed or wounded, and with but cannoneers enough to man a section, he pushed his gun to the fence in front, and was killed while serving his last canister into the ranks of the advancing enemy."[45]

Cushing's classmate George Woodruff (#16, June) was mortally wounded on Cemetery Ridge. The commander of the artillery brigade, John Hazard, reports,

> First Lieut. George A. Woodruff, commanding Light Company I, First U.S. Artillery, fell, mortally wounded, on July 3, while the rebel lines, after a most successful and daring advance, were being pushed back in destruction and defeat. To the manner in which the guns of his battery were served and his unflinching courage and determination may be due the pertinacity with which this part of the line was so gallantly held under a most severe attack. Lieutenant Woodruff was an able soldier, distinguished for his excellent judgment and firmness in execution. . . . He expired on July 4, and, at his own request, was buried on the field on which he had yielded his life to his country.[46]

In a letter written on July 4, Emory Upton said, "Lee's attack yesterday was imposing and sublime. For about ten minutes I watched the contest, when it seemed that the weight of a hair would have turned the scales."[47]

Woodruff was the second 1861 graduate—his friend Edmund Kirby was the first—to die commanding Battery I, First U.S. Artillery. But this time the Army of the Potomac was victorious, as a comment from a classmate in the opposing army indicates. On July 4, on Seminary Ridge, Confederate Colonel Garnett says, "The rain fell throughout the day in cold, chilling sheets that added still more to the feeling of depression that pervaded the army. The gloomy day was drawing to a close when Gen. A. P. Hill stopped to warm himself by my bivouac fire. I saw plainly that his spirit was gone, and that he made no effort to hide the fact. Presently, without a word of comment upon the result, he turned sorrowfully toward me and said: 'Colonel, we must return to Virginia and prepare to try it again.'"[48]

The return to Virginia started that day. Kilpatrick and Custer pursued, the former writing about it eight years later: "At daylight on the morning of the 4th, I received . . . from General Pleasanton . . . an order directing me to march with all haste across the mountains, and strike . . . burn bridges,—obstruct the roads."[49]

Charles Francis Adams Jr. of the First Massachusetts Cavalry remarked on July 12, 1863, "We have done our work decently, but . . . Kilpatrick is a brave injudicious boy . . . who will surely come to grief."[50]

Henry du Pont—who had served as assistant adjutant general at Fort Hamilton, New York, from April 1862 to July 4, 1863—wrote on the same day from a camp near Harrisburg, Pennsylvania. Du Pont had taken command of Light Battery B, Fifth U.S. Artillery on July 5. He told his father, "After incessant labors here for the last week the Battery is at length equipped and we march this evening via railroad to Chambersburg and there to the front to join Couch's army which is co-operating with Meade in his movements against Lee. . . . A great deal of responsibility devolves upon me in this going right into action with a Battery of recruits who have never fired a single shot and then too to be supported by these miserable militia—However if we get in, we will have to do the best we can."[51]

In the same letter, du Pont said, "In all probability I think we will be engaged though we may be either too late for the fight or held in reserve." The whole Federal army was too late. On the night of July 13, the Army of Northern Virginia, which had its back to the river, crossed the Potomac at Falling Waters and Williamsport and returned to its state. Some of the things it left behind—besides its sense of invincibility—are listed in a report by John Edie (#14, June), who became acting chief ordnance officer of the Army of the Potomac, succeeding his classmate Daniel Webster Flagler (#5, June), who had that position at the time of the battle. Edie's list includes "collected by—Lieut. Morris Schaff, Ordnance Department: 19,664 muskets, 9,250 bayonets, 300 sabers, and 26 artillery wheels."[52]

On July 18, Henry du Pont observed, "Lee having been allowed to get away by Meade, the stampede is pretty much over."[53] Orville Babcock wrote in his diary on July 27, 1863, "Lee safe across the Potomac. Heard of the death of Woodruff & O'Rorke."[54]

6

The Boy Generals

The most obvious (if not the most attractive) quality in a boy general was ambition. On August 31, 1863, Colonel Thomas L. Rosser suspected (inaccurately) that Jeb Stuart was keeping him from becoming a general. "I have always liked Gen. Stuart," Rosser told his wife, "and have supported him in every instance and it is very hard for me to believe that he would desert me—I am now one of his oldest Colonels and I feel that I . . . deserve promotion."[1]

On September 13, 1863, LeRoy "Deacon" Elbert (#28, June), who was born in Ohio like his friend Custer, died of a fever on the Mississippi River.

On the same day, from a camp near Martinsburg, West Virginia, Henry du Pont wrote to his mother on one of his favorite subjects—his dislike of volunteer officers. Du Pont says he has "a prejudice . . . against having my battery destroyed by the absurdities and gross ignorance which in a place like this you meet at every turn. For instance the A.A.A.G. here informs me that my Battery having rifled guns would be the very thing they wanted to send out on cavalry scouts!! When I have a battery of mounted artillery!! I seriously believe he dont know the difference between horse artillery & mounted artillery. As a matter of course I could not keep up with the cavalry and if we fell in with any rebel cavalry in superior force, these gentlemen would scamper off and leave my battery to be taken."[2]

As early as September 16, 1863, Rosser told his wife, who lived in eastern Hanover county, "You may look out for a raid very soon I think, for the Yankee Cav'y can manage our cav'y so easily that they can ride over our country whenever they choose—This is a very sad thought to me." In the same letter, Rosser says,

> Stuart sent me very kind messages by one of my officers a few days since, but I know the measure of his friendship only too well now to be trifled with by

him longer—I have determined to leave his Command and *nothing* will keep
me—Col Willis, an old West Pointer, told me today that he had just been
speaking with Gen. Fitz Lee about my promotion and Lee could not understand why it was that I had not been promoted, and remarked to Willis that
I was the most "*skillful* and *efficient* officer in Battle, he ever saw" This is a
compliment that I feel very proud of, but I have always known that Gen.
Lee had this opinion of me. But Stuart Stuart Stuart! I am done with him!.
. . . Please don't let any one know how I feel . . . I don't speak of it myself—
I am cheerful and speak of Gen. Stuart as usual—I will never give him an
opportunity of deceiving me again.[3]

The next day, September 17, Harvard zoologist Theodore Lyman gave an
often quoted description of Custer. "This officer," Lyman observed, "is one
of the funniest-looking beings you ever saw, and looks like a circus rider gone
mad!" Yet Lyman goes on to say, "His aspect, though highly amusing, is also
pleasing, as he has a very merry blue eye, and a devil-may-care style."[4]

In Georgia, on September 20, 1863, Custer's classmate John Herbert Kelly
distinguished himself again, even against George Thomas, "The Rock of
Chickamauga." Kelly led a brigade in the assault on Snodgrass Hill. Major
General Simon B. Buckner reported, "Upon Brigadier-General Preston and
his brigade commanders—Brigadier-General Gracie and Colonels Trigg and
Kelly—I cannot bestow higher praise than to say that their conduct and
example were such as to convert a body of troops (but few of whom had
before been under fire) into a division of veterans in their first battle."[5] Kelly,
born on March 31, 1840, was promoted to brigadier general on November
16, 1863, the youngest Confederate general at the time of his appointment.

Kelly's example was also mentioned by the division commander, William
Preston, who said, "During the struggle for the heights, Colonel Kelly had
his horse shot under him. . . . He animated his men by his example, and"—
most importantly—"with unshaken firmness retained the ground he had
won." That was something even Joseph B. Kershaw's superb brigade could
not do. He also paid an enormous price, as can be seen in Preston's report-
ing, "Colonel Kelly took into action 876 officers and men . . . and lost 300
killed and wounded."[6] Kelly's casualties are a reflection of the huge losses
Braxton Bragg reported (2,312 killed, 14,674 wounded, 1,468 missing) in
driving General William S. Rosecrans's Army of the Cumberland off the
Chickamauga battlefield and back to Chattanooga.

Eight days after the major Confederate victory at Chickamauga, Henry A.
du Pont told his father about that part of the Federal response that he had
seen. From Martinsburg, West Virginia, du Pont writes,

We have been stirred up here a little by the passage of the 11th and 12th Army Corps through here via the Baltimore and Ohio R.R. Their supposed destination is Chattanooga. They come direct from the Army of the Potomac and have been going through for three days. . . . We have sustained a heavy defeat in the West much more disastrous than the newspapers here generally made out. Battery "H" of the 5th was taken and almost destroyed. . . . They are extremely anxious to keep this movement of troops quiet, but I see that the newspapers have already got hold of it. Here they wont let any one out of the town on this account. Hooker is assigned to the command of the two Corps and Slocum has for this reason resigned—Howard of the 11th passed through here yesterday morning. I fired a salute for him with the Battery. . . . I have yet to see in what the eminent generalship of Halleck consists. I have talked to a great number of the officers passing through here. I have yet to see one who is not a McClellan man out and out.[7]

On September 24, 1863, Colonel Rosser told his wife,

I had a long conversation with Gen. Stuart today who endeavored to explain to me why I had not been promoted. His arguments I thought quite silly. He seems to hate the way he has treated me, but that is too late now you know. He recommended me for Brig. Gen. of any command that I can be transferred to stating that I have *no* superior on the "field of Battle" and all that, which does very well but I think I can do all that I desire without his aid. Gen. *Ewell* invited me to take position of chief of artillery with the rank of colonel on his staff. Gen. Pendleton wants me made Brig. Gen. of artillery—Let them do what they will, I can get a position almost any where—Gen. R. E. Lee seems quite anxious to do something for me—seems to sympathize with me very much and so does Fitz. I saw the old Gen. several days ago & he said that he was very anxious to give me a good command.

On the letter's last page, after telling his wife that the enemy has been guilty of rape, Rosser says, "keep yourself armed at *all times*, and use them if necessary."[8]

Returning to promotion two days later, Rosser says, "Stuart gave me his word as a man that if I would remain with him that I should have the next position of Brig at his disposal, but when will there be another appointment? and again this is but repeating what he promised long ago—I can't respect Stuart as a *gentleman* and I think that the sooner I leave him the better for us all—I know what Fitz Lee thinks of me. He thinks that if he loses me there will be a *pillar* gone—& he can't afford to lose any of his & Stuart's supports."[9] In any case, Rosser received the promotion—that Stuart had always supported—to brigadier general on October 10, 1863 (to rank from September 28).

Rosser's classmate Wright Rives was in poor health on October 18, 1863, when he wrote another letter to Andrew Johnson, which shows how well he knew the military governor of Tennessee, whom Rives would later work for in the White House: "I am perfectly willing to accept a position in your office, although I will lose rank by it, yet I am willing to do that and have something to do rather than keep my present rank and obtain a sick leave. . . . If you consent telegraph to the Secy of War on the receipt of this and also to me. If I do not hear from you by Thursday, I shall consider that I am not needed[.] Yours in haste Wright Rives."[10]

A friend of Custer's, General Pierce M. B. Young, wrote about West Point in the Civil War in the *Atlanta Constitution* in 1893 and mentions meeting Custer at Buckland Mills on October 19, 1863:

> I never met face to face in shock of battle, any of my former comrades, but we were often opposed to each other in battle. I several times recognized with my glass General Custer. He was always in full uniform and always wore long hair. There had existed between Custer and myself, a warm friendship, which I am happy to say the war never interrupted in either of us. We had been roommates for a time at school, and always friends. We met several times after the war, and renewed our warm friendship. There was a pleasant incident that occurred during one of the cavalry fights just after the Gettysburg campaign. It happened at Buckland mills, ten or fifteen miles north of Warrenton. We had been marching nearly all night in the direction of Warrenton. My brigade was marching in rear next to the enemy. It was a little after dawn and the enemy had attacked us in the rear. I drove him off and was just moving off, when one of Stuart's aids dashed up and said General Stuart sent him to say that a regiment had been sent to relieve me, and that I must come to him in person immediately at the Hunton house, which was near the mill. When I entered the house General Stuart was at breakfast and two beautiful girls were attending him. They were the two Misses Hunton. He presented me and they invited me to breakfast. Stuart finished and left me, telling me not to be long, as we were forming on the other side of the creek and the enemy might catch me. When I was about through a shell exploded over the house and my courier called out: "They are coming, sir, we must hurry or be cut off from the bridge." I left the young ladies and the breakfast with many regrets, saying I would return, mounted my horse and rushed for the bridge just in time to get over safely. We retired slowly toward Warrenton, sending Fitz Lee's division down the creek. We set a trap for our friends, the enemy, and they walked into it. As soon as we left the mill, Custer's command came up. Custer himself rode up

and politely asked the young ladies to have breakfast prepared. They told him breakfast was on the table, a confederate general had just left it. He inquired all about who had been there. The ladies told him that General Stuart and myself had just left, but I had not finished my meal and it was now on the table. Custer said: "Very well, ladies, Young and I are friends. I will take his breakfast." So he took it and enjoyed it. He chatted on gaily, telling the young ladies of our former intimacy, and when he had finished he said: "Now young ladies be so good as to have something prepared for dinner for myself and staff, as I am likely to be about here till after dinner."

Stuart's ruse worked well. We attacked in front and flank at a charge, and as the boys say, "wiped him up." As Custer passed he stopped a moment at the gate, saying: "Ladies, give Young my compliments and tell him I took his breakfast. He can take my dinner, and please give him this picture of myself and tell him to send me his," and he galloped away, for he was crowded. Gallant Custer, he lost his life in that dreadful massacre by the Indians. He has been criticized by some, but he made his record fighting soldiers as brave and accomplished in the art of war as the world ever saw.[11]

On November 1, 1863, General Rosser wrote a few lines on trading with the enemy. "I have sent to Baltimore," Rosser told his wife, "for some little things I suppose you want. If there is anything you particularly want from the North, please let me know immediately and I will endeavor to procure it."[12]

Emory Upton shared some reflections on the art of war with his sister, after first giving his location on November 6, 1863. "We are again," Upton said in a letter from Warrenton, Virginia, "around this 'secesh' town, which we left about September 12th. We then marched to the Rapidan. The rebel fortifications appearing too formidable, Meade did not attack. Lee then began a series of manoeuvres which (I can, but ought not to criticize) threw us back behind Bull Run. Lee fell back immediately without trying to force battle. We followed up leisurely to this point, where we arrived October 20th." Upton admits,

> I sometimes get discouraged because of our not accomplishing decided results, but patience is a military as well as a social virtue, and therefore I continue to hope. I am reading "Plutarch's Lives," and I can not fail to see the charm success lends to military life. Victorious in every battle, courage rewarded in every struggle, who could not follow a Caesar or a Napoleon? Success begets confidence and resolution, which is a battle half won. No soldier in the world can equal the American, if properly commanded. . . . You know not the good a single word does a soldier when he is under fire. He feels that his commanding officer is directing him and looking at his actions.[13]

Emory Upton praises one of his classmates in his *Military Policy*, noting, "At Knoxville, November 29, 1863, Benjamin with but 300 men, repulsed the assault of four brigades of Longstreet's corps."[14] In his tenacious defense— including the use of wire and ice—of Fort Sanders (or Loudon, as it was also called), Samuel Benjamin (#12, May) took only thirteen casualties while giving the Confederates over 800. Since this book is particularly interested in classmates as authors, an unusual review of Benjamin's work by Douglas Southall Freeman is noted. Samuel Nicoll Benjamin had a rare distinction, according to Freeman, who said, "The report of Lieut. Samuel L. [*sic*] Benjamin (O.R., 31, pt. 1, pp. 341–44) might be read to advantage by every soldier as an example of the manner in which the splendor of a great exploit can be ruined in the telling."[15]

Readers can decide for themselves what to make of the following long excerpt from Benjamin's report of his defense of Fort Sanders. It was written at West Point on December 20, 1863. Benjamin says of his report to Major General Burnside (which he signs "your friend"):

> It is miserably written, but I had to hurry it, as I am very busy, and could hardly get time to write at all; so please excuse mistakes and all deficiencies. . . . On the 29th, I rose early, roused and warned all the men, and had every one posted, watching for the attack. A little after 6.30 A.M. the enemy opened furiously on the fort, with over twenty guns, and also swept the parapets and rained through the embrasures a heavy fire of musketry from the crest of the ridge 80 to 100 yards off. I went about the fort enforcing strict silence, and seeing that the men were kept close against the parapet, ready to rise and fire. So well had I protected the fort with traverses . . . no one was hurt by this fire except one cannoneer. In about twenty minutes the cannonade slackened . . . at the same time a heavy column charged on a run. . . . They burst through the abatis. . . . They lost many at the entanglement, and in less than two minutes from their appearance, they were in the ditch, attempting to scale the parapet. As they endeavored to surround the fort, the two guns in the bastion poured triple rounds of canister in their faces (not 10 yards from them), and I soon had the flank gun firing through the ditch and across the salient. They climbed the parapet continually, but only to be shot as they gained the top, the men being ordered to fire at none except those on the parapet. I also threw shells with my own hand in the ditch, to explode among them. After a while they began to fall back, but another column coming up, the assault was pushed more savagely than ever, and three of their flags were planted in our parapet. At length they again fell back in great confusion. . . . We took over 250 prisoners unhurt, 17 of them

commissioned officers (we were not 250 strong in the fort). . . . In the fort we lost 13 men, 8 killed and 5 wounded.

General Ferrero was in the little bomb-proof, and I did not see him outside, nor know of his giving an order during the fight.[16]

Edward Ferrero had been the dancing teacher at West Point. Two days later, Henry du Pont wrote, "The news from the West is very gratifying."[17]

In the middle of December, du Pont sent a private to Delaware to pick up a horse and sent instructions to his family on class distinctions in the Regular Army. "As to the man," du Pont tells his father, "I would like to have him treated well of course, but it would be injurious to discipline. . . . For instance do not invite him to take a meal with the family, etc, etc. At the same time I would not like him sent to the kitchen and treated like a servant."[18]

About the same time, du Pont told his mother, "I see by the papers that there is a scheme afloat to add to the Regular artillery sundry volunteer regiments just as they stand. I can hardly think such an outrageous thing as this can succeed. It is bad enough to be ranked I think by volunteer colonels even for the war especially in my own arm, but to have a host of captains etc over me permanently would be far worse. After all my luck in promotion has turned out rather poor."[19]

Du Pont's classmate Thomas Rosser obviously had much better luck in promotion, which was much faster in the Confederate cavalry than the Federal artillery. Rosser also had that monumental confidence and drive that seem to come to people who think they have done everything themselves. In a letter of December 30, 1863, written at Mt. Jackson in the Shenandoah Valley, Rosser tells his wife, "Tomorrow I march against the enemy. Fitz Lee is going along in Command, and of course will get all the credit. I will endeavor to do my duty and inasmuch as my Brig: will compose the greater part of the Command, I feel that the expedition will end well."[20]

Nine days later, from New Market, Virginia, Rosser told his wife, "I have just returned from an expedition across the mountains, cold & frostbitten, Brig: used up & men broken down, I am almost without a command. Fitz Lee went along but I did as usual all the work—my Brig: captured a wagon train of forty wagons—500 head of cattle, 300 horses and mules & about one hundred prisoners."[21] Despite Rosser's often expressed feeling that he did not get all the credit he deserved, Rosser and Fitz Lee got along well, remaining friends after the war, even after Rosser left the Democrats and quarreled with many other Confederates.

7

Custer, Rosser, and du Pont

On January 1, 1864, the famous Confederate diarist Mary Chesnut quoted Pierce Young, of the class of June: "General Young says, 'Give me those dare-devil dandies I find in Mrs. C's drawing [room]. I like fellows who fight and don't care what all the row's about.'"[1] The head of the class of May, Henry A. du Pont, recalled where he was that day when he wrote *The Campaign of 1864* in the Valley of Virginia sixty years later: "The first day of January, 1864, found me in camp at Martinsburg, West Virginia, in command of Light Battery B of the Fifth Regular Regiment of artillery . . . stationed along the Baltimore & Ohio Railroad for the protection of that important line of communication between Washington and the West."[2]

On February 9, 1864, General George A. Custer married Elizabeth Bacon in Monroe, Michigan. She had told him, "I want you to wear your full-dress uniform. I have changed my mind about not wanting ostentation."[3]

In Mississippi with General Sherman on the Meridian campaign was Custer's classmate Joseph C. Audenried (#17, June), who receives a sketch in Sherman's *Memoirs*. "Colonel J. C. Audenried," says William T. Sherman, "was a graduate of West Point, class of 1861, served . . . on the staff of General Sumner until his death, March 31, 1863; soon after which he was sent with dispatches to General Grant at Vicksburg. In July, 1863, General Grant sent him with dispatches to me at Jackson, Mississippi. Impressed by his handsome appearance and soldierly demeanor, I soon after offered him a place on my staff, which he accepted, and he remained with me until his death, in Washington, June 3, 1880."[4]

Sherman recalls how they spent the evening of February 12, 1864:

Intending to spend the night in Decatur, I went to a double log-house . . . and fell asleep. Presently I heard . . . pistol-shots. . . . My aide, Major Auden-ried, called me and said we were attacked by rebel cavalry, who were all around us. I jumped up and inquired where was the regiment of infantry I had myself posted at the cross-roads. He said a few moments before it had marched past the house . . . and I told him to run, overtake it, and bring it back. Meantime, I went out into the back-yard, saw . . . horsemen dashing about. . . . Gathering the few orderlies and clerks that were about, I was preparing to get into a corn-crib at the back side of the lot, wherein to defend ourselves, when I saw Audenried coming back with the regiment, on a run, deploying forward as they came. This regiment soon cleared the place and drove the rebel cavalry back.[5]

Judson Kilpatrick would be sent to Sherman after an unsuccessful raid on the Confederate capital. On the night of February 28, 1864, Kilpatrick, with 4,000 cavalry, set out to free the Union prisoners in Richmond. Custer led an astonishingly successful diversionary raid toward Charlottesville, which pulled Jeb Stuart's cavalry toward him and away from Kilpatrick. At 6 P.M. on March 1, near Madison Court House, Custer reported, "Since yesterday morning I have marched 100 miles."[6] Two days later, Custer wrote, "My command returned to its camp without having suffered the loss of a man."[7] Anyone who dismisses Custer as an incompetent who could not handle a regiment should ask how many generals could have operated as well in the rear of the Army of Northern Virginia.

Ulric Dahlgren—a twenty-one-year-old colonel who had lost his lower right leg in the Gettysburg campaign—handled the detailed planning for the attack on the Confederate capital and commanded a strike force of five hundred of Kilpatrick's men, which separated on February 29 and was supposed to ride into Richmond almost unopposed from the south. But heavy rain and high water prevented Dahlgren from crossing the James. Although Dahlgren's plan was complicated—the two Federal columns were supposed to communicate by flares—it was also a good one since it did not divide the columns equally, but instead still left Kilpatrick with a large enough force to break through the Richmond defenses. On March 1, Kilpatrick reached Richmond, hesitated before some five hundred defenders, and finally retreated. Dahlgren was killed the next night; papers he carried with instructions to kill Jefferson Davis set off an endless controversy. It is easy to believe that if Custer—or Dahlgren—had been commanding the raid on Richmond, he would have smashed through the vastly outnumbered Confederates and entered the city.

Dahlgren's father, who commanded the South Atlantic Blockading Squadron, wrote a Memoir of Ulric Dahlgren, and his stepmother, novelist Madeleine Vinton Dahlgren, wrote a Memoir of John A. Dahlgren, which has excerpts from the admiral's diary, including one for March 12, 1864, that says, "General Kilpatrick came on board to see me." Of course they talked about Ulric Dahlgren's orders. According to the admiral's journal, "The General said it was basely false that his order contained anything of killing Davis or burning the city. The General had read it over with Ully more than once."[8]

In a letter written at Meade's headquarters in March, Colonel Theodore Lyman remarked, "Behold my prophecy in regard to Kill-cavalry's raid fulfilled. I have heard many persons very indignant with him."[9] The next month, Kilpatrick joined Sherman in the West.

On March 9, 1864, Ulysses S. Grant became lieutenant general, and on March 28, Elizabeth Custer—referring to her husband by his family nickname, "Autie"—told her father, "We traveled from camp to Washington by the special train put on for Genl. Grant. Autie introduced me, and I had the honor of a short conversation with the distinguished man. . . . I was the only lady, and he was so considerate he went out on to the platform to smoke his cigar, fearing it might be disagreeable to me, till Autie begged him to return." In her letter from Washington, Mrs. Custer also says,

> I can't tell you what a place Autie has here in public opinion. . . . It astonishes me to see the attention with which he is treated everywhere. One day at the House he was invited to go on the floor, and the members came flocking round to be presented. . . . You got his telegram about his confirmation? How glad I am he really is a Boy Gen—I mean, a Brigadier!
>
> The President knew all about him when Autie was presented to him, and talked to him about his graduation.
>
> None of the other generals receive half the attention.[10]

Why did Custer get so much attention? An artist's explanation is given in *Time Exposure: The Autobiography of William Henry Jackson.* That photographer (who would explore Yellowstone with John Whitney Barlow of the class of May) had served for a year in the Twelfth Vermont Volunteers and then returned to a studio in Rutland, Vermont, in 1863. According to Jackson,

> General Grant had been a popular hero from the outset, and, now that the tide had turned, Lincoln was coming in for his share of adulation. We did a profitable business supplying hand-finished portraits of these two. I doubt, though, whether both of them combined ever won more enthusiastic devotion than George A. Custer. Promoted a brigadier of cavalry at the age of twenty-three . . . he . . . never knew anything but brilliant success through-

out the war. The children loved him, the ladies adored him, and all men envied him. All men, that is, except photographers. They loved him too, and never was there a subject who offered more to a retoucher handy with colors. Even then this hero had long mustaches and his famous flowing golden hair. He scorned the blue service uniform and wore instead a green-gray suit of velveteen richly trimmed with gold braid. He likewise spurned regulation headgear and chose a wide-brimmed cavalier hat. All those adornments still did not suffice: a long scarlet tie streamed invariably from his collar. General Custer was the artist's dream beyond compare.[11]

Custer liked the theater. His wife says in an April, 1864, letter, "The President was . . . the gloomiest, most painfully careworn looking man I ever saw. We have sat in a box opposite him at the theatre several times, and reports of his careworn face are not at all exaggerated." In the same letter to her parents, Elizabeth Custer says,

> I . . . will tell you of the President's Levee. Representative and Mrs. Kellogg took me. . . . He—the President—shook hands with me, as with everyone, and I felt quite satisfied and was passing on, but. . . . At mention of my name he took my hand again very cordially and said, "So this is the young woman whose husband goes into a charge with a whoop and a shout. Well, I'm told he won't do so any more." I replied I hoped he would. "Oh," said the prince of jokers, "then you want to be a widow, I see." He laughed and I did likewise. . . . Afterward, meeting one of his Secretaries, I bade him tell Mr. Lincoln he would have gained a vote if soldiers' wives were allowed one.

Mrs. Custer went on to defend her husband's commander, General Alfred Pleasonton—chief of the Cavalry Corps until replaced by Philip Sheridan—against the charge of drunkenness, telling her parents in her letter from Washington, "In this Sodom and Gomorrah everybody drinks."[12]

General Custer may have received more attention than the other boy generals, but he did not receive the Third Cavalry Division in April, 1864, when Judson Kilpatrick was sent to Sherman in the West. Grant wanted his former aide James Harrison Wilson, who explains how he got his division in his book *Under the Old Flag*: "after Grant came east he sent for Sheridan . . . and gave him command of the cavalry corps of the Army of the Potomac. In turn . . . he relieved Kilpatrick . . . while he transferred Merritt, Custer . . . to other brigades so as to make way for my formal assignment to the command of the Third Division. Although Merritt was below me in class standing and Kilpatrick and Custer came out a year later . . . each of them got his general's star a few months before I did. In short, they outranked me as brigadiers . . . my assignment to the command of a division . . . gave particular offense to my seniors of the line and led to hard feelings."[13]

Custer's feelings can be seen in a letter he would write to his wife after the Wilson-Kautz raid. Custer tells,

> My Darling—The papers have no doubt informed you of the disgrace brought upon a *portion* of the Cavalry corps by the upstart and imbecile Wilson. . . . He permitted himself to be cut off, lost all his artillery, burnt his ammunition and wagon trains, abandoned his ambulances filled with wounded. . . . Here is the result of consigning several thousand cavalry to the charge of an inexperienced and untrained officer. . . . Even Genl. Grant in his high and responsible position cannot fail to learn wisdom from this disgrace. Genl. Grant obtained the confirmation of W's appointment by the Senate, but it will require influence even more powerful to satisfy the people—above all, the Army, that this was a judicious measure, in view of his total ignorance and inexperience of cavalry, because he was a favorite staff officer of Genl. Grant, and also it was he who wrote . . . and later has been engaged in writing a history of Genl. Grant's campaign in the West. I hope the authorities have learned from this unnecessary disaster that a man may be a good engineer, but an indifferent cavalry leader. One might as well expect that a person with a good singing voice should necessarily have a talent for painting.[14]

Despite his disastrous raid in Virginia, Wilson would end the war with a superb record as a cavalry commander (defeating—with the help of Emory Upton—Nathan Bedford Forrest at Selma). But Upton was not yet a boy general—or any kind of general—when he told his sister on April 10, 1864, "General Meade has informed me that without 'political' influence I will never be promoted." In the same letter Upton says, "I trust General Grant will sustain his former reputation, and administer to General Lee such heavy blows that he may never recover. I confess I am ready for action. . . . The Army of the Potomac deserves a better name than it has, as we will soon prove."[15]

On April 25, 1864, Upton told his sister,

> I have received of late many gratifying proofs of the confidence and esteem of both officers and men under my command, and not only in my command, but outside it. The officers of the First Brigade of this division were nearly unanimous in recommending me for promotion, in the hope I might be assigned to that command. Considering that their lives to a great degree would be in my hands, especially in battle, and that no motive other than

their safety and welfare could prompt such an action, is it not the highest tribute men can pay me, that they should select me as their chosen leader in the hour of battle? The compliment is the more gratifying as coming from the New Jersey brigade, preferring me over every colonel from their State. The recommendation will not be forwarded, but it will serve to show the opinion of the officers of this division. Would the President consult the views of my superior officers, whose reputation depends upon my conduct to a certain degree, or those officers whose lives are in my hands in action, my promotion would not be withheld. I ought to have had it a year ago.

Upton adds in the same letter, "We are expecting to move soon. Our army is in fine condition, and I have no doubt that the bloodiest battle of the war will be fought in a few days. General Grant is well liked, and, as he is taking time to prepare his campaign, there is strong probability of his success."[16] A biographical sketch of Grant by a member of the June class, Colonel John J. Garnett, C.S.A., notes, "The policy of Grant was to move all of the armies at the same time, so that his enemy would not be able to reinforce either one of his armies by troops taken from the others."[17] On May 4, 1864, the Army of the Potomac crossed the Rapidan, and on the next two days there were heavy casualties in the Wilderness. Charles Henry Brightly (#29, June), commander of the Fourth Infantry, was mortally wounded on May 6, 1864. He died in Philadelphia on June 9.

Brightly's classmate Garnett comments on Grant's next move: "as he had never been content with a drawn battle he determined to push 'on to Spottsylvania.' The Army of the Potomac from that moment entered upon a new career; hitherto it had in no single instance fought its battle through, but henceforth it was determined never to turn back. . . . From that day forth, although baffled, delayed, and staggered, it held its way onward through the terrible times of Spottsylvania, North Anna, Tolopotomy, Cold Harbor, and the investment of Petersburg, sternly and courageously, for a whole year, meeting the enemy in almost daily battle."[18] Grant comments on Emory Upton's assault on the Mule Shoe at Spotsylvania on May 10, 1864, where Upton tried out his new infantry tactics designed to reduce casualties. Grant writes in his Memoirs,

Wright also reconnoitred his front. . . . He then organized a storming party, consisting of twelve regiments, and assigned Colonel Emory Upton, of the 121st New York Volunteers, to the command of it. About four o'clock in the afternoon the assault was ordered, Warren's and Wright's corps, with Mott's division of Hancock's corps, to move simultaneously. The movement was prompt, and in a few minutes the fiercest of struggles began. The battle-field was so densely covered with forest that but little could be seen, by any one person, as to the progress made. Meade and I occupied the best position we could get, in rear of Warren. . . . Upton with his assaulting party pushed forward and crossed the enemy's intrenchments. Turning to the right and left he captured several guns and some hundreds of prisoners. Mott was ordered to his assistance but failed utterly. So much time was lost in trying to get up the troops which were in the right position to reinforce, that I ordered Upton to withdraw; but the officers and men of his command were so averse to giving up the advantage they had gained that I withdrew the order. To relieve them, I ordered a renewal of the assault. By this time Hancock . . . had returned. . . . His corps was now joined with Warren's and Wright's in this last assault. It was gallantly made, many men getting up to, and over, the works of the enemy; but they were not able to hold them. At night they were withdrawn. Upton brought his prisoners with him, but the guns he had captured he was obliged to abandon. Upton had gained an important advantage, but a lack in others of the spirit and dash possessed by him lost it to us. Before leaving Washington I had been authorized to promote officers on the field for special acts of gallantry. By this authority I conferred the rank of brigadier-general upon Upton on the spot, and this act was confirmed by the President. Upton had been badly wounded in this fight.[19]

Upton's friend and classmate, Henry du Pont, wanted to present an account of his own battles in Virginia, particularly New Market. Du Pont remarks that the Union commander in the Shenandoah Valley, General Franz Sigel, had only one inaccurate sentence on his battery in a chapter in *Battles and Leaders*. "Except as just stated," du Pont remarks in his book *The Campaign of 1864*, "Sigel's article does not make any other reference to the Regular battery and he is absolutely silent in regard to the part it took in covering the retreat of the Union forces, which was apparently due to his habitual carelessness and lack of information in regard to the details of his command."[20]

Du Pont later remarks, "Although the battle of Newmarket was of comparatively little importance, either with respect to the numbers engaged or the results attained, it was an episode of the Civil War which has always aroused special interest in Virginia, largely due to the fact that the youthful cadets of the Virginia Military Institute had participated so valiantly in that engagement."[21] Du Pont's part in his first fight began that Sunday, May 15, 1864, when his six cannon "moved to the front at a sharp gallop, arriving on the battlefield between 2:30 and 3:00 P.M."[22]

As du Pont describes it,

No general officer was in sight, but I was at once pounced upon by a number of young and inexperienced staff officers who proceeded to give me (upon their own initiative but in the names of Generals Sigel or Stahel) the most absurd and contradictory orders with respect to putting the battery in position. In speaking of the youth of most of these officers, it occurs to me that I myself was not twenty-six at the time, but common sense, reenforced by eight years of continuous military instruction and military discipline, made it easy to reach an instant decision as to what ought to be done, and, although under fire for the first time in my life, I then and there made up my mind to ignore the conflicting instructions and to take such measures as seemed right and proper. . . . I had to depend entirely upon myself *and did not receive a single order, either directly or indirectly, from any military superior!*[23]

In addition to not having anyone above him, du Pont had no one on his flanks:

The battery was in the open and entirely without support, but a thick curtain of smoke which hung over the field prevented the Confederates from discovering this fact, and it seemed necessary to risk the loss of some of my guns in order to cover and protect the retreat of the Union troops. The leading platoon (two guns) under Second Lieutenant Charles Holman, was at once put in position close to the turnpike and on its west side, and instantly opened fire. Taking advantage of this, I ordered the other four pieces to fall back and put the center platoon, commanded by First Sergeant Samuel D. Southworth, in position some five or six hundred yards to the rear and immediately on the east of the turnpike, with orders to open fire as soon as he was unmasked by Holman. Indicating a slight swell of the ground at about the same distance still further to the rear, I instructed Second Lieutenant Benjamin F. Nash, commanding the left platoon, to go into position at that point. These dispositions, known in the tactics of that day as retirement "by echelon of platoons," consumed but a very few moments, when I galloped back to the front and remained with Lieutenant Holman's pieces which continued to fire with great rapidity and precision until we found ourselves entirely alone, with not a single Federal soldier in sight save the members of our own battery.[24]

Sigel's army retreated and du Pont adds an observation in his book: "In addition to Sigel's many shortcomings, both in strategy and grand tactics, the military administration of his command was very far from working smoothly and efficiently. His spectacular appearances on horseback surrounded by a brilliant but largely incompetent staff and followed by a cavalry escort, did not succeed, as he had apparently hoped would be the case, in inspiring the confidence and good will of those under him."[25]

In a letter of May 17, 1864, du Pont was even harsher, telling his father, "Every thing has been very much mismanaged in my opinion. Sigel commanded in person—nearly all of the infantry ran at the first fire and left the artillery to be captured—I only wish that I could get out of this."[26] Sigel was out on May 19, 1864. The new Union commander in the Department of West Virginia was General David Hunter, class of 1822. Du Pont told his mother on May 24,1864, "Hunter has made me Chief of Artillery of the Dept. and in consequence I am continually occupied. . . . Professionally I am much better off than before and, as in addition I personally disliked Sigel and had no confidence in him, I am much pleased at the change of commanders."[27]

On June 1, 1864, Emory Upton's anger was noted by one of his surgeons. Within a mile and a half of Cold Harbor, Daniel Holt notes, "General Upton, from some cause, *very* wolfish. Threatens to turn *every surgeon in the Division out of office*! I pity the poor fool."[28] On June 3 at Cold Harbor, Alexander Duncan Moore—who had resigned from the June class on April 22, 1861, and was now colonel of the Sixty-sixth North Carolina—was mortally wounded.

On June 5, 1864, Emory Upton wrote a pessimistic letter to his sister, adding, "The fatigue of the campaign hardly disposes one for letter-writing." From the headquarters of the Second Brigade, Upton said,

> We are now at Cold Harbor, where we have been since June 1st. On that day we had a murderous engagement. . . . My brigade lost abut three hundred men. My horse was killed, but I escaped unharmed. Since June 1st we have been behind rifle-pits. . . . I am very sorry to say I have seen but little generalship during the campaign. Some of our corps commanders are not fit to be corporals. Lazy and indolent, they will not even ride along their lines; yet, without hesitancy, they will order us to attack the enemy, no matter what their position or numbers. Twenty thousand of our killed and wounded should to-day be in our ranks. But I will cease fault-finding, and express the hope that mere numbers will yet enable us to enter Richmond.[29]

Arthur Henry Dutton (#3, June) died on June 5, 1864, from a wound received at Bermuda Hundred, Virginia, where he was colonel of the Twenty-first Connecticut Volunteers in the Eighteenth Corps. General William T. H. Brooks said, "It is not improper to make here a report of the death of the colonel of this regiment, Col. A. H. Dutton, then in command of the brigade, who was mortally wounded while making a reconnaissance in front

of our lines near Port Walthall, just as this corps was about to join the Army
of the Potomac. The service has lost no more accomplished officer than
Colonel Dutton."[30] Dutton was a brevet brigadier general and dead at
twenty-five.

After describing the Federal victory on June 5, 1864, at Piedmont, Virginia—where Confederate General William E. "Grumble" Jones was outnumbered (by some 8500 to 5600), defeated, and killed—Henry du Pont
mentions two cadets he had known at West Point who were also there. The
second was a member of the June class:

> Although I did not learn of his death until long afterwards, among the killed
> on the Confederate side was Major Richard Brewer, of Annapolis, Mary-
> land, with whom I had been at West Point for several years. Hearing, how-
> ever, that Colonel William H. Browne, of the Forty-fifth Virginia infantry,
> who also had been with me at the Military Academy and whom I knew per-
> sonally very well, was wounded and a prisoner, I went to see him. He had
> received medical attention and been made as comfortable as possible on the
> ground and did not seem to me to be very seriously injured. Having acted as
> brigade commander on the extreme left of the Confederate line, Browne
> talked almost exclusively about the tactical dispositions of the opposing
> forces, insisting that the Union infantry had not been well handled, as it
> should have attempted earlier to turn the left flank of the Confederates,
> which was their vulnerable point. Not having been on that part of the field,
> however, I was unfamiliar with the ground and could say but little. As we
> both looked forward to his long captivity as a wounded prisoner, I inquired
> whether he had any funds, his reply being, "Not one cent," upon which I
> gave him all the money I then had in the world, consisting of a $10 bill.
> As our column was just beginning the march to Staunton early on the fol-
> lowing morning, I heard, to my surprise and very great regret, that Browne
> had died of his wounds during the night.[31]

A few days later, Henry A. du Pont entered the college town of Lexington, where Washington College, now Washington and Lee, has a plaque
dedicated to him. Du Pont says,

> upon reaching Lexington before noon on the 11th, were met by a straggling
> infantry fire from the cadet barracks of the Virginia Military Institute. . . .
> We remained at Lexington for two days and a half, during which time every
> building connected with the Institute was burned to the ground by General
> Hunter's order, save the quarters of the superintendent, Colonel F. H. Smith,
> which were spared on account of the illness of a member of the Smith fam-
> ily. With several other officers, I took part in saving some of the personal

effects of Mrs. Gilham, wife of one of the professors of the Institute, by carrying out of her house with our own hands tables, sofas and other articles of furniture just before the building was set on fire. Mrs. Gilham, whose brother [Julis Hayden] was an officer of the United States Regular Army, was in great distress and we were only too glad to assist her in every way in our power. Among those who helped I can only recall Captain William McKinley, afterwards President of the United States.[32]

Fifty years later, du Pont was a United States senator introducing a bill to reimburse the Virginia Military Institute for the damage caused when General Hunter burned it down. Another senator asked him, "What was the general's idea in burning those buildings?" Du Pont replied, "The general was a very peculiar man. His father was a Virginian. [Laughter]. That did not make him a peculiar man. But, if you will allow me to finish my sentence, his mother was from Princeton, N. J.; his father was a clergyman. I do not think he was in pleasant relations with his southern relatives, of which there were a great number. He had a most extraordinary idea of how to put an end to armed resistance."[33]

In August of 1864, General Philip Sheridan—who also had an idea of how to end armed resistance—took command in the Valley. From Harpers Ferry, Emory Upton told his sister on August 9, "A new campaign will be inaugurated to-morrow under the command of General Sheridan. . . . General Sheridan has the appearance of great nerve, and hitherto has been quite successful. For one, I am better pleased with his appearance than that of any other commander under whom I have served. How humiliating was the reverse at Petersburg, and how disgraceful on the part of division commanders to abandon their troops! I have never been reckless, but I am sure it is a praiseworthy quality when so few of our higher commanders expose themselves as much as duty requires . . . so, whatever I may do, you must not attribute it to rashness, but to a soldier's sense of duty."[34]

The "inevitability" of Confederate defeat after Gettysburg and Vicksburg was not at all clear to the participants. In September of 1864, Thomas Rosser still thought the South would win, telling his wife, "I am a soldier by profession and may be compelled to remain in the Army after the war."[35] There would, of course, be no after the war for him in the army unless the Confederacy won. That it did not was to a large degree determined by Sheridan's campaign in the Shenandoah Valley. The crucial timing of the Valley campaign of 1864—right before the presidential election—gives it (and Henry du Pont's account of it) an importance out of all proportion to the numbers of troops involved.

Members of the June 1861 Class in Order of Class Standing

Unless otherwise noted, all photographs are courtesy of the Gilder Lehrman Collection on deposit at the Pierpont Morgan Library, New York. GLC 5084

1.

Patrick Henry
O'Rorke

2.

Francis Ulric
Farquhar

3.

Arthur Henry
Dutton

4.

Clarence Derrick

5.

Daniel Webster
Flagler

6.

Thomas Carr
Bradford

7.

Richard Mason
Hill

8.

William Hamilton
Harris

9.

Alfred Mordecai

10.

David Hillhouse
Buel

11.

Stephen Carr
Lyford

12.

Alonzo Hersford
Cushing

13.

Charles Carroll
Parsons

14.

John Rufus
Edie

15.

Lawrence Sprague
Babbitt

16.

George Augustus
Woodruff

17.

Joseph Crain
Audenried

18.

Julius Walker
Adams

19.

Peter Conover
Hains

20.

Francis Henry
Parker

21.

Joseph Pearson
Farley

22.

Joseph Boyd
Campbell

23.

Henry Erastus
Noyes

24.

Philip Halsey
Remington

25.

Not shown:
William Duncan
Fuller

26.

Justin E. Dimick

27.

James Pierre
Drouillard

28.

Leroy S. Elbert

29.

Charles Henry
Brightly

30.

Eugene Carter

31.

Samuel Peter
Ferris

32.

George Owen
Watts

33.

Frank A. Reynolds

34.

George Armstrong
Custer

John Herbert Kelly

*Left West Point before graduation
to join the Confederacy*

(*Courtesy of the Alabama Department
of Archives and History, Montgomery,
Alabama*)

Felix Huston Robertson

*Left West Point before graduation
to join the Confederacy*

(*Courtesy of the Massachusetts Commandery
Military Order of the Loyal Legion and the
US Army Military History Institute*)

Pierce Manning Butler Young

*Left West Point before graduation
to join the Confederacy*

(*Courtesy of the Massachusetts Commandery
Military Order of the Loyal Legion and the
US Army Military History Institute*)

Sheridan fought Jubal Early at the third battle of Winchester (also called Opequon) on September 19, 1864. Du Pont says, "I took part in this battle as chief of artillery of the Army of West Virginia (Crook's corps) and, so far as many of the features of this conflict were concerned, was either a participant or a personal observer."[36] After a Confederate counterattack, du Pont recalls, "Crook instantly ordered his whole staff to ride back at a gallop and hasten his corps forward, and as I was starting with the others he turned to me and said: 'It is not worth your while to go. Send your officer.'"[37]

As a result, du Pont had an excellent vantage point for this battle, noting, "there were only four persons left on the rounded eminence. . . . On his horse and to the front sat General Sheridan, silent and immovable: a few feet behind him were General Crook and myself, and immediately in rear of us was my orderly, Bugler Richard Wende."[38]

Du Pont heard the name of his friend Emory Upton mentioned and that of General David Allen Russell. "Major George A. Forsyth of General Sheridan's staff," du Pont reports, "galloped up and reported to the commander-in-chief that Russell had been killed, but that Upton, with his brigade, had struck the Confederate line in flank and arrested its forward movement. This last piece of information was a tremendous relief and the arrival of Crook's corps was now awaited with comparative serenity."[39]

Where du Pont was not an eyewitness he had a good source:

Turning now to that portion of the conflict entirely hidden by the trees from the rounded eminence on which Sheridan had taken his position, my narrative is based upon the very detailed account given me personally upon a number of occasions by my friend and classmate at West Point, the lamented Upton. His statement, which is confirmed in every particular by the official reports, was substantially as follows:—

"As you know, I belonged to the Sixth corps and was in command of the Second brigade of Russell's First division which constituted the second line of battle of our corps, my brigade consisting of the Sixty-fifth and One hundred and twenty-first New York Volunteers, together with Mackenzie's Second Connecticut heavy artillery serving as infantry. . . . When the Nineteenth corps and most of our Third division gave way and broke to the rear, General Wright, commanding the Sixth corps, ordered our second line of battle to move to the front and my brigade then advanced in two lines, the Second Connecticut in the first line. Soon afterwards, our West Point classmate, Colonel Jacob Ford Kent of Wright's staff, directed me to move to the right. I obeyed the order, marched my brigade, still in two lines of battle, by the right flank, crossed the turnpike and halted my second line in a narrow strip of timber and again faced it to the front, but continued the movement of my first line beyond the right and towards the rear of the second, and placed it in an oblique position to the advancing enemy. As soon as the Confederates came within two hundred yards, I ordered Mackenzie to fire, upon which the enemy fell back in great disorder. Then forming my whole brigade in line I continued, upon my own initiative, to strike the enemy in flank, driving him back and inflicting heavy losses in killed and wounded. Russell had fallen, although I did not know it at the time, and while I had received no orders I saw that the only thing to do was to change the direction of my brigade so as to take the Confederate line in flank, and this I did as rapidly as possible."

According to du Pont, "Upton's military instincts and professional ability prompted him, without a moment's hesitation, to make the proper dispositions and to deal a blow which shattered the Confederate advance and changed the whole aspect of the battle. Upton, be it said, never received the full credit to which he was justly entitled, as his own official report is naturally free from self-laudation, and Russell, his division commander, who undoubtedly would have done him full justice, had met a soldier's death." Perhaps because he felt Sheridan had not given Upton enough credit, du Pont adds, "Upton, entirely upon his own initiative, had done the right thing at the vital moment."[40]

Another classmate is mentioned in a description of an assault on the Confederate flank by Isaac Hardin Duval. "With a tremendous shout," du Pont recalls,

which resounded along the lines of the Nineteenth corps, our Second division rushed forward to the charge, but at that very instant a body of cavalry suddenly loomed up in the distance on the right flank of Duval's line of battle. . . . Crook with his staff at once rode towards them to ascertain whether they were friends or foes. Upon drawing nearer, we made out that they were Federal soldiers, and in a few moments recognized General Merritt, commander of Torbert's First cavalry division. Among the officers of Merritt's staff, was another classmate of mine, his aide-de-camp, Captain McQuesten [#39 May], whom I had not seen since we left the Military Academy in May, 1861; but as we were all riding at a gallop, we were only able to exchange a very few words: he was killed, poor fellow, about an hour later in the splendid charge made by Merritt's cavalry division.[41]

James McQuesten was from New Hampshire. In the twentieth century, Adelbert Ames remembered, "McQuesten, modest, generous, brave, was killed in battle."[42] A member of Custer's class was wounded in that battle.

Clarence Derrick (#4, June) had been dismissed on July 16, 1861, for ten-dering his resignation in the face of the enemy. Derrick was lieutenant colonel of the Twenty-third Virginia at Opequon, where he was captured.

In September of 1864, Thomas Rosser was sent to the Shenandoah Valley to reinforce General Jubal Early. "I am not very anxious to go to the Valley now," Rosser had told his wife on September 15, 1864, "for Fitz Lee has had such bad luck over there and his force now so weak that my part of the work would be very heavy if I were to go, and again, there is nothing to eat for man or beast."[43]

In addition to that problem, Rosser and Early developed a hatred for each other that only increased in the postwar years. In one letter to his wife, whom he wanted to visit, Rosser says, "I fear that I will have great difficulty with Gen Early . . . about indulgency & the like—he is so perverse and mean—He remarked when I saw him about going home that he has always had great difficulty with army women. . . . But I will go somehow or other."[44]

Custer commanded Sheridan's Third Cavalry Division and had the chance to do what Rosser had done to him at Trevilian Station on June 11, 1864, when Rosser captured Custer's headquarters, letters, and clothes. In a the-atrical scene at Tom's Brook, Custer rode out in front of his line, took off his large hat, and bowed to Rosser. After that he attacked him and wrote about it in a letter to his wife, which she included in her *Boots and Saddles*. "Rosser said," according to Custer's letter of June 26, 1873,

> the worst whipping he had during the war was the one I gave him the 9th of October, when I captured everything he had, including the uniform now at home in Monroe. He said that on the morning of that fight, just as the battle was commencing he was on a hill on our front, which I well remem-ber, watching us advance. He was looking at us through his field-glass, and saw and recognized me as plainly as if I had been by his side. I was at the head of my troops—all of which I remember—and advancing to the attack.
>
> Rosser said as soon as he recognized me he sent for his brigade com-manders and pointed me out to them, saying, "Do you see that man in front with long hair? Well, that's Custer, and we must bust him up to-day."
>
> "And so," General Rosser continued, "we would have done had you attacked us as we thought you intended to; but instead of that you slipped another column away around us, and my men soon began calling out, We're flanked! we're flanked! then broke and ran, and nothing could stop them."[45]

Nothing would stop Rosser's promotion to major general (on November 4, 1864, to rank from November 1), not even his defeat by Custer at Tom's

Brook. Henry du Pont mentions hearing Rosser at Cedar Creek. Du Pont says, "the Confederate attack began between 4:30 and 5:00 A.M. on the 19th of October, 1864." His account shows the surprise of Early's attack and that it was a Confederate classmate who woke him up: "I was aroused by some distant firing on our extreme right which was caused by Rosser's demonstration on the Back Road . . . as the firing did not cease I jumped up, put on my clothes, ordered my horse, called the chief bugler and directed him to sound the 'reveille.'"[46]

Du Pont remembers, "Although it did not occur to me that we were going into immediate battle, I felt some anxiety while standing in front of my tent waiting for my horse which was promptly brought by Private Charles Tucker (who was taken prisoner and afterwards died in captivity at Salisbury, North Carolina). No particular mount having been designated, he brought my grey mare, almost white, which, needless to say, on account of her conspicuous color, would not have been ridden from choice during a general engagement."[47]

Du Pont galloped down to the camp of Battery B to try to save his guns. He would get the Medal of Honor for Cedar Creek and gives this account of his battery:

Although there was not a single commissioned officer in the ravine on duty with the battery, the drivers, in spite of a very heavy fire, were making extraordinary efforts to harness and hitch their horses. . . . Everyone displayed the utmost calmness and courage and there was not the slightest disorder or confusion. First Sergeant Webb was in command and was loyally assisted by Quartermaster Sergeant Sauthoff, Stable Sergeant Rogers and all the other non-commissioned officers of the battery. I have never seen a more striking illustration of the discipline and devotion of the patriotic soldiers of our Regular Army than was afforded on that day by the enlisted men of Light Battery B, Fifth United States Artillery . . . largely by their exertions the battery was extricated while almost within the enemy's grasp and the greater part of its materiel saved."[48]

Du Pont says later,

Night had now fallen and the battle was over, the next task being to provide food and water for my exhausted men and horses. . . . At this juncture I suddenly realized that I was almost completely worn out mentally and physically; that I had not tasted food for more than twenty-four hours; that I had been almost continuously in the saddle since the Confederates attacked us between 4:30 and 5:00 o'clock in the morning. . . . The only recourse was to seek food and shelter at the headquarters of my corps which were with Army Headquarters at the Belle Grove house. Upon arriving there, one of the first persons I met was General Torbert of Delaware, commander of our cavalry corps, who lost no time in telling me that General Ramseur was mortally wounded and lying in the house, which information so acutely shocked and distressed me that I forgot for the time my own necessities and hastened upstairs to see him.[49]

Confederate General Stephen Dodson Ramseur, a North Carolinian, was a member of the class of 1860. Ramseur was at Union headquarters after being captured by Custer. Du Pont says, "Ramseur and I had been on terms of most friendly intimacy during the four years we served together at West Point, and although his own surgeon and adjutant-general were present, he turned to me in his suffering and never relinquished his grasp of my hand until the anaesthetic given to relieve his agony had rendered him unconscious, which condition continued until the end came."[50]

One explanation for Early's eventual defeat by Sheridan was given by Rosser, who did not care for either of them: "Sheridan's success in the Valley against Early was not due to his skill as a general so much as to the fact that Early misunderstood his true character. Early handled his army as infantry against cavalry, while Sheridan handled both his cavalry and infantry as *infantry*, and instead of the sabre and pistol, for which Early appeared to have great contempt, he encountered everywhere the most improved long-ranged rifled-musket or rifled carbine, in the hands of dismounted cavalry or infantry."[51]

Grant had sent Sheridan to clear the valley of Rebels. Grant himself was with the Army of the Potomac. His aide Horace Porter, class of 1860, gives an account of Orville E. Babcock of the May class and the general-in-chief at Hatcher's Run on October 27, 1864. Porter says,

General Grant, as was his constant practice, wished to see the exact position of the enemy with his own eyes. He . . . called on one aide-de-camp, Colonel Babcock, to accompany him, and rode forward rapidly . . . a shell exploded just under his horse's neck. The animal threw up his head and reared, and it was thought that he and his rider had both been struck, but neither had been touched. The enemy's batteries and sharp-shooters were both firing. . . . The telegraph-lines had been cut, and the twisted wires were lying about in confusion upon the ground. To make matters more critical, the general's horse got his foot caught in a loop of the wire, and as the animal endeavored to free himself the coil became twisted still tighter. . . . Babcock, whose coolness under fire was always conspicuous, dismounted, and carefully uncoiled the wire and released the horse. The general sat still in his saddle, evidently thinking more about the horse than of himself, and in the most quiet and unruffled manner cautioned Babcock to be sure not to hurt the animal's leg.[52]

On November 13, 1864, Grant sent a telegram from City Point, Virginia, to General Meade, which was of particular interest to a classmate of Babcock's and member of Meade's staff, Campbell Dallas Emory (#38, May). Grant told Meade, "please inform Capt Emery that his brother is in Hampton Roads a prisoner aboard the Florida . . . if he wishes to do so permit him to visit his brother."[53] Emory's brother was Confederate Assistant Surgeon Thomas Emory, who was aboard the C.S.S. *Florida* when it was captured near Brazil by the U.S.S. *Wachusett* on October 7, 1864. Emory's father was Federal General William Hemsley Emory. His great-great-grandfather was Benjamin Franklin.

On November 23, 1864, Orville Babcock told an uncle that General William Babcock Hazen had asked him about his family history. Babcock includes a brief sketch of himself in which he mentions, "I have been in the field since May 1861. Was on Genl McClellan staff as Engineer—during his command . . . and have been with Gen. Grant since last April. I have never been wounded but twice—and but slightly either time."[54]

Babcock's classmate John Whitney Barlow gives an account of his own experiences that year: "I left our comfortable quarters at Brandy Station late in February, '64, for a few months' tour of duty at West Point and next . . . was transferred to the West, joining Gen. Sherman's armies near Marietta, Georgia." The Atlanta campaign would have enormous political impact, since it was taking place only months before the presidential election. Barlow describes the fight in July that took place two days after he became chief engineer of a corps: "On the 22d occurred the battle of Atlanta, one of the sharpest of the war, in which the 17th Corps covered itself with glory by repulsing five different charges of the enemy from both front and rear. These reckless charges in which, it was said, whiskey furnished a part of the inspiration, cost the rebels 2,000 men killed on the slope of Bald Hill.[55]

The high cost to the Federals as well that day was noted by Barlow:

In the beginning of this fight, the gallant McPherson met a soldier's death. . . . The Army of the Tennessee . . . was again put in march under Gen. Logan, and making a long detour to the extreme right on the opposite side of Atlanta, at Ezra Church it again encountered the weight of Hood's forces on the 28th. This was the third time that Hood had gallantly tried, by leaving the trenches filled with militia and throwing his massed veterans upon a fraction of our line, to gain an important advantage. But the desperate bravery of his men was each time unavailing. Here, as on the 22d, his losses were enormous. In front of one of our regiments armed with Spencer rifles, I saw, after the enemy fell back, almost an entire regiment of dead, including the colonel. So near together and in such good line were the bodies, that a person could have walked its whole length without touching ground.[56]

In his *Memoirs*, William T. Sherman recalls Judson Kilpatrick's zeal in August of 1864:

On the 16th, I . . . ordered strong reconnoissances forward from our flanks. . . . Kilpatrick . . . displayed so much zeal and activity that I was attracted to him at once. . . . I summoned him to me, and was so pleased with his spirit and confidence, that I concluded to suspend the general movement of the main army, and to send him with his small division of cavalry to break up the Macon road about Jonesboro', in the hopes that it would force Hood to evacuate Atlanta. . . . Kilpatrick got off during the night of the 18th, and returned to us on the 22d, having made the complete circuit of Atlanta. He reported that he had destroyed three miles of the railroad about Jonesboro', which he reckoned would take ten days to repair. . . . On the 23d, however, we saw trains coming into Atlanta from the south.[57]

The same raid is described in the *Autobiography of Oliver Otis Howard*. Howard says, "Sherman tried one more raid, using the energy of our sanguine Kilpatrick. That general made his march with promptness, but soon came back."[58] Howard also has some reflections on Kilpatrick, noting politely, "Two days after Kilpatrick's return one would hardly believe that he had been defeated at all." While praising Kilpatrick's "optimistic nature and fearless enterprise," Howard also points out, "His memory and his imagination were often in conflict."[59]

Kilpatrick's habit of exaggerating his accomplishments has been widely noted. His "aversion to the unpleasant truth" in his official reports "makes corroboration necessary," notes a student of Kilpatrick after doing a dissertation on him.[60] But it was in his appreciation of publicity that Kilpatrick may have been on to something new. E. A. Paul of the *New York Times* stayed with Kilpatrick's Third Division after Hanover in the Gettysburg campaign. Kilpatrick understood the power of the press. In the next century, army officers even more skillful at cultivating the media—but with much more meager combat records than Kilpatrick—would go to the top.

Yet General Howard gave a very favorable account of Kilpatrick in August of 1864, saying,

The night of the 26th my move began. My army (of the Tennessee) was at the time 25,000 strong. . . . When day dawned we were beyond the reach of danger from the rear. This march was the first that I had made in conjunction with Kilpatrick. He cleared my way as rapidly as he could of the enemy's cavalry and artillery with it. . . . I shall never forget that march. The country was mostly covered with trees . . . so that it was exceedingly hard to maneuver any considerable body of horsemen. Having now to do with cavalry, I was apprehensive of a surprise, particularly when the horses were crowded together in narrow roads; so I became quite happy and satisfied to see how Kilpatrick managed. He kept his guard so far out that all the irregularities of a cavalry bivouac did not much disturb him.[61]

Kilpatrick has, of course, received an enormous amount of criticism. Historians still write about his "serious deficiencies of both intellect and character."[62] Yet it is worth noting that some of the generals he worked for, Howard and Sherman, were "quite happy and satisfied" with how he managed.

Kilpatrick's classmate General Rosser remarked to his wife in September of 1864, "Poor Hood has ruined himself by accepting the Command of the Army of the West—He was engaged to marry Miss *Preston* of S.C. Gen. Hampton's niece, but the impression now is that she will not accept him."[63]

After Sherman took Atlanta on September 2, 1864, he planned the March to the Sea. In October, General James H. Wilson was put in charge of all of Sherman's cavalry in the Military Division of the Mississippi. But for the March to the Sea, Sherman chose Kilpatrick. Wilson said, "In asking me to outfit his division Sherman said with perfect frankness, but apparently without intending to disparage him: 'I know Kilpatrick is a hell of a damned fool, but I want just that sort of a man to command my cavalry on this expedition.'"[64]

Sherman had over sixty thousand men divided into two powerful columns. Henry W. Slocum commanded the left wing, which had the Fourteenth and Twentieth Corps, and Oliver Otis Howard the right, with the Fifteenth and Seventeenth Corps. Howard reports, "We left White Hall November 15, 1864. . . . Kilpatrick's cavalry, about 5,000 horsemen, had already reported to me, and were sent during the first of 'The March to the Sea' to clear my front and watch my right flank as we wandered southward."[65]

Kilpatrick, constantly skirmishing—with Joseph Wheeler, who had been two years ahead of him at West Point—protected Sherman's flanks. Sherman would later tell Kilpatrick on December 29, 1864, from Savannah, "But the fact that to you, in a great measure, we owe the march of four strong infantry columns, with heavy trains and wagons, over 300 miles, through an enemy's country, without the loss of a single wagon and without the annoyance of cavalry dashes on our flanks, is honor enough for any cavalry commander."[66]

Of course, it also helped that Confederate General John Hood took his army off to Tennessee and out of Sherman's way. According to John Pelham's friend William Blackford, "Hood was a gallant man but weak in the upper story . . . leaving Sherman loose to march one way while he marched the other; was there ever such folly in the history of war?"[67]

An actual massacre of over a hundred wounded and defenseless black troopers of the Fifth U.S. Colored Cavalry had taken place at Saltville in southwestern Virginia on October 2, 1864, in which troops from the brigade of General Felix Robertson—who had resigned from the June class to join the Confederacy—took part. After the war, Captain Champ Ferguson, commander of a company of bushwackers, was tried and hanged for murder, but General Robertson was never punished by a court.[68]

Robertson was punished by Kilpatrick at Buckhead Creek, Georgia, on November 28, 1864. Robertson described what happened to him in a ten-page letter written in 1895 to another Confederate veteran, Major George K. Miller:

> orders soon came to report to Gen. Wheeler at Atlanta. . . . By this time, Sherman had begun his march from Atlanta to the sea. I found Gen. Wheeler at Macon. . . . Kilpatrick, with his Cavalry, left the protection of Sherman's Infantry, and started for Augusta, Georgia. Wheeler soon discovered the movement, and bent all his great energies immediately upon Kilpatrick, and at night-fall of the first day, we drove him out of the village of Waynesboro. So sharp had been our advance that Kilpatrick despaired of reaching Augusta, and here made a sharp turn to the right, with a view of again sheltering himself from Wheeler's Cavalry, behind Sherman's Infantry.
>
> During the night at Waynesboro Wheeler directed me to take command of the advance guard, and force Kilpatrick to a fight. From daylight, we crowded Kilpatrick, and at Buckhead Creek, forced him to a halt and to form line of battle across the road, which line I promptly charged with such soldiers as I could assemble from the skirmish line; we broke the line, and went with it through the swamp of Buckhead Creek, pell mell. As I rode into the column, with my revolver in hand, I looked for some insignia of rank, with the purpose of bestowing my attention upon the highest officer then present. Kilpatrick passed within five feet of me, but had his back to me, was wearing a blouse, and no insignia of rank w[h]atever, exposed to view. I did not shoot him, but turned my attention to a lieutenant, who

seemed to be in command. I fired at him with, I supposed, fatal effect. . . . I then continued to fire, until I had emptied my pistol, and then drew my sabre, and began some sabre practice. Although my sabre had been well ground a few days before, the long gallop had dulled its edge against the mettle scabbard; and I found it impossible to force the point through the Yankee jackets while the wearers were travelling the same direction in which I rode.

I then endeavored to thrust the sabre into the exposed part of the neck, and I succeeded very well, in that way, in doing some execution. As soon as I would finish disposing, with my sabre, of one man, I would spur my horse forward and reach another. This process had continued a little while, but unfortunately, my sabre strokes made no [some?] noise, and some Yankee on my left gathered sufficient presence of mind to shoot me. The bullet struck me in the left elbow, and carried away pieces from two bones, and left me useless for further fighting. When I felt the shot, I raised myself in my stirrups for the purpose of cutting down the man who had shot me, and delivered with my full force a swinging blow on the head of my adversary. So great was the force of my blow that my stirrup leather broke, and I was about to fall to the ground; but caught, with my right heel, on the cantel of my saddle, and succeeded in regaining my upright position. By this time my horse was in full gallop, carrying me along with my fleeing enemies, my left hand useless and my sabre in my right hand; but by taking the reins of my bridle in my teeth, I was enabled to get a fresh hold with my right hand, bring my horse to a stop, and as soon as the rush of fugitives had passed by, I turned and rode to the rear. I had gone but a short distance when I met Gen. Wheeler and our main body. . . . Kilpatrick had formed a strong line on the south side of Buckhead creek, and I left Gen. Wheeler, with my comrades, to give the requisite attention to Kilpatrick, while I went to the nearest farm-house to have my wounds dressed. As I rode back to the farmhouse, I met Dr. Frank Lynch, who was Wheeler's surgeon, and most of the other surgeons of the Corps, all of whom I well knew. These gentlemen carefully examined my wound, and the opinion of the majority was, that my arm should be amputated. Dr. Frank Lynch, however, took a more cheerful view, and thought it might be saved. When they reported their disagreement to me, I Promptly decided in favor of Lynch's opinion, and in a very few moments, he had performed the necessary operation.[69]

The surgeon succeeded; Robertson lived until 1928, the last surviving Confederate general.

Ending the War

The last surviving Union general, Adelbert Ames, of the class of May, lived until 1933, the opposite of Felix Robertson in every way. Ames commanded the Federal infantry division that stormed Fort Fisher, "the Gibraltar of the Confederacy," which guarded the South's last major open port, Wilmington, North Carolina. Ames read his own account of the capture of Fort Fisher to chapters of a veterans group—the Military Order of the Loyal Legion of the United States—in the 1890s, and one of them published it.

The first expedition to Fort Fisher (December 7 to December 27, 1864), commanded by Benjamin Butler (who would become Ames's father-in-law) had failed and returned to Fort Monroe, Virginia. The second expedition took place in January 1865, with General Alfred Terry in command of army operations and Admiral David Dixon Porter again in charge of the naval operations. Ames commanded the Second Division of the Twenty-fourth Corps, and his commander, General Terry, would also be Custer's commander in the Little Bighorn expedition. Ames quotes from General Terry's report on Fort Fisher and also from his subordinates, saying, "I have called up the actors themselves, and have let them speak in their own words."[1]

Ames reports,

I had thirty-three hundred picked men in my division. General Paine had the same number in his. There were added a brigade of fourteen hundred men under Colonel J. C. Abbott and two batteries of light artillery of three and six guns each. Colonel Comstock, who represented Grant on our first expedition, returned with ours on the second.[2]

The troops were landed on the 13th, some two miles north of the fort. Upon landing the first work on hand was to establish a line of breastworks from the ocean beach to the river to keep the enemy in the direction of Wilmington from interfering with our operations.

Terry, Comstock and I were in a small advanced outwork about half a mile from the fort. My able and gallant Adjutant General, General Charles A. Carleton, has made the following record: "General Terry turned to General Ames and said: 'General Ames, the signal agreed upon for the assault has been given.' General Ames asked: 'Have you any special orders to give?' General Terry replied: 'No, you understand the situation and what is desired to be accomplished. I leave everything to your discretion.' Thus was given me the unrestricted command of the fighting forces.

At once I directed Captain Lawrence of my staff to order Curtis, commanding the First Brigade, to charge, striking the parapet at the end nearest the river.[3] The palisade had been sufficiently broken and shot away by the fire of the navy to permit the passage of the troops.

Captain Lawrence heroically led the charge of that part of the brigade which advanced at this time. He was the first through the palisade, and while reaching for a guidon to plant on the first traverse, his hand was shot away and he was dangerously wounded in the neck, but with this lodgement on the first traverse, the force of the charge was spent. I quickly ordered Colonel Pennypacker's brigade, which was close at hand, to charge and sweep down the parapet to the ocean.

I will not attempt a description of the battle. It was a charge of my brigades, one after the other, followed by desperate fighting at close quarters over the parapet and traverses and in and through the covered ways. All the time we were exposed to the musketry and artillery of the enemy, while our own Navy was thundering away, occasionally making us the victims of its fire.

Major O. P. Harding, who came out of the fight in command of the Second Brigade, reports: "Colonel Pennypacker was seriously wounded while planting his colors on the third traverse."[4]

Let me say, in passing, that Colonel Pennypacker's conduct in leading his brigade with the colors of his own regiment, placed him second to none for gallantry that day. It would be difficult to overestimate the value of his example to his brigade.

Entering the fort and passing to the rear of the parapet at the west end, I made an examination of it from that position, and decided to use my third brigade, Colonel Bell's, with its left by the parapet, right extended south and west inside the fort, and charge into the angle formed by the land and sea faces. I ordered Bell forward with his brigade. . . . Unfortunately Colonel Bell was killed in the advance, gallantly leading his brigade.[5] The part of his brigade which reached me was in a somewhat disorganized condition. I formed it as best I could for the charge. Owing to the obstructions of the demolished quarters of garrison and the fire of the enemy from the front . . . and from the right, as well as the fire of our Navy, the advance was checked.

The men were in a very exposed position, and as no advantage could be gained there I ordered them to join the other troops in pushing seaward on the land-face of the fort.

Owing to the contracted space in which the fighting was done, brigade and regimental formations were impossible. What was accomplished was through the heroic efforts of small bodies of officers and men.

From time to time I sent to Terry, who was in the earthwork half a mile away, reports of the progress I was making.

I had previously learned that the sailors and marines who had made an attack on the sea angle had been quickly repulsed.

As the sun sank to the horizon, the ardor of the assault abated. Our advance was but slow. Ten of my officers had been killed, forty-seven wounded, and about five hundred men were killed and wounded. Among the killed was one brigade commander, the other two were wounded and disabled. I now requested Terry to join me in the fort. It was dark before he and Comstock arrived. I explained the situation.

Colonel Abbott's brigade, which had been relieved from its position in the line facing Wilmington, by the defeated sailors and marines, had been ordered to report to me.[6]

Ames quotes from the report of Colonel Abbott, whose brigade turned the tide and took the rest of the fort. After that Ames says, "It was ten o'clock. The task set for us at half-past three was finished. Our work was done."[7]

On February 1, Sherman entered South Carolina, but Confederate leaders still did not realize that they had lost the war. Three of them—Alexander Stephens (vice president of the Confederate States), John A. Campbell (former justice of the United States Supreme Court), and R. M. T. Hunter— attended a peace conference with Lincoln and Seward at Hampton Roads on February 3, 1865. Orville Babcock of Grant's staff had escorted the Confederate commissioners through the Union lines. But, of course, the peace conference failed. The Confederates would not recognize the authority of the Federal government (or that it was time to surrender on the best terms they could get).

Henry du Pont, in Cumberland, Maryland, remarked to his mother on February 3, 1865, "The peace rumors seem to occasion very little interest here save among the citizens. I cannot see for my part how people can induce themselves to believe in the probabilities that the war can be ended by diplomacy. Lee's army the real Southern Confederacy, must be crushed by force of arms before in my opinion we can hope for the end of the war. I trust that the next campaign will accomplish this."[8]

Emory Upton's part in the end of the war can be best told by his last commanding officer, James Harrison Wilson, who led an invasion of the Deep South in the Selma, Alabama, campaign. Wilson had 13,500 men, the largest mounted force of the war. But it was the way in which Wilson and Upton used cavalry that was remarkable and resembled the armored cavalry of the next century. They moved fast—three hundred miles in less than two weeks—never giving the opposing commander, Nathan Bedford Forrest, a chance to concentrate his scattered forces. More extraordinary for an all-cavalry force, Wilson's corps (often fighting dismounted) stormed heavily fortified positions that seemed impregnable to cavalry.

Wilson mentions Upton's wounding while commanding infantry at Winchester on September 19, 1864: "His wound was so severe that he was entirely disabled by it till the middle of December following. Meanwhile I had been assigned to the task of . . . commanding the Western cavalry, and had been promised the assistance of a few good officers from the Army of the Potomac. I had asked for Upton at the head of the list, and as soon as he was able to travel he joined me in midwinter at Gravelly Springs, Alabama. . . . His wound was not yet entirely healed, but he at once assembled his division and set about its instruction with all his accustomed industry and enthusiasm."[9]

Upton was given the Fourth Cavalry Division of the Cavalry Corps of the Military Division of the Mississippi. "When he reported to me," Wilson recalls,

he remarked that he had no doubt of his professional capacity to manage cavalry as well as either artillery or infantry, but he expressed considerable anxiety as to his standing with his division until he should have commanded it in action and shown both officers and men that he was neither afraid nor lacking in dash. He feared that the rigid discipline he would exact and the constant instruction he would give might for a while make him unpopular, but he felt sure that he would remove all prejudice of that sort at the first action in which he should lead his division. The result was as he anticipated in every respect, except as to his unpopularity. The division to which he was assigned was composed of veterans, who saw from the start that his was a master-hand. Both men and officers responded promptly and cheerfully to every demand he made.[10]

One of the places where they responded was Montevallo, Alabama, forty miles north of Selma. Wilson says, "I reached Montevallo at one o'clock on March 31. Upton, having the lead, occupied the place at dusk the evening before and by the time he had given me . . . the enemy's probable position,

Long's division and LaGrange's brigade of McCook's division, free from all wheels except those of their batteries, had closed up."[11]

According to Wilson, "Forrest was in our front. . . . True to his own rule, he was striving . . . to strike the first blow. But we had anticipated him and, as soon as advised of his advance, I ordered Upton, who was fully ready, 'to sail in!' . . . his skirmishers from both brigades were already in line and, to add to their weight, the splendid regular battery was thrown well to the front, followed by Winslow, Noble, Benteen. . . . The enemy was checked, his formation broken, and his whole line overthrown and in retreat."[12]

General Forrest, Wilson says,

> selected a new position . . . some five miles south of Montevallo, and . . . made another stand. . . . But Upton . . . attacking both center and flanks, soon lifted him from his new position and drove him in confusion down the Selma road, till darkness put an end to the pursuit. . . . Upton, flushed with victory, bivouacked that night fourteen miles south of Montevallo. . . . Both officers and men . . . had gained for themselves and for the corps a moral supremacy over the enemy which they never lost. They had fairly "got the bulge on Forrest" and his followers and held it till the end. . . . on April 1 Upton . . . had the good fortune to capture a rebel courier . . . he found three dispatches, which he sent me without delay. The first was from Forrest. . . . I now knew exactly where every division and brigade of Forrest's corps was, that they were widely scattered and that if I could force the marching and the fighting with sufficient rapidity and vigor, I should have the game entirely in my hands.[13]

At the battle of Ebenezer Church, Wilson says, "Upton with his entire division was soon abreast of Long. Both commanders knew their business perfectly, and with their men all on the field together, without delaying to reconnoiter the enemy's position . . . or to ask for instructions, they threw forward a strong dismounted skirmish line, which at once became hotly engaged. In the midst of the rattle . . . Upton sent Alexander with two mounted regiments . . . to catch the enemy in flank and drive him in confusion from the field. . . . Forrest's whole line was overborne and driven from the field."[14]

Upton describes how he used his cavalry division against Bedford Forrest in his report of May 30, 1865: "Whether mounted or dismounted, but one spirit prevailed, and that was to run over the enemy wherever found or whatever might be his numbers. Nothing but the impetuosity of the charges, whereby the enemy was not given time to defend himself, can account for the small list of casualties."[15]

Upton's role in storming Selma was explained by Wilson: "an English civil engineer named Millington, who had been employed on the fortifications at Selma, gave himself up to Upton, and . . . at Upton's request prepared an accurate pencil sketch of the trace and profile of the works." Wilson further recalls the advantage of having an infantry general with him—and not just any infantry general: "Upton and I spent an anxious hour considering every possible aspect of the case. He had had unusual experience and success with infantry in just such work and from Marye's Heights to the Dead Angle at Spottsylvania had never failed to break through the entrenchments he had attacked. He was, therefore, my main dependence."[16]

Giving his assessment of his officers (and himself), Wilson says, "Upton was a veteran who needed no supervision. . . . Long was a good soldier, but had had no experience except with cavalry, and up to the time he fell under my command had seen but little good military team work." Wilson also lists "Alexander, Winslow, Noble, Garrard, Peters, Benteen, Young, and Eggleston, the splendid colonels of Upton's division."[17]

At Selma, on April 2, 1865, at 5 A.M., according to Wilson's account,

Upton, hearing the noise of battle to his right . . . waited for neither signal nor orders, but made his way through the brush, across the swamp, carrying the works in his front. . . . Upton, with true military instinct, was under full headway . . . while Long, to the right, swept over . . . driving Forrest and Armstrong from their outer entrenchments. . . . Upton was doing his work well . . . sweeping everything before him. He also broke through the inner line, putting the enemy after a headlong charge again to flight. Orders were sent to press his advantage, but upon such an occasion and to such a man orders were hardly necessary.[18]

In the east, according to John J. Garnett's sketch of Ulysses S. Grant, "The siege of Petersburg, which was neither a siege nor investment, but a continual menace, drew rapidly to a close in the Spring of 1865. In the later part of March, having fully matured all his plans, Grant gave the orders which put his forces in motion."[19]

On April 1, at Five Forks, Sheridan broke the Confederate lines with his cavalry (which included Custer's division) and Gouverneur Warren's Fifth Corps, taking 4500 prisoners and forcing the evacuation of Richmond and Petersburg the next day. The Confederate collapse at Five Forks was hastened by the absence of their leaders, George Pickett and Fitz Lee, who had gone to General Rosser's shad bake. In *The Sunset of the Confederacy*, Morris Schaff says these generals "were engaged in planking shad on the north bank of Hatcher's Run, two miles or more in the rear of their resolute but greatly outnumbered troops. Although the fire was quick and heavy, it was completely smothered by the intervening timber, and . . . before Fitz Lee, Pickett and Rosser got to the front the day was lost; so at least the story was told to me by my friend Rosser."[20]

Yet at High Bridge on April 6—after a week of disasters for Robert E. Lee's retreating Confederates—Rosser won the last victory of the Army of Northern Virginia. But James Dearing (who had been in West Point's D Company with Rosser and Custer) was mortally wounded, the last Confederate general to die from a combat wound.

At Federal cavalry headquarters, Sheridan sent a dispatch to Grant dated April 8, 1865, 9:20 P.M.: "I marched early this morning . . . on Appomattox Station, where my scouts had reported trains of cars with supplies for Lee's army. A short time before dusk General Custer, who had the advance, made a dash at the station, capturing four trains of supplies. . . . Custer then pushed on toward Appomattox Court-House, driving the enemy, who kept up a heavy fire of artillery, charging them repeatedly and capturing, as far as reported, twenty-five pieces of artillery and a number of prisoners and wagons. . . Custer is still pushing on. If General Gibbon and the Fifth Corps can get up to-night we will perhaps finish the job in the morning."[21]

As already noted, some form of the word "push" was often used to describe Custer. His friend Tom Rosser praised "Custer, who was by far the best cavalry general the North produced during the war."[22] Of course, his many enemies could say, after Custer's Last Stand, that he pushed too hard.

Rosser said in a letter about himself, "the greatest triumph of my military career . . . was the successful charge which I made at Appomattox Courthouse on the 9th of April, 1865, when after General Robert E. Lee had decided to surrender the Army of Northern Virginia . . . to General U. S. Grant, about 5 o'clock in the morning, at the head of my command, composed of my division (McCausland's and Dearing's Brigades) and Fitz Lee's Division . . . I took these hungry, wasted, and worn out brigades forward . . . rode over a brigade or more of the enemy, captured the Lynchburg road and left that fatal field in triumph, refusing to surrender either myself or my command to the enemy."[23] Rosser also ended a speech to a reunion of the Maryland Line with his favorite line—"THE CAVALRY Never Surrenders!"[24]

At Appomattox Court House on April 9, Lee was escorted through the Union lines by Orville Babcock, of the class of May, in order to meet with Grant in Wilmer McLean's parlor. Custer was there, with other Union generals. After the surrender, Grant left for Washington. The formal surrender was taken on April 12 by Joshua Chamberlain, who had been Adelbert Ames's lieutenant colonel in the Twentieth Maine. Now a distinguished and frequently wounded major general—"I am not of Virginia blood; she is of mine"[25]—Chamberlain honored the Army of Northern Virginia with a salute—order arms to carry arms—before it stacked its arms. He also said, "How could we help falling on our knees, all of us together, and praying God to pity and forgive us all!"[26]

Three days later, Henry du Pont wrote to his father from Cumberland, Maryland: "This morning we have all been profoundly shocked by a despatch from Washington announcing the assassination of the President. I can hardly realize that it can be true & still hope that it may turn out to be without foundation. . . . I think that Grant's terms to Lee were entirely too lenient and was much disappointed when I read them. Public opinion however seems to endorse them."[27]

PART TWO

Postwar Lives

9

Adelbert Ames:
Reconstruction Governor

From the summer of 1866 until June of the next year, Adelbert Ames traveled in Europe and kept a three-volume "Journal While Abroad." In his diary, he records his views on race, Reconstruction, President Johnson, and the role of an army officer in a republic.

In Berlin, Prussia, on August 24, 1866, Ames says, "At half past eleven this morning I saw about five or ten thousand soldiers reviewed by the King." After praising the horses and men, Ames said, "The officers were quite ridiculous in their bearing and step. I refer to the company officers on foot; they bore themselves in such a manner and stepped so very high (sole of the foot horizontal) as to make caricatures of themselves. . . . The King looked like an elderly man—one about sixty-five years old—as he is. I saw no *King* in him. But in all the officers and men I saw 'Dutchmen' as they are called in America. Someone was constantly reminding me of the Germans in the 11th Corps with which I once had the honor to serve!"

Ames sees a connection between parade ground and opera in Prussia, saying, "I find, at the theaters and operas that the more swagger, gesticulation and mouthing the better pleased the audiences. As a consequence of this, or rather this the consequence, the people only see that which is natural in what an American can but regard as unnatural and extravagant. In this connection can much be said of the German character."[1]

On August 29, Ames left Dresden, Saxony, for Prague, Bohemia, where he reports, "I first went to the American Consul's. . . . I next rode to the Jewish quarter of the city. There are some twelve thousand of them here. A Jewish synagogue interested me much. The most recent part of it is six hundred years old—the oldest, about a thousand. Formerly the oldest part used to be underground, there placed for the safety which was found in the secrecy of those who worshipped."[2]

In an entry for Zurich, Switzerland, September 3, Ames says, "After dinner, I read New York papers . . . I see, our worthy President wishes to trust the people . . . he is . . . joking. . . . Not for years has such an important public measure been attempted without consulting the people, as his reconstruction policy."[3]

At Berne, Ames writes on September 9, 1866, "This morning I attended divine service at the British Chapel. . . . I saw in the hall an old friend and comrade in arms—General Paine, who commanded the division of colored troops which went at the same time with me and my division to the first and second attacks upon Fort Fisher. . . . We . . . chatted the afternoon away."[4]

On September 15, 1866, at Vevay, Switzerland, Ames reports, "Tonight I discussed 'negro suffrage' with an American—advocating what I consider the only true policy—which is that the negro ought not to be allowed to vote; but I was not at all satisfied with the way I presented my side of the case."[5]

At Heidelberg ten days later General Ames gives his opinion of Andrew Johnson, noting,

> the President and the congressional party have openly declared war against each other. . . . I do not know as I care much how much injury Mr. Johnson may do his own cause. . . . He may soil his own garments, but I seriously object to his trailing his presidential mantel in the mud. On the other hand, his opponents do not seem to hesitate at anything. Their violence and excesses cause me sorrow . . . I feel with them and do not like to see them . . . injure their cause. I feel that I would like to participate in the campaign which is being . . . carried on between them. . . . I approve of the policy of taking a half if the whole is unattainable. Yet, I know many say unless we have all we will take nothing. This is illustrated by those who in the present crisis cry for negro suffrage. Foolishly, they would let such a plank in a platform be a source of great insecurity—fatally so. But I do not believe in negro suffrage.[6]

Ames changed when he later lived in Mississippi and saw how blacks were mistreated.

The next day, in Heidelberg, Ames saw another example of the appeal of the Confederacy overseas: "At the dinner table today, I made the acquaintance . . . of two English ladies. . . . Like all Englishmen—or nearly all—they sympathized with the southerner, and expressed the hope that 'poor President Davis would soon be released!'"[7] But Jefferson Davis would remain a prisoner in Virginia until 1867.

General Ames says on October 1, 1866,

By the English papers, I see . . . reports from America indicate that John-son's policy is losing favor with people—a dispatch—which I hardly believe—says that the New York Times pronounces the "President's policy a failure." Should this be true, his leadership has gone forever and he will only be president long enough to serve out Mr. Lincoln's unexpired term. I see the London Times advocates the extension of suffrage to the negro, this step it advises the people of the south to take. . . . The ratification of the Acts of Congress by the people will so strengthen the congressional party that the president will be powerless—and the South will be taught that a bloody war of four years cannot be indulged in by them without results they have no right to expect to avoid—which will doubtless be far different from what they have received at the hands of Mr. Johnson.

Ames adds, "And, on the other hand, I am of the opinion the party in Con-gress holding the control of affairs in its hands will go too far in the other direction and insist upon conditions that the best of loyal men will disagree to."[8] Two days later, he adds, "I find nearly every American I meet here a sup-porter of the congressional party—or radicals, as they are called."[9]

In November, Ames watched Emperor Napoleon III review his troops, remarking, "I saw that in the Prussian soldier which nothing here appears to equal—a solidity and intelligence which *should* have weight in battle. Yet, on no occasion have I seen such intelligent men as I saw in our own armies."[10]

On November 10, 1866, Ames and two friends set out for the Bois de Boulogne. "We had not gone far," Ames reports, "when we met the Emperor and Empress. . . . I am of the opinion that one can see as much extravagance and folly in New York as here." Ames ends his entry by noting, "The evening was spent in a room where hung a portrait of Jefferson Davis at the present time a resident of Fortress Monroe."[11]

Ten days later, Ames says, "At dinner I met a young gentleman just from Yale College who is unable to find in Paris anything superior to what the United States can produce. A short visit to one of the places of low life fill him with bitterness because it is not bad enough—even New Haven can equal it."[12]

On December 9, 1866, Ames has a long entry on a large party, saying, "This evening I was at the American Minister's and saw there among others the Duke of Seville . . . there was Lord Lytton (formerly Sir Edward Bulwer Lytton). Certainly his face has never done him any favors. It was one of the most unpleasant I have noticed for many a day. I was conversing with a daughter of one of our poets, William Cullen Bryant . . . he looked the farmer rather than the poet and scholar. . . . I had a short conversation with Mr. Bryant and thought he spoke less easily and fluently than I had expected. However, I had no good opportunity to judge."[13]

The next day, Adelbert Ames records his observations on Paris and compares that city (unfavorably) to a warship in a way that shows his interest in liberty and hatred of censorship. Ames says in Paris,

> Nothwithstanding this is the second city in population in the civilized world, it is ruled with the vigorous hand one finds generally only on ships-of-war. In the latter case, it is necessary to a great degree, inasmuch as all are confined to a very small space and because the various distinctions must be preserved. Here, however, one has actually less liberty than there. A censorship over everything and government spies succeed in probing to the depth of every person's affairs, and often to the very root of all one's opinions and feelings.[14]

In January of 1867, Ames says,

> The most elegant gatherings of Americans abroad are at such places as our Minister's receptions. . . . In the evening, I went to the Dix's . . . and until nearly midnight the gathering remained. At that time, I went to the hotel with some Americans—young ladies and their ma'mas—and drank champagne and so forth—after which, about half past one o'clock in the morning, I went with friends to the masked ball at the opera. Here, I found some of my young lady acquaintances—Americans—who had gone to see that grand carnival of folly. Much to my surprise, they remained till nearly morning, witnesses of many things I would not like friends of mine to see. . . . But then, I suppose in this, as in other things, each one has his or her particular tastes.[15]

In his entry for January 17, Ames gives his opinion of a ball given by Napoleon III, noting, "After we had waited too long, the Emperor came into the room. . . . His face is not a pleasant one. To me, the characteristics were cunning and stolidity. In his manners, there was a stiffness and heaviness I had not expected—and which I cannot account for unless it is the privilege of rulers to assume a dignity which gives the appearance of stupidity."[16]

In Nice on January 30, 1867, Ames says, "I called upon a Mr. Kennedy of Maryland today." Ames recounts part of his conversation with John P. Kennedy, who had served with Andrew Johnson in the House of Representatives: "We discussed at some length the President and his policy. He said that Johnson when in the House was regarded as one of the lowest politicians of the democratic party; and that he made himself particularly obnoxious to his associates by his rudeness and coarseness."[17]

General Ames was invited to a ball on board the USS *Colorado* in Nice and remarked, "Owing, perhaps, to the inspiriting effects of many American flags, uniforms and faces, I took the decks to dance, which amusement I indulged in more than I had since I left West Point."[18] Ames has an entry for Florence, noting on February 14, 1867, "I called upon our great American Sculptor, Hiram Powers. He showed me all his works and insisted upon talking politics. Now, as a general thing I like politics, but he was too much for me. He is a true republican and loses his temper when he speaks of that 'traitor' Johnson who 'doubtless had an interest in the murder of Lincoln.'"[19]

In London, on March 23, 1867, Adelbert Ames went to a dinner party given by Charles Francis Adams: "This evening, I dined with our Minister, Mr. Adams. There were but eight or ten persons present. The manner of Mr. Adams is rather cold and formal. He does but little to make his callers at ease. He is quite notorious as an actor of this role. He is a small man and resembles his father, John Quincy Adams, very much."[20]

Two days later, General Ames says, "I presented a card from the United States Minister to the doorkeeper of the House of Commons and was ushered into the small and uncomfortable gallery of the House of Commons. The speaker of the evening was Mr. Gladstone. . . . Mr. Disraeli . . . made remarks. I was very fortunate to have been present."[21] Ames was fortunate the next day, too. He says in his entry for March 26,

> In the evening, I went with friends to hear Charles Dickens read some of his own writings. One of the two pieces was Pickwick's trial and, more especially, Sergeant Buzfuz's address to the jury. St. James Hall was crowded by a very intelligent audience. He read well—he certainly knows better than anyone how to render his own works—but to my thinking and that of some of my friends, he did not do as well as others have. I remember a classmate's speaking this same speech. He was a very fat fellow who could not do or say anything, whatever his intention, without appearing ludicrous and provoking mirth. The effect produced upon his audience was far greater than that which followed Dickens' efforts. I would not go to hear him again—but am glad I have heard him once—for it is very gratifying to see so prominent a writer and to hear him read what we all love to often read. But a good comedian would have done Charles Dickens better than Charles Dickens could do himself. He is a writer, not an actor.[22]

On April 22, 1867, in an entry written in Killarney, Ames says, "Before leaving London I told our Minister, Mr. Adams, of my proposed visit to Ireland, when he smilingly said it was possible that I might be arrested as a Fenian. . . . So, by his suggestion, I took a letter from his secretary to consuls in Ireland."[23] General Ames was not arrested as a Rebel.

In Paris, on May 29, 1867, Ames went to a reception given by the American Minister, General Dix. Ames left with a friend and says, "At the 'Palais a l'industrie' we stopped to see the paintings. . . . . While there, we saw the Emperor of the French. . . . A few paces off, we raised our hats—he, seeing it, lifted his, also. A compliment he did not pay the crowd, generally—the attention paid us was, we thought, because he detected in us the characteristics of Americans. He is quite a short man, but now inclined to be stout. His walk was any other than a military one."[24]

Bearing—good posture—was one of Ames's lifelong obsessions. Ames's granddaughter Pauline Ames Plimpton remembered his extremely erect walk. Mrs. Plimpton said that when his grandchildren shook hands with him, he made them "look him in the eye."[25] In some ways, Adelbert Ames did not change from the time when he was the young colonel of the Twentieth Maine.

After returning from his year in Europe, Ames served in the South. He was acting assistant inspector general in Arkansas and Mississippi and then in command at Vicksburg. Still called "general," his regular army rank was lieutenant colonel in the Twenty-fourth Infantry. Ames received a new title on June 15, 1868, when he was appointed provisional governor of Mississippi by Ulysses S. Grant, then secretary of war, who was using the power of the Reconstruction Act to replace a governor. To protect blacks required the use of federal troops, which in turn brought criticism of Reconstruction in the North as well as South. The man who was thrown out of the governor's mansion, Confederate General Benjamin Grubb Humphreys, had previously been thrown out of the class of 1829 after a riot at West Point.

Grant became president on March 4, 1869, and the next day appointed Ames to an additional post, commander of the Fourth Military District. On April 29, 1869, Ames ordered all persons competent to serve on juries, without respect to race, color, or previous condition of servitude. He also lowered the poll tax and guarded polling places with troops. In the election of November 30 through December 1, 1869, blacks voted in large numbers, and the regular Republicans won, with James Alcorn defeating Louis Dent, who was Grant's brother-in-law but not his choice for governor.

The new legislature met in January of 1870 with the unusual task of choosing three United States senators. For the term that would end in 1871— Jefferson Davis's former seat—Hiram Rhoades Revels, of Indian and African descent, was chosen. Governor Alcorn was picked to succeed him for a full six-year term. Blacks considered Ames an ally, and he was elected to the senate for the term ending in 1875.

The Senate debated for several months whether Ames was a resident of Mississippi. Ames had signed his own credentials, and that upset his opponents: "I, Adelbert Ames, Brevet Major-General United States Army, provisional governor of the State of Mississippi, do hereby certify that Adelbert Ames was elected United States Senator by the Legislature of this State on the 18th day of January, 1870."[26] On April 1, 1870, by a vote of forty to twelve, the Senate allowed Ames to take his seat.

In the Senate gallery, during the impeachment trial of President Johnson in 1868, Adelbert Ames met Blanche Butler. Their courtship included riding, walking, and listening to her father trying to convict Andrew Johnson of high treason. Benjamin Butler's daughter was an auburn-haired beauty and the belle of Washington. On July 21, 1870, at St. Ann's Episcopal Church in Lowell, Massachusetts, Ames married Blanche Butler. There were six hundred guests; one of the groomsmen was Major Adelbert Rinaldo Buffington (#7, May).

Ames told his wife in a letter written on May 21, 1871, "Yesterday after dinner, for the want of something else to do, I went to the President's grounds to hear the music. . . . I walked about nearly all the time while there with Senator Wilson. I got him to talk of Senatorial times when Sumner was beaten over the head by Brooks. All M.C.s went armed then. He wore two pistols and he said so accustomed to such scenes did he become he felt almost inclined to open fire. Not his words, his idea."[27]

Blanche Ames's first child, Butler, was born in 1871. Mrs. Ames did not like the hostile climate in Mississippi—complete with heat, epidemics, and bullets (sometimes fired near the governor's mansion)—and she and her son usually stayed in Lowell.

In Natchez on November 4, 1872, Senator Ames says, "Tomorrow will be election day. . . . Were the world half so solicitous about the Judgement Day there need not have been such a deep anxiety about tomorrow." Ames adds, "I shall go to the city hall tonight to speak, after which I shall go home and read Mark Twain's *Roughing It*."[28] The next day Adelbert Ames voted for the first time in his life and helped President Grant and his running mate, Henry Wilson, win in Mississippi.

In Vicksburg, on June 29, 1873, Senator Ames described his campaigning to his wife: "Yesterday afternoon I strolled around the streets . . . called on the foreign element. . . . Among the Germans I found very intelligent men.

One elderly man was very interesting. I spoke of the oppressions suffered by the Israelites in Europe, at the same time showing my sympathy for them and then stated we ought not treat the colored men of the South in a similar way. My remarks upon the Jewish question to him opened the discussion and he discoursed very fluently but not as a Jew, though he stated his parents were Jews."[29]

Black politicians wanted Ames to run for governor in 1873, and Mississippi's Republican convention nominated him on a ticket with three blacks. They were candidates for lieutenant governor, A. K. Davis; superintendent of education, T. W. Cardozo; and secretary of state, James Hill. In the general election, Ames faced Senator Alcorn, who was running for governor as an independent Republican with Democratic support.

In a letter from Booneville, Mississippi, on the campaign trail, dated October 1, 1873, Adelbert Ames tells his wife,

This is a white county, and the colored people did not have a fair chance to hear us yesterday, the room not being large enough for all, they were the ones to be crowded out. So last evening the colored people met in their church over the hills, a half mile away, to hear some of our speakers. There were present some thirty or forty colored men and women. It was a pleasant, yet a sad sight. This having been the scene of the Ku Klux outrages, the colored people have been deprived of almost every right, and their joy was apparent when they could meet away by themselves to hear the gospel preached by such speakers as are along with me. I imagine early Christians met and worshipped in the same manner—there was a sentinel to guard our building. It was sad because it showed how much they had been oppressed, and how eager they were for light. The church we were in was not half built. It was covered in, but there were no windows, and the stars shone through the cracks. They were so poor they could not complete the building. Yet they sat and cheered and laughed in turn, probably enjoying the meeting more than meetings are enjoyed even when the audience sit on velvet cushions.[30]

Ames won the election for governor by about 20,000 votes out of some 120,000 cast. He resigned from the Senate on January 10, 1874, and his inauguration as governor of Mississippi took place in Jackson on January 22, 1874. In his inaugural address, Governor Ames recommended compulsory free public schools, encouragement of manufacturing, diversification of crops, and expansion of land ownership by blacks.

Mississippi's most serious problem was violence, especially in Vicksburg, where whites were arming themselves before the local election in August.

On July 31, 1874, Governor Ames told his wife, "I have tried to get troops, but the President refuses. It is thought he wants the support of the Southern Democrats for a third term."[31]

Two days later, from Jackson, Mississippi, Ames tells his wife, "I received my pistol by yesterday's mail. . . . I do not imagine it will be of any use. However I will carry it as of old." Ames adds, "You perhaps have seen my telegram to the President. So I feel you know where I am and what I am doing. The condition of affairs in Vicksburg is beyond description. The Democrats by force of arms control everything."[32] The election was won by the Democrats on August 4, 1874.

Governor Ames notes on October 16, 1874, "Inside my house and myself all is well; but Republican disasters in Ohio and Indiana and the gradual and seemingly certain falling away of Republican states in the South makes us all a little gloomy and full of forebodings of a like fate."[33] By November 4, 1874, the foreboding of October had become a reality for Ames. Writing from the Custom House in New Orleans, he tells Blanche Ames, "The telegraphic dispatches this morning proclaim the defeat of your Father for Congress. They also assert that the Democracy have triumphed in every quarter. . . . The old rebel spirit will not only revive, but it will make itself felt." Ames could understand that Confederate veterans would continue to fight while a Yankee general and Benjamin Butler's daughter lived in their state. What he could not understand was why so many in the North were unwilling to fight: "The great reaction at the North is an enigma to me. I cannot understand it. . . . What a revolution. . . . A Democratic congress! And the war not yet over."[34]

Mississippi was already a battlefield, reaching a peak at Vicksburg on December 7. Whites had control of the city but blacks still controlled the county government. A black posse marching toward Vicksburg to reinstate a sheriff who had been indicted and driven out was attacked by whites with the loss of close to three hundred lives.

In a letter of December 14, 1874, Blanche Ames tells her mother, "Say to Father that we are in the midst of warlike times. . . . We pull down the shades and close the blinds at night, lest some foolish person might think it well to fire in." Before getting her daughter's letter, Sarah Hildreth Butler had written, "Political life is but a game of chance, hardly worth the struggle."[35] The violence continued in 1875. Ames remarked, "The old rebel armies are too much for our party."[36] He wanted Federal troops and could not understand why public support for it no longer existed, even in the North.

In a letter dated October 12, 1875, Governor Ames told his wife, "Yes, a *revolution* has taken place—and a race are disfranchised—they are to be returned to a condition of serfdom—an era of second slavery. . . . The nation should have acted but it was 'tired of the annual autumnal outbreaks in the South'—see Grant's and Pierrepont's letter to me. The political death of the Negro will forever release the nation from the weariness from such 'political outbreaks.' You may think I exaggerate. Time will show you how accurate my statements are."[37]

Adelbert Ames said in October of 1875, "Next year will be worse than this. . . . A year or two will end it all."[38] He was right. The Democratic campaign of fear and fraud worked. With many Republican leaders in hiding, and many blacks prevented from voting, the Democrats swept the election. Blanche Ames told her mother on December 8, 1875,

> I do not see that there are any favorable signs for our remaining here long. It is folly to say that they cannot find grounds for impeachment. Of course we know that there are none. But it is easy enough to concoct any number sufficient for their purpose. . . . The Democrats are determined to get rid of Gen'l Ames and if they should not succeed in impeaching him, they would not hesitate to assassinate. . . . At night in the town here, the crack of the pistol or gun is as frequent as the barking of the dogs. Night before last they gave us a few shots as they passed the Mansion yard, by way of a reminder. I do not think they fired at the windows, only discharged the guns to disturb our slumbers.[39]

In the new legislature that met on January 4, 1876, twenty-six of thirty-seven senators were Democrats as were seventy-seven of 116 representatives. The legislature immediately began planning the impeachment of the governor, as Blanche Ames had predicted.

There were rumors in Mississippi that Benjamin Butler might come to the state to try to help his son-in-law. Instead Butler hired lawyers who had the right credentials to deal with Ames's enemies. One was Roger Pryor, the secessionist editor and Confederate general, who got credit for working out a deal that had been proposed to him by Blanche Ames. If the Democrats dropped the impeachment charges, the governor would resign. On March 28, the articles of impeachment were dismissed by the legislature; on March 29, 1876, Adelbert Ames resigned. He left Mississippi and never returned.

Ames began a third career at forty as a businessman. He invested in flour mills with his father and brother in Minnesota. He spent some time in that state but more in Massachusetts, which his wife preferred. In 1878, "Little" Blanche was born. The next year the family moved to New York City, where

Ames went into the wheat commission business. In 1880, Adelbert Jr. was born and two years later Jessie, who would help edit the family letters, *Chronicles from the Nineteenth Century*. The family moved to Highlands, New Jersey, where the young children were tutored by their parents. In *Adelbert Ames*, his daughter Blanche says, "he insisted that his boys should go to college and his girls, also, long before higher education for women was an accepted custom."[40] The older girls went to Bryn Mawr and the younger ones to Smith.

Their father went to war, again, in 1898. The Spanish-American War began in April and would be over by August. The president was appointing generals, and on April 26, 1898, Ames wrote a letter to Governor George Boutwell of Massachusetts asking for a recommendation: "Will you write to President McKinley recommending me for appointment as a General, and stating Grant's opinion of me as set forth in your letter to Gov. Wolcott?"[41]

The *New York Times* of June 21, 1898, noted that "Adelbert Ames, who has been nominated to be Brigadier General, was graduated from West Point in 1861."[42] Ames wrote in his diary: "Left New York . . . July 6, 1898 bound to Santiago de Cuba . . . on board . . . Gen. G. V. Henry. . . . Gen. Henry was a classmate of mine at West Point, my junior in Civil War, but now my senior."[43] With General Ames was his son Adelbert; his oldest son, Butler, a West Point graduate as well, also served.

Ames received command of the Third Brigade of the First Infantry Division, containing three regiments of Regulars, the Ninth, Thirteenth, and Twenty-fourth, which was black. In a letter to his wife of July 14, 1898, from Fort San Juan, Ames says, "I have just seen Gen. Kent, Division Comd. who told me that if this city does not surrender today the Secretary of War has ordered an assault."[44] In addition to being his division commander, J. Ford Kent was his classmate.

Joseph Wheeler, a Confederate cavalry general, got along well with Ames. On July 15, 1898, General Ames told his wife, "I stopped to chat with Gen. Wheeler. He said he had been up till 1:30 this morning negotiating with the Spaniards. . . . And he also said he recommended to our commissioners that I be made Governor General of this Province upon surrender; and that the appointment would make it necessary that I be promoted to Major General. He was very kind in other utterances to the effect that I should have been one of the first M.G.s."[45]

Disease had killed more Americans than battle, and on August 3, 1898, there was a meeting on medicine. Ames reports, "All the Surgeons and some of the Generals talked and Roosevelt and I made speeches."[46] Theodore

Roosevelt, like Custer, had a flair for publicity. Ames thought someone only reading newspapers would think most of the troops in Cuba were Roosevelt's Rough Riders.

On August 25, 1898, Ames was appointed commander of the First Division and of Camp Wikoff, Montauk, New York. Three days later he wrote a letter to his mother, Martha Ames, in which he tells her, "Blanche, Sarah, Little Blanche, Adelbert and Jessie are sitting in my tent. . . . They left Boston in the yacht 'America' last Wednesday. . . . Butler was recommended for Colonel by his regiment and by three generals. . . . Two of these generals, Wilson and Henry, were friends of mine." Ames adds, "I command . . . one third of the infantry of the regular army. . . . I rather like this business. It recalls old war times when I was a youth."[47]

The old war would also be recalled in a letter Ames wrote in August of 1898: "I regret that I cannot accept your kind invitation to the Reunion of the 20th Maine. . . . The differences of dates of my two commissions as Brigadier General by Lincoln and McKinley is just thirty five years, yet when I reached the trenches on Fort San Juan hill and found myself among soldiers and heard the bullets and shells that period of more than a third of a century was obliterated and I was again a youth. . . . Please give my kindest regards to Chamberlain."[48] But the first colonel of the Twentieth Maine was not able to attend the reunion, since he was on active duty.

Ames was sent south in the fall to help select a site for a military base. In November in Summerville, South Carolina, Ames says, "I am surprised at the great change in public sentiment here as compared to what I have known. In this town are two or three union flags on residences. Some of its young men are in the S.C. regiments. One or two natives are at home on furlough wearing our uniform. I am treated with great courtesy."[49]

Ames explained his popularity, noting, "Every one expects to make a harvest out of us. I expect they will. . . . This change of base is of great financial benefit to these southern localities. It is not exactly war. It has the smell of politics about it. But the people here like it. Again, I say, this war with Spain in many and devious ways is obliterating Civil War animosities."[50]

General Ames was honorably discharged on January 3, 1899. He lived quietly in Tewksbury, Massachusetts, until he read *The Spirit of Old West Point* in 1908. The author, Morris Schaff (class of 1862) was a cadet from Ohio, like Custer, whose closest friends were from the South. There are some unflattering references to New England cadets in his book—even though Schaff now lived in Boston—and Ames immediately fired off an eight-page letter. He received a paragraph reply from the author and this P.S.: "Changes determined upon before the receipt of your letter, will appear in the next printing."[51]

In 1918, Ames wrote to a colonel at West Point and asked, "Will you be so kind as to give me the addresses of my classmates."[52] Adelbert and Blanche Ames spent the winters at Ormond Beach, Florida, where Ames had someone his own age to play golf with, John D. Rockefeller. The *New York Times* of April 4, 1928, has an account of one of their games under the headings, "Rockefeller . . . Beats General Adelbert Ames in Farewell Golf Game . . . Gives Dimes."[53]

On April 13, 1933, Adelbert Ames died at his home in Florida. In 1956, his name would appear in Senator John F. Kennedy's *Profiles in Courage*, which says, "No state suffered more from carpetbag rule than Mississippi. Adelbert Ames, first Senator and then Governor, was a native of Maine, a son-in-law of the notorious 'butcher of New Orleans,' Ben Butler. . . . He was chosen Governor by a majority composed of freed slaves and radical Republicans, sustained and nourished by Federal bayonets . . . two former slaves held the offices of Lieutenant Governor and Secretary of State."[54] Instead of being praised for having an integrated administration and being a courageous civil rights hero, Ames received that criticism in *Profiles in Courage*.

Senator Kennedy received a letter from Governor Ames's daughter, which begins, "I wish first to introduce myself. I am Blanche Ames Ames, wife of former Professor Oakes Ames, daughter of General Adelbert Ames and grand-daughter of General Benjamin F. Butler, Governor of Massachusetts. I think you know my grandson, George Ames Plimpton."[55] Blanche Ames asked Senator Kennedy to make corrections in future editions "for your own sake as well as mine."[56] But he replied on July 13, 1956, saying, "It is not anticipated that *Profiles in Courage* will go through another printing and thus there will be no opportunity to make changes in the text."[57]

After learning of plans for a televised version of *Profiles in Courage* in 1963, Mrs. Ames wrote to President Kennedy, since it would be a good opportunity "to bring your views into accord with the trend of modern historical interpretation of the Reconstruction Period."[58] Theodore Sorensen, special counsel to the president, answered Mrs. Ames on White House stationary on August 5, 1963, saying, "The President has asked me to reply to your very thoughtful letter . . . his present duties do not make it possible for him to undertake additional research and revisions with respect to his book. . . ."[59]

If others would not set the record straight, Blanche Ames would. Her daughter Pauline Ames Plimpton remarked, "For her to have an idea was to act."[60] The result was a six hundred-page biography, *Adelbert Ames, 1835–1933: General, Senator, Governor*. After Blanche Ames died in 1969, her family continued to defend her father's record in Mississippi. Her son-in-law Francis T. P. Plimpton told the *Brockton Daily Enterprise*, "She felt strongly about it because he was just trying to do what we're trying to do today—he was determined to make sure the Negroes had their full legal rights."[61]

10

George Armstrong Custer:
Little Bighorn

The postwar road to Little Bighorn began in Texas in 1865, where Custer commanded a reorganized cavalry division of troopers wanting to go home and, for the first time, was unpopular with the men he led. Custer's command was part of General Philip Sheridan's army near Mexico. Custer seemed to have been an exception to the usual problem of being promoted beyond one's depth. He was, paradoxically, a very successful brigade and division commander in the Civil War; it was a regiment that gave him trouble, long before he led part of it into Custer's Last Stand.

Youth had obviously not prevented Custer from successfully handling the command responsibilities of a general when he was twenty-three and twenty-four. It could, of course, be easily argued that he was a better officer at that age than when he got himself wiped out at thirty-six. Custer's personality, or more likely his behavior, which had obviously not held him back in the Civil War, either changed to some degree, or, in the changed circumstances of regimental command, caused problems. It is remarkable that the same man was very popular with his command when it was large (a brigade or division) but could not retain that popularity when it was reduced.

One explanation is that, in the smaller circle of a regiment, everyone knew him. In some ways it is easier to hide unattractive qualities, such as favoritism and arrogance (or at least their unpleasant consequences), when most of the officers do not really know their commander. A lack of fairness can be more harmful to morale and cohesion in a small unit, and Custer was especially clannish. More than in most regiments, factionalism was a problem in the Seventh Cavalry, which had its pro- and anti-Custer factions, with the former consisting heavily of old friends and relatives. Custer outdid most in nepotism. Killed with Custer at Little Bighorn were two brothers

(Tom and Boston), a brother-in-law (James Calhoun), and a nephew (Autie Reed). For "whatever errors he may have committed,"[1] to use General Terry's words, he had paid for them.

Custer rejoined the Regular Army when he was mustered out of the Volunteers on February 1, 1866. Still called general, he reverted to his regular rank of captain in the Fifth Cavalry and took a pay cut from $8,000 a year to $2,000. But Mexico still had a war, and Custer was offered the rank of general in the Mexican army at a salary of $16,000 in gold.

Grant wrote a letter of introduction for Custer, saying on May 16, 1866, "This will introduce to your acquaintance Gn. Custer who rendered such distinguished service as a Cavalry Officer during the War. There was no officer in that branch of service who had the confidence of Gn. Sheridan to a greater degree than Gn. C. and there is no officer in whose judgement I have greater faith than in Sheridans."[2]

Despite that endorsement, the secretary of state, William Seward, opposed the idea, so Custer had to give up plans for Mexico. But four new U.S. cavalry regiments were being created, numbered seven through ten. The Ninth and Tenth Cavalry were black regiments, and Elizabeth Custer has an illustration by Frederic Remington called "Negroes Form Their Own Picket-line" in her *Tenting on the Plains*.[3]

Custer became lieutenant colonel of the Seventh U.S. Cavalry in July of 1866. Since the colonels, Andrew Jackson Smith and then Samuel Davis Sturgis, were hardly ever with the regiment, Custer led the Seventh until his death. In an often quoted remark, Custer says, "If I were an Indian, I often think I would greatly prefer to cast my lot among those of my people who adhered to the free open plains rather than submit to the confined limits of a reservation, there to be the recipient of the blessed benefits of civilization, with its vices thrown in."[4] Custer adds, "At best the history of our Indian tribes, no matter from what standpoint it is regarded, affords a melancholy picture of loss of life."[5]

The origins of the Indians intrigued Custer, who thought they might be Jewish. "Many of the Indian customs and religious rites," according to Custer, "closely resemble those of the Israelites. The 'medicine man' of the tribe, who is not, as his name implies, the physician, but stands in the character of high priest, assumes a dress and manner corresponding to those of the Jewish high priest."[6]

Custer's Seventh Cavalry, stationed at Fort Riley, Kansas, took part in General Winfield Scott Hancock's expedition against the Indians in 1867.

Hancock's heavy force included artillery, infantry, and reporters. The *New York Herald* sent Henry Morton Stanley—who had served in the Confederate army and the Union navy—before he went to Africa to say, "Dr. Livingston, I presume?" But Hancock's expedition was not a success for the commanding general or for Custer, who managed to get himself court-martialed on eight counts.

Custer's defense counsel at the court martial was a classmate from West Point, Charles Parsons of the Fourth Artillery. Parsons would leave the army for the ministry, but his calling was not law. Custer was convicted on all counts, including shooting deserters and leaving his command (in order to be with his wife), but was only suspended without pay for one year.[7]

After being restored to regimental command, Custer won the battle of the Washita on November 27, 1868, which gave him a reputation as an Indian fighter and much criticism. In the east especially, Custer was criticized for attacking the village of Black Kettle in the Indian Territory, now Oklahoma. In the army, Custer was criticized for leaving the field without knowing the fate of the regiment's major, Joel Elliott, and nineteen men (who were wiped out, including Sergeant Major Kennedy). This increased the feud in the Seventh Cavalry between the pro- and anti-Custer factions. One of Custer's strongest supporters was Lieutenant (often regimental adjutant) William Winer Cooke, the son of a wealthy physician in Hamilton, Ontario, where he would be reburied after Little Bighorn.

The leader of the anti-Custer faction in the Seventh was Captain Frederick William Benteen, later brevet brigadier general. He wrote a letter to a friend denouncing Custer for abandoning Major Elliott, which was published (without his name) in the *St. Louis Democrat* (February 9, 1869) and the *New York Times* (February 14, 1869). A fuming Custer told his officers he would horsewhip the author. Benteen gives an account of this "congeniality" in the Seventh Cavalry in an 1896 letter to Theodore Goldin, who had been an enlisted man. "I . . . drew my revolver," Benteen recalled, "turned the cylinder . . . returned it lightly to holster . . . you can imagine what would have happened had the rawhide whirred!"[8] Benteen acknowledged his authorship, and Custer, wisely, did not carry out his threat.

Benteen had been a colonel during the Selma campaign, whose commander, General James Harrison Wilson, thought highly of him.[9] So did a future superintendent of West Point; General Hugh Scott, who served as chief of staff at the beginning of World War I, says, "I found my model early in Captain Benteen, the idol of the Seventh Cavalry on the upper Missouri in 1877, who governed mainly by suggestion; in all the years I knew him I never once heard him raise his voice to enforce his purpose. . . . If he found this kindly manner were misunderstood, then his iron hand would close down quickly."[10]

In 1869, Custer had a brilliant success by freeing two women who had been captured by Indians. In addition to the Seventh Cavalry, Custer also had the Nineteenth Kansas Volunteer Cavalry, commanded by Samuel Crawford, war governor and author of *Kansas in the Sixties*. Not only was Custer able to control the volunteers, but getting the hostages back alive was unusual. He used skill, patience, and some kidnapping of his own—threatening to hang three chiefs—and was successful. The women were treated with great enthusiasm when they returned, which was not always the case with former hostages, some others thinking they would have been better off dead.[11]

Custer left Kansas in 1871, when the Seventh Cavalry served on Reconstruction duty in South Carolina, Louisiana, and Kentucky. The Custers and two companies of the Seventh lived in Elizabethtown, Kentucky, where the general spent his time suppressing the Ku Klux Klan, smashing distilleries, and buying horses.

Custer was also building a reputation as a sportsman. From 1867 to 1875, Custer wrote fifteen letters for the New York sports magazine *Turf, Field and Farm*, using the name "Nomad."[12] Sometimes his topic was buffalo hunting, and in 1872, General Sheridan ordered Custer to escort Grand Duke Alexis of Russia on a buffalo hunt. The guide was Buffalo Bill Cody, whose flair for publicity equaled Custer's.

In 1873, the Seventh Cavalry was sent to the Dakota Territory. The regiment marched from Yankton, near Nebraska, to Fort Abraham Lincoln, which was being built on the west bank of the Missouri, five miles downstream from Bismarck. Elizabeth Custer was usually more critical of Indians than her husband. She wrote her books as a widow. And, of course, General Custer did not know, when he wrote *My Life on the Plains, or Personal Experiences with Indians*, that they would kill him.

Elizabeth Custer explains her double danger: "I had been a subject of conversation among the officers, being the only woman who, as a rule, followed the regiment, and without discussing it much in my presence, the universal understanding was that any one having me in charge in an emergency where there was imminent danger of my capture, should shoot me instantly."[13]

In July and August of 1874, General Custer led an expedition through the Black Hills of Dakota. Sacred land to the Sioux, white men had no business being there, according to treaty. But Custer rode through with the Seventh Cavalry, two companies of infantry, a photographer, miners, and professors from Yale, including George Bird Grinnell. Custer's engineers mapped the terrain, the miners found gold, and Custer named mountains after General Alfred Terry and himself.

Serving on the frontier could be excruciatingly boring; to survive you had to know how to kill time. An army officer had a choice of becoming an alcoholic or a scholar, according to one professor at West Point. At the end of 1874, Custer studied military history and worked on his Civil War memoirs, writing at a table in his library, which also had a gun rack. On the walls were some of the results of his favorite pastime: mounted heads of antelope, bison, and bear, and enlarged heads (mounted photographs) of his favorite generals, McClellan and himself.

In the autumn of 1875, the Custers went east on leave and, Mrs. Custer recalls, "spent most of the winter delightfully in New York. . . . Every one seemed to vie with every one else in showing appreciation of my husband during that winter. At the Century Club he received from distinguished men the most cordial congratulations on his essay into the literary field. They urged him with many an encouraging word to continue the work. Some of the authors he met there were double his age, and he received each word they said with deep gratitude."[14]

Custer also talked to Congressman Hiester Clymer's committee (March 29 and April 4, 1876) which was investigating corruption in the War Department of Secretary William W. Belknap. Custer's testimony about kickbacks for post traderships, although largely hearsay, was very critical of the secretary and the president's brother Orvil. Democrats were delighted; the president was not. Without the intervention of Custer's superiors (especially Generals Sheridan and Terry) and the anti-Grant press, Custer would not have been allowed to take part in the Great Sioux War of 1876.

Elizabeth Custer described the departure of the Seventh Cavalry from Fort Lincoln on May 17, 1876, saying, "when our band struck up 'The Girl I Left Behind Me,' the most despairing hour seemed to have come. All the sad-faced wives of the officers who had forced themselves to their doors to try and wave a courageous farewell, and smile bravely to keep the ones they loved from knowing the anguish of their breaking hearts, gave up the struggle at the sound of the music."[15] Clearly, while that lilting tune may have improved the troops' morale, it seems to have had another effect on their wives, one saying, "To this day that tune makes the cold chills run through my body."[16]

After forced marches, the Seventh Cavalry—some six hundred officers and enlisted men plus about a dozen civilians and thirty-five Indian scouts—found Sitting Bull's village in the valley of the Little Bighorn. Custer had turned down General Terry's offer of four troops, or companies, of the Second U.S. Cavalry. On June 25, in another display of overconfidence, Custer divided his command in four ways, even more than usual in Indian fighting, and attacked *against the advice of his scouts.* Forced onto ground that was unsuitable for cavalry tactics and that was not within supporting distance of the other battalions, Custer, as we all know, ran out of luck. Two hundred and ten men and officers were killed, and Companies C, E, F, I, and L were annihilated when Custer's command was wiped out.

Custer has been blamed for everything imaginable, but it is significant that the person who perhaps hated him the most, Benteen, only blamed him for one mistake. Frederick Benteen asked Theodore Goldin, "Now, isn't that the whole and sole reason that we were so badly beaten? i.e. the regiment being broken up into four columns, and none of the four within supporting distance of either of the others, (without any orders even to be such a support to any) true? . . . That is all that I blame Custer for—the scattering, as it were, (two portions of his command, anyway) to the—well, four winds, before he knew anything about the exact or approximate position of the Indian village or the Indians."[17] Benteen, in the opinion of many of the survivors, saved the other seven companies of the Seventh, and he was angered that he and Reno were criticized—by Custer's friend Rosser, among others—for not rescuing Custer. They could have easily ended up like Custer. That they avoided his fate was in large part the result of the rest of the regiment winding up in one place, which Benteen notes: "Tell me, please, was there any generalship displayed in so scattering the regiment that only the merest of chance, intervention of Providence—or what you will—saved the whole 12 troops from being 'wiped out.'"[18]

To a remarkable degree, Benteen's analysis was shared by the *Army and Navy Journal,* which even notes that "by chance" Benteen and Reno combined forces. Perhaps most remarkable, "A Glance at the Recent Disaster" was published on July 22, 1876. It is more balanced than most commentary on Custer, then and since. How does one prepare for circumstances that have almost never occurred before? Given what Custer knew at the time, his decisions and aggressive tactics made sense. As the article notes, they were not those of a commander ignorant of his profession.

In a reference to Custer's quarrel with President Grant—who had briefly removed Custer from command of the Seventh—the *Army and Navy Journal* says,

It has been asserted that, smarting under the wounds which preceding events had inflicted upon his pride, Custer dashed recklessly into this affair for the purpose of eclipsing his superior officers in the same field, regardless of cost or consequences. This, it seems to us, is going much too far. Custer was doubtless glad of the opportunity to fight the battle alone, and was stimulated by the anticipation of a victory which, illuminating his already brilliant career, would make him outshine those put on duty over him in this campaign. But his management of the affair was probably just about what it would have been under the same circumstances, if he had no grievance. His great mistake was in acting in mingled ignorance of, and contempt for, his enemy. He regarded attack and victory in this instance as synonymous terms, the only point being to prevent the escape of the foe. Under this fatal delusion he opened the engagement, with his command divided into four parts, with no certainty of co-operation or support between any two of them. Three companies, under Benteen, were off on the left, ordered in, it is true, and by chance arrived in time to aid Reno. One company, under MacDougal, was in rear with the pack train. Reno was sent to the left bank of the river to attack the enemy with three companies, while Custer with the other five companies not only remained on the opposite bank from Reno, but went back—of the bluff, and three miles lower down the stream, thus placing mutual support, in case of necessity, out of the question. . . . Neither ambition, nor wounded vanity, prompted these . . . fatal dispositions, nor were they due to lack of knowledge of the principles of his profession. They proceeded, as heretofore stated, from a total misconception, which Custer shared with others, in relation to the numbers, prowess, and sagacity of the enemy he was dealing with.[19]

Walt Whitman was more sympathetic in "A Death Sonnet For Custer" from *Leaves of Grass*:

The fall of Custer and all his officers and men. . . .
Desperate and glorious, aye in defeat most desperate, most glorious,
After thy many battles in which never yielding up a gun or a color,
Leaving behind thee a memory sweet to soldiers,
Thou yieldest up thyself.[20]

Another poem was written for the *Tribune* by Edmund Stedman, a poet with a seat on the New York Stock Exchange—"the Bard of Wall Street"—who produced fifty lines on the "wild young warrior."[21]

Buffalo Bill gave up acting (temporarily) and became a scout for the Fifth U.S. Cavalry. After killing Yellow Hand at War Bonnet Creek, according to his autobiography, he yelled, "The first scalp for Custer," but was back in the theater in the fall, publicizing Custer's legend and his own.[22] The grand finale of Buffalo Bill's Wild West Show was a reenactment of Custer's Last Stand.

Custer was reburied at West Point on October 10, 1877. Lincoln's secretary, John Hay, wrote a poem called "Miles Keogh's Horse," which was "the only living thing" to survive Custer's Last Stand. Comanche, the wounded hero horse, was the object of a special order by Samuel Sturgis, the colonel of the Seventh Cavalry, whose son James (class of 1875) was killed with Custer. To ride or strike Comanche was a court martial offense, and he was not to be put to any work. Hay adds that Sturgis's order proves

> That the sense of a soldier's worth,
> That the love of comrades, the honor of arms,
> Have not yet perished from earth.

Hay, who became secretary of state, explains Custer's fame by observing, "Custer, / In his disastrous fall, / Flashed out in a blaze that charmed the world."[23]

Elizabeth Custer's idealized account of her husband and her marriage appears in her *Boots and Saddles* in 1885. Two years later, Mark Twain's Charles L. Webster & Company published Mrs. Custer's next book, *Tenting on the Plains*, or *General Custer in Kansas and Texas*, with ten signed illustrations by Frederic Remington. In the winter of 1887, Mrs. Custer went to a dinner party with Robert Louis Stevenson at Lake Saranac, New York. In 1898, she became a member of an artists colony at Onteora, New York, in the Catskills, where one of her neighbors was Mark Twain. Candace Wheeler recalls "a luncheon. . . . We were a company of perhaps a dozen authors, editors, writers, artists, and the like. . . . Mrs. Custer looked across the table. 'Why,' said she, 'we are all working-women; *not a lady among us!*'"[24]

In 1912, the movie *Custer's Last Fight* appeared, directed by John Ford's older brother Francis, who also played the general. One of Mrs. Custer's young friends was the future actress and author Cornelia Otis Skinner, who received an inscribed copy of *Boots and Saddles* with the enclosed note:

April 18 [1919]

Dear Miss Skinner

Thank you for your note and the feeling that between the lines there is such evidence of friendship. . . . I want . . . you to feel that I can be called upon if there comes a time you need me

—affectionately Elizabeth B. Custer[25]

The address on Mrs. Custer's letter to Miss Skinner is 71 Park Avenue. Mrs. Custer bought an apartment on the ninth floor of the red stone building near 38th Street, which was still there in the 1990s when the Cosmopolitan Club, of which she was a member, had an exhibit of her books. She spent the winters in Florida at Daytona Beach. Elizabeth Custer died on April 4, 1933, and was buried at West Point. Franklin D. Roosevelt was president and the army chief of staff was Douglas MacArthur. When General MacArthur entered Tokyo at the end of World War II, the Seventh Cavalry was his escort.[26]

Custer's image had begun to change about the time of his wife's death, reflecting changing attitudes towards Indians and the military by authors, artists, journalists, and filmmakers. His heroic reputation was turned on its head as he became the symbol of everything bad the United States had done to the Indians. Each interpretation reveals something about the interpreter and the times, if not about Custer.

Two of the most memorable pro-Custer films were made at the beginning of World War II. Olivia de Havilland plays Elizabeth Custer in *They Died With Their Boots On*; the boy general is Errol Flynn, who is killed by Anthony Quinn, playing Crazy Horse. In *Santa Fe Trail*, Custer is played by Ronald Reagan. "The United States Cavalry," according to Bosley Crowther's review in the *New York Times*, "comes whooping to the rescue not once but twice—and beautifully."[27]

Movies maintained Custer's international reputation. In the Falkland Islands War, young British officers described a particularly sharp fight by saying it was like Custer's Last Stand. During the Gulf War, when a journalist asked General Norman Schwarzkopf about his reluctance to attack, Schwarzkopf reportedly said, "If the alternative to dying is sitting in the sun for another summer, then that's not a bad alternative. I'm not rushing into battle. I'm not General Custer."[28]

Writers like to talk about the complexity of their subject. That could be a mistake in Custer's case. As many have said, he was a brave cavalryman whose luck ran out in the valley of the Little Bighorn. Maybe there is less there than meets the eye.

Thomas Lafayette Rosser:
Custer's Rebel Friend

After breaking out at Appomattox Court House on April 9, Rosser was captured at "Courtland," his wife's house, on May 2, 1865, and taken to Richmond. He was soon released after the Federals learned that he had not
surrendered at Appomattox and therefore could not be violating the parole
that Confederates who were there received. On May 2, 1867, he lectured at
Cooper Institute in New York on "The Last Days of the Army of Northern
Virginia," expressing disappointment that more New Yorkers had not come
"to hear what a rebel had to say," while emphasizing that the war was not
brought on by military men.[1]

In 1868, Rosser got a job on the Pittsburgh and Connellsville Railroad. His
postwar career was described by Custer, who says, "When the war ended,
Rosser, like many of his comrades from the South . . . at once cast about him
for an opportunity to begin anew the battle, not of war, but of life. Possess-
ing youth, health, many and large abilities, added to indomitable pluck, he
decided to trust his fortunes amidst his late enemies, and repaired to Minnesota."[2]

Rosser began working on the Lake Superior and Mississippi Railroad in St.
Paul in 1871 as an ax-man, but quickly worked his way up. Later that year,
the Northern Pacific hired Rosser as assistant engineer and as division engineer in charge of surveys and construction in Dakota and Montana Territo-
ries. Rosser led the engineering party in an 1871 survey of the Yellowstone.

Custer's article on the 1873 Yellowstone expedition notes, "The engineers
and surveyors of the Northern Pacific railroad were under the direction and
management of General Thomas L. Rosser."[3] Custer's cavalry protected
them. Mrs. Custer says, "The general wrote me that he was lying on the
buffalo-robe in his tent, resting after the march, when he heard a voice out-

side asking the sentinel which was General Custer's tent. The general called out 'Halloo, old fellow! I haven't heard that voice in thirteen years, but I know it. Come in and welcome!'"[4]

Custer told his wife, "Well, I have joined the engineers, and am having such pleasant visits with General Rosser. We talk over our West Point times and discuss the battles of the war. I stretch the buffalo-robe under the fly of the tent, and there in the moonlight he and I, lying at full length, listen to each other's accounts of battles in which both had borne a part. It seemed like the time when we were cadets together, huddled on one blanket and discussing dreams of the future."[5]

Usually, when classmates met after the war, the one from the North helped his friend from the South. Here the roles were reversed, since Custer was under arrest for insubordination. But Rosser convinced the commander of the expedition, Colonel David S. Stanley—who hated Custer—that the Northern Pacific would want Custer leading the cavalry.

During the summer expedition, Rosser and a small group were surrounded by Indians; but he held out until the U.S. cavalry arrived. Three years later, after Little Bighorn, Rosser sent a letter to a newspaper, often reprinted, blaming Custer's subordinates for the disaster. Rosser concluded, "I knew Gen. Custer well; have known him intimately from boyhood; and being on opposite sides during the late war we often met and measured strength on the fields of Virginia, and I can truly say now that I never met a more enterprising, gallant or dangerous enemy during those four years of terrible war, or a more genial, whole-souled, chivalrous gentleman and friend in peace than Major General George A. Custer."[6]

In 1881, Rosser was hired by James J. Hill to become chief engineer of the Canadian Pacific Railway (CPR). Rosser had become rich by speculating in town lots along the railroads he was building—and his engineers believed he had permission to do the same while choosing the route across Canada— but the CPR's (later Sir) William C. Van Horne fired Rosser and pulled a pistol on him in the Manitoba Club in Winnipeg.[7]

Rosser bought an estate, Rugby Hall, near Charlottesville, Virginia. According to Custer, "The manly course adopted by Rosser after the war, his determined and successful struggle against adversity, presents a remarkable instance of the wonderful recuperative powers of the American character."[8] Rosser became a consulting engineer for the Charleston, Cincinnati, and Chicago Railroad, which was formed in 1886 to build a line through Appalachia. But he was unable to repeat his success in the west.

In 1889, Rosser had two controversial speeches published because "these addresses . . . have occasioned so much malignant criticism from individuals, and the press, North and South."[9] Rosser calls McClellan's aide, the comte de Paris and author of a four-volume *History of the Civil War*, a "princely 'Tramp'" and talks about what he inherited from "his imbecile grandfather, Louis Phillippe."[10]

There was something in Rosser's speech to offend every group:

> The conflict to-day is between the individual . . . and corporate power sustained by the government. . . . This conflict which may well be called the *irrepressible* is not witnessed in the *rebellious* South. It is confined to the 'loyal' North, and a most singular anomaly will, ere long, be witnessed—capital fleeing from the North and seeking the protection of the Southern people whom that capital has heretofore endeavored to enslave; because here in the South the capitalist will find . . . his rights will be respected and his property, however ill-gotten, and liberty, however ill-deserved, will be protected . . . and to the astonished world will be revealed the fact that the rebels of the South and their descendants will be the only defenders of the American Union, Equality and Liberty given us by the Constitution of 1787.[11]

In Rosser's view, the line back to the Founding Fathers in Philadelphia ran through Confederate Richmond, not Washington. He tried and failed in 1892 to get the Democratic nomination for Virginia's Seventh Congressional District. He finally got a good job (and almost got out of debt) in 1898 when President McKinley appointed Rosser brigadier general of United States Volunteers during the Spanish-American War. He was given an infantry brigade—the Fourteenth Minnesota, Second Ohio, and First Pennsylvania—which he drilled during the summer of '98 before being honorably discharged in November. Rosser described to Senator John W. Daniel of Virginia the "metamorphosis of sentiment that occurred in me . . . I was ordered to Chickamauga Park . . . I took an oath to defend the flag which I had so often fought and bled to dishonor . . . I experienced a strange sensation . . . many of the splendid boys . . . were the sons of Union soldiers I had met in the bloody battles of the Civil War."[12]

In 1900, Rosser became a Republican and in 1905 was appointed postmaster of Charlottesville by President Theodore Roosevelt. Mrs. Custer refers to Rosser becoming a symbol of reconciliation in the Spanish-American War, noting, "how indebted our country was to the prompt act of patriotism on the part of General Rosser, General Wheeler and General [Fitzhugh] Lee, when our country was obliged to enter into a foreign war. It grows upon me what a wonderful cementing of the South and the North resulted from the act of these three patriots."[13]

In keeping with the symbolism of national reconciliation, after he died on March 29, 1910, Rosser's obituary photograph in the Richmond *Times-Dispatch* the next day showed him wearing the uniform of a general of United States Volunteers, with "U.S.V." on the collar.

John Whitney Barlow:
Explorer of Yellowstone

John Whitney Barlow is remembered not for a battle but for a park. His *Report of a Reconnaissance of the Basin of the Upper Yellowstone in 1871* was published by Congress, which set aside land the next year for the first national park.[1] From his headquarters in Chicago, General Philip Sheridan had sent Barlow, his chief engineer, to map the Yellowstone Basin. Barlow shared a cavalry escort with the leader of another expedition, geologist Ferdinand V. Hayden.

Barlow left Chicago on the morning of July 2, 1871. The Northwestern Railway took him over the prairies of Illinois and Iowa, and he reached the Missouri River the next morning. After a ferry boat ride and a ride on the Union Pacific, Barlow says, "We celebrated the 4th of July in crossing the main divide of the Rocky Mountains."[2]

Changing at Corinne, Utah, to a stage coach, Barlow's party headed for Fort Ellis, Montana. "A stage ride," Barlow remarks, "at best, is a cheerless experience, but the Montana route particularly has usually been considered almost unendurable. The heat, the dust, the crowded condition of the stage, and above all the loss of sleep for three or four nights and days, it is said, reduces the traveler to a state bordering on insanity." He adds, "We were more fortunate, perhaps, than others, inasmuch as our first day was cool," and they reached Virginia City "after several changes of conveyances, generally for the worse."[3]

At Fort Ellis, Barlow found Hayden and his escort, Company F, Second U.S. Cavalry. *The Great West* by Hayden has a picture of eminent American explorers and artists, including Custer and himself.[4] On July 16, they started, but by the next day, according to Barlow's diary, "the mules and drivers behaved better."[5]

On Warm-Stream Creek, Barlow saw a boiling brook and warm mineral springs, where invalids had formed a camp. Barlow also tried the warm water, saying, "Many of the basins have the size and shape of bathtubs. The temperature varies in the different pools from fifty degrees all the way up to one hundred and eighty, so there is no difficulty in finding a bath of suitable temperature." Barlow adds, "Toward evening I enjoyed a bath among the natural basins of Soda Mountain. The temperature was delightful, and could be regulated at pleasure by simply stepping from one basin to another. They were even quite luxurious, being lined with a spongy gypsum, soft and pleasant to the touch."[6]

The explorers' food was improved by one of the artists Hayden had brought along, Thomas Moran, who, according to photographer William Henry Jackson, knew a new way to bake trout.[7] The great falls of the Yellowstone Barlow claims are as beautiful as any place on earth, the water of the upper fall "spreading out at the bottom with the grace and beauty of a lady's ballroom costume."[8] Half a mile below was the crest of the lower fall with a drop of 350 feet.

After crossing prairie, Barlow saw another soda mountain: "Approaching nearer, I found jets of smoke and steam issuing from the face of the hill, while its other side was hollowed out into a sort of amphitheater, whose sides were steaming with sulphur fumes, the ground hot and parched with internal fires. Acre after acre of this hot volcanic surface lay before me, having numerous cracks from whence were expelled, sometimes in steady, continuous streams, sometimes in puffs like those from an engine, jets of vapor. I ascended the hill, leaving my horse below fearful that he might break through the thin rock-crust, from which hot fumes were sure to issue."[9]

Barlow also found "a large boiling spring, emitting strong fumes of sulphur and sulphureted hydrogen, not at all agreeable. Near this was a spring having regular pulsations, like a steam-engine; giving off large quantities of steam, which would issue forth with the roar of a hurricane. This was, in reality, a steam volcano."[10]

The next day Barlow found a mud volcano. He says, "The surface of the bottom is in a constant state of ebullition, puffing and throwing up masses of boiling mud, and sending forth dense columns of steam several hundred feet above the surrounding forests." Trees one hundred feet away were covered with mud. At a different spot on the same day, Barlow "enjoyed a steam bath at the mouth of the cavern-spring. The water was much too hot for bathing, and the stones upon which I stood would have burnt my feet but for the precaution of keeping on my shoes."[11]

Some geysers shot a column of water two hundred feet high. Old Faithful was photographed in action by Hayden's photographer, William Jackson, who was impressed that Hayden never seemed to rest, noting, "Even the Indians, some of whom regarded him as insane, were awed by Hayden's industry. They named him Man-Who-Picks-Up-Stones-Running."[12]

The entry in Barlow's diary for July 29 notes, "Sounds resembling a human voice calling for help were heard at intervals through the night; it is supposed they proceeded from the throat of a species of panther, called the American lion. I saw the skin and claws of one of these animals at Bottler's Ranch. I judged that an encounter with one would not be altogether safe." He mentions meeting a large grizzly bear and cub and says, "not being armed or mounted we made a safe detour of the monster."[13]

In addition to writing in his diary and collecting rocks, Barlow named a mountain after his boss. Mount Sheridan is a ten thousand-foot snow-covered peak. The next day he named Mount Hancock.

Leaving Yellowstone on August 28, Barlow was back in Chicago on September 15, 1871, in time to have his office burned in the Chicago Fire. Photographs were destroyed and Barlow's report was delayed, but a summary appeared in the Chicago Journal of January 13, 1872, and it helped promote Yellowstone. At the end of the month, the Senate passed a bill to establish Yellowstone National Park; the legislation passed the House in February and President Grant signed it on March 1, 1872.

General Sheridan ordered his chief engineer to join another expedition the next summer, when the Northern Pacific Railroad sent a surveying party down the Yellowstone River. Barlow accompanied the cavalry escort with verbal orders from Sheridan to keep a diary.

In 1874, Barlow became superintending engineer for Long Island Sound. He was promoted major of engineers in 1879 and lieutenant colonel in 1884. Two years later, he was in charge on the Tennessee River, opening the Muscle Shoals Canal in 1890. From 1892 to 1896, Barlow commanded the American engineers on the International Boundary Commission, resurveying the Mexican border from El Paso to the Pacific. John Barlow became a colonel in 1895 and rose to general and chief of engineers on May 2, 1901. He retired the next day.

Barlow had outlived the woman he married in 1861, Hessie McNaughton Birnie. In 1902, he married Alice Stanton Turner of New London, Connecticut, and they made their home in that navy town. Interservice rivalry did not bother Barlow; some of his best friends were admirals. The Barlows went on a tour of the Holy Land, where John Barlow died in Jerusalem on February 27, 1914. General Barlow's body was sent back to Arlington and the river he had guarded as a young lieutenant in the Army of the Potomac.

Henry Algernon du Pont:
Businessman, Senator, Author

After the Civil War, Henry Algernon du Pont remained in the artillery and served on a board (with his classmate Emory Upton) to assimilate tactics for artillery, infantry, and cavalry. Du Pont married Mary Pauline Foster in 1874, left the army in 1875, and lived in Europe for a year. He then became head of the sales division of E. I. du Pont de Nemours & Co. He was president and general manager of the Wilmington & Northern Railroad from 1879 to 1899. In 1889, when his father died, Henry and his brother William had four-fifths of the shares of the Du Pont partnership. But Henry du Pont did not succeed his father as head of the firm because his younger brother would not support him.

In 1895, Henry A. du Pont was the largest stockholder in his family's chemical company and a candidate for the United States Senate. After four months and 177 attempts, the Delaware legislature elected him by a one-vote margin; but the Senate, after a year, then rejected du Pont's credentials by one vote.

In 1899, du Pont, who thought the family firm should incorporate, became a vice president of the new corporation. In 1902, Henry du Pont, who was regarded as the head of the family, was instrumental in preventing the family business from being sold to Laflin & Rand. Instead the business was turned over to another generation of du Ponts, Alfred, Coleman, and Pierre. According to Alfred's biographer, Henry du Pont accomplished it "with the commanding dignity of person that was his greatest asset."[1]

Henry du Pont was also the family biographer. He edited in French the *Mémoires* of the family's founding father, Pierre Samuel du Pont de Nemours (1739–1817), the French statesman, philosophe, and friend of Thomas Jefferson. It includes an account of the storming of the Tuileries (August 10, 1792) by Du Pont de Nemours, who was a member of the King's Guard, and a reminiscence of Louis XVI, who said on that day, "Ah! Monsieur du Pont, we always find you where we need you."[2] The *Mémoires* were published in Paris in 1906, with footnotes and a preface by Henry du Pont.

H. A. du Pont also mentions his great-grandfather in his book on his uncle, *Rear-Admiral Samuel Francis Du Pont, United States Navy: A Biography.* S. F. Du Pont (the only grandson of Du Pont de Nemours to spell his name with a capital D) did not have a hard time getting into the navy. His grandfather, who left France when Napoleon returned from Elba in 1815, wrote to Thomas Jefferson, who wrote to James Madison. H. A. du Pont observes, "Jefferson's confidence as to the probable action of President Madison was fully justified . . . Samuel Francis Du Pont, then a few months over twelve years of age, was appointed midshipman . . . this appointment being accompanied by another to the Military Academy at West Point."[3]

On June 13, 1906, Henry du Pont was elected to the United States Senate, where he served as chairman of the Committee on Military Affairs from 1911 to 1913. In 1914, he introduced legislation to compensate the Virginia Military Institute (VMI) for the damage it suffered when his commanding officer, General David Hunter, burned it down. His legislation said, "Be it enacted . . . That the Secretary of the Treasury be . . . directed to pay to the Virginia Military Institute . . . $214,723.62 . . . for the damage and destruction of its library, scientific apparatus, and the quarters of its professors in June, eighteen hundred and sixty-four, by the military authority of the United States."[4]

At a Senate hearing on February 7, 1914, du Pont said,

the history of my connection with the bill under consideration is this: I was chief of Artillery of Gen. Hunter's command, which was operating in the valley and took possession of Lexington on the 11th of June, 1864. Gen. Nichols, the superintendent of the Virginia Military Institute, knowing this, came to see me and made some inquiries about the destruction of the property of the institute at that time. Most of the buildings . . . were entirely burned down . . . by order of Gen. Hunter. I told Gen. Nichols that at the time I was very much opposed to the destruction of the institute buildings, as I thought it was a wholly unnecessary destruction of private property and not justified by the rules of war . . . and that this opinion was generally concurred in by all the officers with whom I came in contact. I remember, among others, that the late President McKinley, who was there, being one of the staff officers, expressed the same views. . . . After hearing what I had to say, Gen. Nichols asked me if I would introduce a bill for the relief of the institute and mentioned that there was a precedent for such action in the case of the William and Mary College.[5]

Du Pont's legislation passed, and he was asked to give out the Jackson-Hope medals at VMI's 1915 commencement, which he did, along with remarks on the joys of competition. Du Pont expressed "deep appreciation of the very warm welcome . . . in striking contrast . . . to the reception upon my previous visit to Lexington during the Civil War."[6]

The head of the class of May 1861 lived long enough to criticize Winston Churchill in a pamphlet called *The Real Stanton*. Of course, du Pont only knew about the Churchill of World War I. According to du Pont, "during the world's great conflict . . . the ideas of a minister, Lord Winston Churchill, who, like Stanton, thought he knew it all, were not only responsible for disaster in Belgium, but brought about the humiliating military reverses of the Dardanelles campaign. A British officer . . . has . . . said . . . 'it was absurd to think that Churchill had the right to assume the functions of a supreme naval commander.' To this we may add that it was equally absurd for Stanton to assume the role of a Grant or Sherman."[7]

On March 21, 1925, Colonel du Pont attended the West Point Graduates' Dinner in Washington, D.C., where he was asked to give a speech as the oldest one there, and told his "Brother Graduates of the Military Academy: During the Presidential campaign last autumn I made a few addresses—these being the last I would ever make, as I then supposed. . . . I want to say to General Pershing, as well as to every West Point graduate in this room, that by far the finest and most interesting military spectacle I have ever beheld was the march through New York City of the composite regiment which represented our American army in France." Du Pont—who would die on the last day of 1926—ends his speech with a call "to measure up as nearly as possible to the standards of former days . . . with a patriotic love and affection for our common country."[8]

14

Judson Kilpatrick:
Playwright and Diplomat

The cavalryman became a diplomat on December 1, 1865, when Kilpatrick accepted an appointment as U.S. minister to Chile from President Andrew Johnson. Kilpatrick married Louisa Valdivoso, niece of the archbishop of Santiago, on November 3, 1866. Kilpatrick served in Chile until August 1868.

Although "being naturally a politician"—according to James Harrison Wilson, who did his sketch in Cullum's *Biographical Register*—Kilpatrick did not fulfill his enormous ambitions, which may have included the presidency.[1] But he kept trying and dabbling in politics, first in one party, then the other. During the 1872 presidential campaign, Kilpatrick, who had been a Republican, worked for the Democratic candidate, Horace Greeley.

In his literary career, Kilpatrick had more success. He edited *Our Magazine: A Monthly Periodical of Interesting Family Reading* and corresponded with leading authors. Kilpatrick was extremely popular on the lecture circuit, giving talks on such subjects as "The Irish Soldier in the War of the Rebellion."[2] Kilpatrick's play about West Point cadets in the Civil War, *Allatoona*, written in 1875 with J. Owen Moore, was revised by Christopher Morley as *The Blue and The Gray or, War Is Hell* (1930).[3] It played fifty-two performances at the Old Rialto in Hoboken, New Jersey. "Naive and vivid as a Currier and Ives print," according to Morley, "it has seemed to us worthy of preservation in our own special cedar-chest of Americana. I think it has improved with age, for it deals with a great tragic issue which has kept all its romance and lost its bitterness."[4]

In his postwar career, Kilpatrick often seemed restless and unable to find a suitable outlet for his ambition and aggression. Returning to the Republicans, he was a delegate to the Republican National Convention in 1880 and an unsuccessful congressional candidate from New Jersey. "He was twice rewarded for his services and failures," James Wilson remarked, "by the appointment of minister to Chile."[5] In 1881, President James A. Garfield sent Kilpatrick back to Chile. As U.S. minister again, Kilpatrick fought with the U.S. minister to Peru, General Stephen A. Hurlbut, the first commander in chief of the Grand Army of the Republic. Peru and Chile were at war and the U.S. minister to each took the side of the country to which he was accredited. Each died at his overseas post, Kilpatrick in Santiago de Chile of Bright's disease in December 1881. He is buried at West Point, under a tombstone with a top hat.

Kilpatrick is mentioned in *Black Knight, White Knight*, by Gloria Vanderbilt, who is his great-granddaughter. His granddaughter Lady Thelma Furness introduced the Prince of Wales (who became Edward VIII and Duke of Windsor) to her friend from Baltimore, Wallis Warfield Simpson.

15

Orville E. Babcock:
The Rise and Fall of Grant's Secretary

For gallant and meritorious services in the field, Babcock had been brevetted brigadier general, U.S. Army, on March 13, 1865. After the war, Babcock stayed with Grant. The advantages to the young officer of being an aide to the commanding general of the army were obvious. Less obvious, at least to historians, was what Grant saw in Babcock and why he remained so loyal to his aide for so long. But Grant's high regard for Babcock was shared by many in the army, including Sherman. He was intelligent (third in the class of May, ahead of Ames and Upton), personable, and capable of handling delicate high-level assignments.

On April 19, 1866, Grant told General Henry Halleck, commander of the Military Division of the Pacific, that he was sending Babcock on an inspection trip. Babcock noted in his diary on May 2, 1866, "Bid St. Louis good morning and good bye, taking the M.P. RR for the Pacific. . . . Genl. Sherman . . . on the same train making it very pleasant. He (Genl. S.) is a very brilliant man. . . . He wishes me to pay particular attention to the Mormon question, to get at the true state of affairs."[1] Babcock also shows why he seemed the perfect aide to one of the most married of presidents in his entry for May 5—"Wrote also to Mrs. Grant—to Kent."[2]

In Utah, in a revealing entry dated June 30, 1866, Babcock asks, "How could Genl. Conner build such a mill, own a ranch, several silver mines, etc. on a Brig. Genl. pay."[3] After attending a party on July 3, Babcock remarked, "Brigham was very pleasant to me, particularly so. Introduced me to Mrs. B. Y. (35th). . . . I think these people who avoid the Mormon women as prostitutes do much harm. They are not whores. To associate with them will do much to break up their doctrine of polygamy." Yet the next day he wrote, "I cannot imagine how a sensible woman can throw off enough of her nature to be a second or third wife. I did not like the look of Brigham's last wife."

The Fourth of July also inspired this thought: "This town like all others on the 4th—drunken men, *national* flags, music . . . noisy and disagreeable."[4]

Like many of his classmates, Babcock had a collection of ranks. He was promoted to colonel (staff) on July 25, 1866. On November 8, 1866, Annie Eliza Campbell of Galena, Illinois, became his wife and the recipient over the years of innumerable affectionate letters. Babcock was promoted to major in the Corps of Engineers on March 21, 1867. He continued to serve as Grant's aide at headquarters until March 4, 1869. When Grant became president on that date, Babcock became his private secretary.

Babcock's office was on the second floor of the White House in an anteroom that led to the president's private office. In order to see Grant, politicians had to go through Babcock. That gatekeeper role, plus his obvious influence with the president, created resentment in many who had at first been impressed by the young officer's attractive personal qualities. He opened letters to the president and in most cases answered them. According to Allan Nevins's assessment of Babcock, "His office was as important as any Cabinet position, and more powerful than most."[5]

The Dominican affair, which was the first major defeat for the Grant administration, also reveals Babcock's influential role. Naval officers had been interested in Caribbean bases and the annexation of Santo Domingo, now the Dominican Republic. But Santo Domingo was also a special interest of speculators. In July and August of 1869, Babcock was in Santo Domingo to report on conditions in that country. He had no diplomatic authority, but that did not stop him from signing a protocol of annexation giving the United States the chance to buy Samaná Bay for two million dollars or the whole country for about twice that amount. Babcock also tried to commit the United States to political and military decisions without the consent of Congress. When Babcock returned to Washington, Secretary of State Hamilton Fish was shocked at what he considered usurpation. What the Senate thought was seen the next summer when it rejected the annexation treaty.

Babcock was, of course, always receiving letters from people who wanted favors from the president. General Franz Sigel wrote to Babcock, saying, "I would be greatly obliged to you for any information . . . relative to St. Domingo."[6] Sigel wrote again on March 1, 1873, "to ask a favor from you. Would you be so kind to remember my friend Genl. *Max Weber*."[7] General Daniel Sickles wrote to Babcock on February 8, 1875, to complain that his application to become a director of the Union Pacific "was overlooked by the Secretary of the Interior."[8]

Like so much else in Grant's administration, the roots of its scandals go back to Lincoln's presidency. There had been suspicions, which became even stronger during Andrew Johnson's administration, that distillers and internal revenue agents were colluding to avoid taxes. More broadly, it was the enormous centralization of power in Washington during the war that made the capital essential for businessmen wanting favors.

It was his involvement with the Whiskey Ring, which at first raised money for politics and then for individuals, that brought Babcock down. He was accused of trying to protect the ring. As Allan Nevins remarks, "The eternal cabal—with Babcock always its centre!"[9] The organizer of the ring was General John A. McDonald, the supervisor of internal revenue in Kansas and the author of *Secrets of the Great Whiskey Ring*, who thought Babcock should have also gone to jail.

Instead, Babcock fought his legal battles with the same coolness he had shown on the battlefield. No matter who was confronting him—even the secretary of the treasury and the attorney general—or whatever the evidence, he never admitted wrongdoing but always came up with explanations for everything, including an incriminating "Sylth" dispatch that was written in his handwriting and seemed to be a warning to the Whiskey Ring in St. Louis.

Orville Babcock Jr. was told by Allan Nevins, "It was a great misfortune, in my opinion, that your father never left a careful statement upon his career in Washington."[10] But what was in the interest of historians was not necessarily in Babcock's interest.

Bluford Wilson—who, as solicitor of the treasury, played a key role in exposing corruption—was examined on July 27, 1876, by Congressman Alexander Cochran of the Select Committee Concerning the Whisky Frauds. According to Wilson, President Grant told him, "If General Babcock is guilty, which I don't believe, he is the most guilty wretch in the world."[11]

Some fifteen years later, Wilson's brother, General James Harrison Wilson, gave an interview to novelist Hamlin Garland in which the same subject came up. General Wilson had been asked by his brother Bluford and by Secretary of the Treasury Benjamin Bristow to tell President Grant what they knew about trusted aides Horace Porter (class of 1860) and Babcock. General Wilson reluctantly did so, telling the president that Porter and Babcock were involved in the Whiskey Ring and were imperiling his reputation. According to Wilson, "He was profoundly moved by what I said. . . . I saw him again, but he refused to believe that Porter was guilty and I don't think he admitted to anyone that Babcock was guilty. He shielded Babcock all he could. He was a deeply affectionate man, and was surrounded by mean, low hangers-on."[12]

On December 9, 1875, Babcock was indicted with the Whiskey Ring for defrauding the Internal Revenue. Reversing the usual practice—in which aides are tossed overboard to protect the man at the top—President Grant went to enormous lengths to protect Babcock and keep him out of jail. General George Patton believed, "Loyalty from the top down is even more necessary and much less prevalent."[13] Even so, Grant's loyalty to Babcock is extraordinary. The president offered to go to St. Louis to be a witness in a criminal trial. Instead, Grant gave a deposition in the White House in which he proclaimed Babcock's innocence; the chief justice signed it; the jury heard it and acquitted Babcock on February 28, 1876.

Babcock received many letters from loyal friends. Daniel Webster Flagler—who began in the class of May but graduated with the class of June due to illness—said, "I think a good deal of that old time at West Point when you used to get out of bed before reveille & run it to the Hospital & read to me & prepare me for my examination."[14]

Babcock also received some surprising support—which notes his own support for civil rights—from John Pelham's oldest brother. A letter dated August 26, 1876, reached Babcock on the letterhead of Charles Pelham, a Washington attorney, announcing, "I have never known a native Southern Republican (I mean a real radical one) who was not your friend, and your friendship for & association with my brother John at West Point, increases my desire to aid you."[15]

Only after Grant was given evidence that Babcock had been speculating in gold (during the days leading up to the Black Friday disaster of 1869) did he let Babcock go in 1876. Historians have been puzzled as to why Grant fought so hard for his aide. Some have suggested that the president thought the prosecutors were really after him. Others have observed that Grant was reluctant to let go of someone who was under fire. According to Hamlin Garland's conversation with James Wilson, Grant referred to Babcock and Horace Porter as "my boys."[16] Mrs. Grant referred to Babcock as "a member of our household" and called him "always civil and obliging and never officious."[17]

After leaving the White House, Babcock became an inspector of lighthouses. He drowned at Mosquito Inlet, Florida, on June 2, 1884, while on an inspection trip. According to his fellow New Englander, Adelbert Ames, "Babcock died at his post of duty after the Civil War. He was one of Grant's favorites. Grant made few mistakes in his friendships."[18]

16

Pierce M. B. Young:
Confederate General and U.S. Diplomat

Between being a major general in the Confederate cavalry and a United States diplomat, Pierce Manning Butler Young served in Congress. He was able to take his seat through the influence of the military governor of Georgia, General George G. Meade, whose son was a West Point friend. General Meade wrote to General Grant on June 3, 1868, saying, "This letter will be handed to you by Gen'l Young late of the confederate army—Gen'l Y—commanded a brigade of cav—in Lee's army, and his name and feats were very familiar to me during the war, but . . . you will find he is all right and it is just such men as he we want down here, as their influence & example are most powerful . . . I know he is loyal to the Union and will do as much to uphold it, and the flag as if the rebellion had never existed."[1]

Grant's endorsement of June 19, 1868, said, "I unite with Gen Meade in recommending the removal of all disabilities in the case of P. M. B. Young to the end that he may be able to take his seat in Congress."[2] What made Meade's influence extraordinary was that one of the congressmen in Pennsylvania was the radical and powerful Thaddeus Stevens, who was willing to do a favor for his state's most famous constituent. Stevens saw Young and had his disabilities—which prevented someone who had taken an oath to the United States and then fought for the Confederacy from serving in Congress—removed. Meade's help was later acknowledged by Young, who expressed in Congress "feelings of gratitude to the great soldier. . . . He signed my first certificate of election, as military governor of Georgia, and by his letters of recommendation I was enabled to obtain my seat in the Fortieth Congress in 1868."[3]

Young was rejected by the Forty-first Congress, but his constituents sent him back and he served again from 1870 to 1875. His contribution was not to individual pieces of legislation but to national reconciliation, of which he was a symbol in Congress. Herman Melville stressed the importance of "Congressional decency" in his "Supplement" to *Battle-Pieces*. "On the floor of Congress," Melville remarked, "North and South are to come together after a passionate duel. . . . Upon differences in debate shall acrimonious recriminations be exchanged? . . . Under the supposition that the full Congress will be composed of gentlemen, all this is impossible. Yet, if otherwise, it needs no prophet of Israel to foretell the end."[4]

Young was well regarded in Congress by Democrats and Republicans, North and South. Even Benjamin F. Butler of Massachusetts, while debating with Young, referred to "his customary fairness."[5] Morris Schaff recalled that Young "as a member of Congress, never failed cheerfully to do all in his power for his old West Point friends."[6] In a book review which is better than the book, Stephen Ambrose quipped, "In the grand southern tradition, the two most important things in Young's life were his mother and his debts."[7]

A conservative "Bourbon Democrat," Young was also a champion of diversification in agriculture and economic development. He voted for the "Salary Grab" Act of 1873, which resulted in unfavorable publicity and his decision not to seek reelection in 1874. That same year he was a member of the Board of Visitors of the United States Military Academy. Young would say, "There is no doubt . . . that the American army is officered by the best educated set of gentlemen of any army in the world today."[8]

Young was a commissioner to the Paris Universal Exposition of 1878 and wrote a "Report on Cotton Culture."[9] After being a delegate to the Democratic National Conventions of 1872, 1876, and 1880, Young was appointed by Democratic President Grover Cleveland to be consul general in St. Petersburg, Russia, where he served from 1885 to 1887. When Cleveland returned to the White House in 1893, he appointed Young United States minister to Guatemala and Honduras. Young died in New York City on July 6, 1896. His body was taken back to Georgia for burial in Cartersville; his train was met in Atlanta by Confederate veterans and the United Daughters of the Confederacy.

Young gave a remarkably accurate prediction of the American role in the world wars of the twentieth century, saying, "The army of the United States is extremely small, really only a skeleton of an army. . . . But it is a nucleus around which an army of millions can be formed in a few months. . . . God grant we may never have to test our strength, but if we do in this day, or in the future, the great republic will be more powerful than any force that can oppose her."[10]

John J. Garnett:
Sketches of Grant and Lee

Robert E. Lee wrote a letter about John J. Garnett on October 18, 1866, that shows that after the war people asked him for advice on every subject. Dr. William Morris of Williamsburg had written to General Lee to find out if rumors about Garnett's troubles during the war were true. The doctor's daughter was evidently considering spending the rest of her life with Colonel Garnett. Lee was as generous as he could be, giving Garnett the benefit of every doubt and giving the doctor what seems like very good marital advice. "I duly appreciate your anxiety in the matter," Lee told Dr. Morris,

> and it would give me pleasure to do anything in my power to serve your daughter, of whom I have the most agreeable recollections. Personally I know but little of Col. John J. Garnett. . . . There were some complaints made against him . . . by his Comdg. officer, Genl. R. L. Walker I believe, in regard to the condition of his battalion; but I think none of a graver character than want of attention, suffering it to deteriorate, and perhaps being absent from his post on one or two occasions. . . . These though serious military offences, do not affect his moral character. Owing to them however, in the winter of 1863–64 as well as I remember . . . and in justice to the claims of others for command, he was relieved from duty with the Army of N. Va., and I think assigned to the Army of Tennessee.
>
> I think you have been misinformed as to his having been brought before a Court Martial for misconduct. I have no recollections of any graver charges against him than those I have mentioned, which may have been attributable more to thoughtlessness and carelessness than to intentional neglect. Having had no opportunity of judging of his character except that afforded by my official relation to him, I can not venture an opinion. That can be better learned from his associates. I trust that the good sense and instincts of your daughter, aided by your advice, will enable her to decide

correctly in a matter so important to her welfare; and I assure her that she has no friend more anxious for her happiness than I am, or one that feels more interest in her future.

with great respect, yr. obdt. svt.

R.E. Lee

The Morris family must have shown Lee's letter to Garnett, who must have been delighted, since he asked the general for a reference. In any case, on December 13, 1866, Robert E. Lee wrote the following letter to John Garnett, who was living in Baltimore.

My Dear Sir:
I regret that I am unable to give you more precise information on the points referred to in your letter of the 8th inst. than that which my memory affords. All my records, papers etc have been destroyed, and I can therefore only speak from general recollection.

You enjoyed the character of a gallant officer in the field, so far as my knowledge extended. . . .

I can not recall to mind any imputations against your courage; but recollect the character you bore for gallantry and skill. . . .

You have it, however, in your own power, in my opinion, to refute all accusations by your future conduct. In this way you can best prove your worth and value. . . .

With my sincere wishes for your success and welfare, I am very respectfully, yr. obdt., svt.

R.E. Lee[1]

Garnett seems to have taken Lee's advice on future conduct. Although a Virginian, Colonel Garnett moved to New York City, where he became a successful editor and publisher. He had a talent for packaging already published material and making money on it several different ways, including selling advertisements. For spectacular public events, he would edit or publish the program, adding a historical or biographical sketch. His skill was in marketing; if he rarely added new material, he was honest in listing his sources, and his publication of programs was valuable.

An example of his work is The Statue of Liberty . . . the inauguration, October 28, 1886, and containing the official programme of the ceremonies. Garnett also did a special edition of the official program without the program (for sale before the statue opened).[2]

Two years later, Garnett delivered a tribute to Robert E. Lee. Nothing in his speech was as interesting as where he gave it—the Southern Auld Lang

Syne Society of Harlem. In the same speech in Harlem, Garnett praises
Jefferson Davis, who had died the month before: "I have been deeply
touched of late in the death of Jefferson Davis, by the generous spirit which
has been exhibited by the journalistic historians of every section of this
country whose duty it is to sit in judgment on the acts of men whose lives are
contemporary with their own. . . . I am pleased to say here to you that I have
noticed everywhere where I had least cause to expect it, a disposition to be
. . . kind."[3] Garnett has nothing new to say about Lee. But he includes several tributes to reconciliation, saying his hero "stands in the galaxy of fame
with Washington, Lincoln, Davis, Grant, Americans all"[4] and calling his
country "the one and indivisible Republic."[5]

    Colonel Garnett also edited another publication in 1890 for the unveiling
of the Lee statue in Richmond. He compiled a *Biographical Sketch of General Robert Edward Lee* from the writings of John Esten Cooke, among others, which Garnett published with the *Programme of the Ceremonies of the
Unveiling of the Equestrian Statue at Richmond, Va., May 29th, 1890*. The assistant marshals that day included Thomas L. Rosser and P. M. B. Young.[6]

    Colonel Garnett produced the same kind of publication for the opening
of Grant's Tomb. Garnett compiled a *Sketch of the Life of General U. S. Grant*,
which he published with *the Programme of the Ceremonies of the Dedication
of the Grant Monument in New York, April 27th, 1897*. The names of four
members of the class of 1861 were taken by posts that marched in the ceremony with the Veteran Grand Division. Custer's name appears twice:
"Custer Post, Department of Connecticut," and "Custer Command No. 4 of
the First Independent Brigade," which also had a "Cushing Command." In
the division of New York City, there was a "Judson Kilpatrick Post," and
Rochester, New York, had an "O'Roake [sic] Post." Last in the line of march
were the Sons of Confederate Veterans.[7]

    Among the Confederate veterans in the class of 1861, John J. Garnett
must have been one of the most successful. He had a country home in Bald-
win, Long Island, and an office on Broadway, where he was the head of the
St. James Publishing Company. Yet in September of 1902, he committed suicide in Ross's Hotel at Sixth Avenue and Fifteenth Street. His wife told the
press she had no idea why.

    The *New York Tribune* said that in Colonel Garnett's possession was a let-
ter from President Theodore Roosevelt offering to help Garnett establish a
benevolent order of Spanish-American war veterans.[8] According to the
page-one article on Garnett in the *New York Herald*, "He was an author and
poet, and was at the time of his death engaged in writing a history of the
West Point Military Academy."[9]

Peter C. Hains:
Bull Run to World War I

Hains became major of engineers and superintending engineer of the Fifth Light-House District in 1870. While engineer secretary of the Light-House Board (1874–1879), he translated Léonce Reynaud's *Memoir upon the Illumination and Beaconage of the Coasts of France*. Hains acknowledged his debt to his father-in-law, noting, "Chapters I and II . . . were translated by Rear-Admiral Thornton A. Jenkins."[1] Hains had married Virginia Pettis Jenkins on November 17, 1864.

In the 1880s, Hains was superintending engineer for river improvements on the Potomac, James, and Shenandoah. Much of his work was in Washington, where he carried out the reclamation of the Potomac flats, converting 650 acres of swamp into Potomac Park, whose south end is still called Hains Point. He was promoted to lieutenant colonel in 1886 and colonel in 1895. In 1898, during the Spanish-American War, he became brigadier general of volunteers and temporary commander of the Third Division of the First Corps. He took part in the capture of Guyama and Las Palmas, Puerto Rico.

From 1899 to 1904, Hains served on the first Isthmian Canal Commission, which picked the best route across Panama. In 1901, Hains predicted, "Japan, a young and vigorous naval power, occupies a favorable geographical position to operate against us in the far east. . . . An attack on the Philippines is within the limits of probability. If successful, Japan might even make a naval demonstration as far eastward as our Pacific coast."[2] Hains concludes, "An adequate defense of a fortified Isthmian canal can be made in no other way than by providing a navy of sufficient power to control the seas at either terminus."[3]

On February 13, 1902, Hains was asked by Senator Mark Hanna, "What line of work have you done?" Without mentioning Vicksburg, Hains replied,

"Well, I have been engaged on public works of various kinds ever since 1863."[4]

In 1903, Hains became a brigadier general in the Regular Army and retired, but he continued to write. Hains described his own career in a 1918 letter that he wrote to update his entry in Cullum's *Biographical Register*: "Under the provisions of act of Congress approved August 29, 1916," he

> was advanced to the grade of Major General, U.S. Army, on the Retired List. When the war with Germany broke out volunteered his services for any duty to which the Government might see fit to assign him, and on September 18th, 1917, he was, by the direction of the President, placed on active military duty and then assigned as engineer of the Norfolk Harbor and River District, in charge of the defensive works at Hampton Roads, Va.; of the improvement of the harbor at Norfolk and its approaches, including Thimble Shoal, and the channel to Newport News; harbor at Cape Charles City and approaches; Nansemond . . . Pagan . . . Onancock, and Blackwater Rivers, Va.; waterways from Norfolk, Va., to the sounds of North Carolina; inland waterways from Norfolk, Va., to Beaufort Inlet, N.C.; Roanoke and Meherrin Rivers, N.C.[5]

A colonel at West Point who wanted a photograph of Hains received a letter of May 17, 1918, asking, "What are you going to do with my photograph? Of course, I will send you one, but would like to know what you are going to do with it. If I am going to be exhibited I want to have a good picture. I have some that are pretty good; some not so good; some taken a few years ago when I was better looking, and a few taken recently. Let me know what you want it for."[6]

The colonel wanted it for an obituary, explaining in an apologetic letter of May 20, 1918, "when in the Annual Report of the Association of Graduates we chronicle these melancholy events, we endeavor to accompany the notice with the best portrait of the individual that we can obtain. We have sometimes great difficulty in obtaining a good one, or even any at all. You will recall that some years ago in the notice of the death of General Custis Lee we used his photograph as adjutant of the Corps of Cadets." George Washington Custis Lee, first in the class of 1854 and eldest son of Robert E. Lee, died on February 18, 1913. The colonel gives another reason why obituaries should be used with care, adding, "We are therefore trying to get photographs which have been selected by the graduates themselves. A great many have sent them to us and a number have even prepared biographical sketches and filed them with us to be used at the right time."[7]

For Hains, the right time would not be while World War I was on and he was on active duty. He told Colonel Robinson in a letter of June 3, 1918, "but am sorry to say I will not be able to attend the graduating exercises on June 11th. . . . It happens that I am on a Board of Engineers, which has an important meeting to take place on the 11th, and I cannot very well get out of it."[8]

Hains also says, "In my former letter . . . I intended to call your attention to Felix H. Robertson, who was an officer in the Confederate Army, and who from last accounts is still in the land of the living. In regard to James P. Parker of my class, who went south, I have never heard anything about him that I remember. Parker was a stout, red-headed fellow, and a very different kind of a fellow from the [Francis Henry] Parker [#20, June] who graduated and was assigned to the Ordnance Department." The Parker who went south was Custer's roommate.[9]

Hains retired again in September 1918. He died on November 7, 1921, at Walter Reed Army Hospital and was buried in Arlington. The journal *Military Engineer* noted his "long and consistently productive service," saying, "In the depth of devotion to his work . . . and in the range of activities, his record has seldom been equalled."[10] It had paid him another tribute when it published, as the lead article in the May–June issue of 1921, his account of "The Vicksburg Campaign."

Emory Upton:
"The Class Genius"

After the war, Upton became the most influential soldier of his class (and almost any other). After commanding cavalry in East Tennessee (July–August 1865) and Colorado (August 1865–April 1866), he became lieutenant colonel of the Twenty-fifth Infantry on July 28, 1866. Upton spent 1866 through 1867 at West Point, instructing cadets while developing new infantry tactics that were based on American, not French, experience.

To cope with the new firepower of infantry and artillery using rifled breechloaders, Upton developed what Russell Weigley called "the first original American system of infantry tactics."[1] Upton promoted a more open order, the use of "fours" (groups of four men), which could be fed into a skirmish line, and later the three-battalion regiment, which was more maneuverable than the traditional American regiment of one battalion.

Upton's *Infantry Tactics: Double and Single Rank* was adopted in 1867 by the United States Army, where it was "hailed as the greatest single advance in tactical instruction," according to T. Harry Williams, "since the work of General Steuben during the Revolution."[2] The adoption of Upton's *Tactics* secured his position as the finest young officer in the army. According to the *Army and Navy Journal*, "he was known more widely through his tactics and other publications than any other officer in the Army, with very few exceptions."[3] The editor of the *Army and Navy Journal*, William Conant Church, was Upton's friend and ally in the campaign for army reform.

In November 1867, Upton took a year's leave and married Emily Norwood Martin of Willowbrook, New York, whose sister was the wife of Upton's friend from the Selma campaign, General Andrew Alexander. They traveled in Europe, where Emily got a lung infection from which she never recovered, and she died in 1870.

Upton had transferred to the Eighteenth Infantry in 1869. He was commandant of cadets at West Point from 1870 to 1875 and wanted to create a
military academy in China. For assimilation with his *Infantry Tactics*, Upton
published *Cavalry Tactics* in 1874 and the next year *Artillery Tactics*, written
with his friend Henry du Pont, who did most of the work on the last. Upton
was the protégé of General William T. Sherman, who thought the U.S.
Army on the frontier might be able to learn something from the British in
India, where a relatively small number of troops occupied a subcontinent.

Upton went on a world tour in 1875 through 1876, publishing his observations and recommendations for reform in 1878 in *The Armies of Asia and
Europe*. But Upton was more interested in European armies than in anything
in Asia, reflecting as well the American military's traditional disinterest in
unconventional warfare. In China, Upton observed, "So harsh is the Government toward its rebellious subjects that its aim appears to be the preven-
tion of rebellion . . . by the practice of cruelty."[4] In India, Upton reports on
the cavalry, noting that the American cavalry experience in the Civil War
was ignored: "As in Europe, so in India, the value of the carbine is but little
appreciated. Apparently indifferent to the brilliant achievements of the
American horse. . . ."[5] In the Austrian army, Upton was delighted to see
interchange between staff and line and promotion by merit, not seniority,
enabling some officers to achieve high command while young.

But it was the expansible Prussian army that most impressed Upton. He
became the latest advocate of an expansible army—a concept appealing to
Alexander Hamilton and John C. Calhoun—in which the whole staff and
basic line organization would be maintained during peacetime so that it
could be quickly converted to war footing. In Calhoun's words, there would
be "nothing either to new model or to create."[6]

Upton has been considered a symbol of the rise of German, as opposed to
French, influence on the American military. But Upton was overly impressed
by the German army and its general staff. The American public had no interest in the German way of conducting war, particularly conscription. It was
his misfortune—and the country's good fortune—that while he was writing
there was virtually no national security threat to the United States that
could justify a large military establishment or scare the American people into
accepting his most important reforms.

Although Upton liked the War Academy in Berlin as a training center for
senior officers, he still maintained that no place he had seen turned out better second lieutenants than West Point. "In all of the academies abroad for

educating officers of infantry and cavalry," Upton observes, "little or no effort
is made to teach them anything pertaining to the science of artillery, or engineering; much less are they taught the tactics and evolutions of the other
arms." In contrast, Upton says, "we have been able, at our Academy, to train
officers equally for engineers, for ordnance, for infantry, for artillery and cavalry, and have given the cadets such a competent knowledge of all the arms
of service that in the late war they were transferred from one arm to another,
frequently serving in all three, with a success and distinction that challenged
foreign admiration."[7] He was, of course, an example of that.

In 1877, Upton became superintendent of the Artillery School at Fort
Monroe, Virginia. His views influenced officers testifying in 1878 before Senator Ambrose Burnside's joint committee on military policy, which introduced a major reform bill. Had it passed, the departments of the adjutant
general and the inspector general would have merged to form a general staff;
there would have been interchangeable service between staff and line; and
staff officers would report to the general-in-chief (ending the independence
of the bureau chiefs). In 1879, the Burnside bill was defeated, and Upton was
extremely disappointed.

While superintendent of the Artillery School at Fort Monroe, Virginia,
from 1877 to 1880, Upton expanded the curriculum to include the use of
artillery with other arms, cavalry and infantry tactics, and military history,
particularly artillery in the Civil War.[8] Upton advocated the need for struc-
tural reform in The Military Policy of the United States, the first scholarly analysis of American military history. He showed the manuscript to William T.
Sherman, Congressman James A. Garfield, and Henry du Pont. Upton
includes examples from military history that he finds supportive of reform,
such as, "the behavior of the regular, or Continental, troops during the Revolution ought to convince every American citizen that a standing army is
among the least of the perils to which our freedom is exposed."[9] In the chapter part entitled "Lessons of the Revolution," Upton also states, "regular
troops . . . are the only safe reliance of a government."[10] According to one of
Upton's controversial remarks, "nearly all of the dangers which threatened
the cause of independence may be traced to the total inexperience of our
statesmen in regard to military affairs."[11] Upton called for an end to the traditional American reliance on a dual military—militia (plus volunteers) and
Regular Army. In an Uptonian system, the Regular Army would have a
monopoly on military force.

Among Upton's papers in Upton Hall at the U.S. Army Military History

Institute at Carlisle Barracks is an unpublished chapter on the "Civil and Military Policy of Rome." Even when writing about the Romans, Upton seems more interested in the future of army reform than the past. Under the heading "Danger of Armies," Upton says, "'Standing armies are dangerous to liberty' is the senseless proverb which usually shapes the military policy of republics,"[12] and later he states "a proverb which as a nation we have sung in chorus since the Declaration of Independence."[13]

Upton was an unhappy man when he became commander of the Fourth U.S. Artillery and the Presidio in San Francisco in 1880. Although the *Army and Navy Journal* noted, "As an Army officer he was regarded as one of fortune's favorites," he committed suicide the next year.[14] There has been endless speculation about the cause: the opinions of three who knew him and who wrote to his friend and biographer, Peter Michie (class of 1863), are included here.

Dr. William Saunders, who was Upton's dentist at West Point, said, "I heard a distinct and regular throbbing in his head. . . . and the general could not sleep unless greatly fatigued. . . . The last time I saw him . . . he exclaimed, 'Cure me of this, and I will give you ten thousand dollars!'" Dr. Saunders concludes, "Whatever may have been the true nature of his fearful malady, we know not, probably never shall."[15]

In July 1880, Upton began seeing a specialist in Philadelphia, Dr. Harrison Allen, who told Michie, "General Upton had a symptom which I had never before seen in a person who had not a tumor growing somewhere in the region of the nose. . . . That symptom was a bloody, chocolate-colored phlegm." Dr. Allen admits, "Respecting the connection existing between the disease and the suicidal mania, I can say little that has the value of evidence. General Upton complained of a dull, dazed feeling about the brows and crown. The sensation was compared to a veil dropping down over his mental faculties. The general conceived that, since this feeling interfered with application, it might become his duty to resign from the army. As he expressed it, he feared he was no longer of use to the Government." Dr. Allen continues, "I think it *probable* that the catarrh was a symptom excited by a slowly-growing tumor . . . which involved the remote recesses of the face, and . . . the membranes of the brain as well. . . . At best, I can but frame a probability."[16]

The possibility considered most likely by historians—nervous depression— was given by Upton's classmate Henry Hasbrouck (#21, May), who also served in Upton's Fourth Artillery in 1881. Hasbrouck wrote to Michie, saying,

he frequently complained about severe headaches . . . that he was frequently
unable to sleep, and after lying down for a while would be compelled to get
up and walk the room for some hours, and until he became so fatigued that
he could get a little sleep before reveille.

Nearer the end I have heard him complain that he had been under the
charge of the best specialists for his catarrhal trouble; that they could give
him no relief; that he never could get cured; that the headaches were getting longer and more painful. He spoke of these things in such a simple,
uncomplaining way, and he was all the time working so hard, and never
neglecting even the slightest detail of a post duty or a drill, that it made but
little impression upon me at the time.

It was Sunday morning, March 13th, that I first realized how much he was
suffering. I happened to be alone with him in his office, and, in answer to
my inquiry about his headache, he broke down completely, laid his head on
his desk, and sobbed. After he was composed I walked with him to his quarters, and was with him all that day and evening, and also Monday evening.
He was very despondent, talked of the loss of his will-power, and of the
respect of the officers of the regiment, spoke much of the failure of his tactics, and particularly of the system of deployment as skirmishers, said if his
system was adopted it would involve the country in disaster in the next war.

All day Monday, the 14th, I was sitting on a court, and was not with him
until evening. He attended to all his duties, and nothing unusual was
noticed by any one except by the adjutant, Mr. Dyer, to whom he had also,
but not to such an extent as to me, spoken of his ill-health and despon-
dency. When I saw him Monday evening he was still depressed, but when
I left him I thought he was in a somewhat more cheerful mood, and he had
given a sort of promise that he would go to Monterey next day. That night
he shot himself. . . . I never thought at the time that his mind was affected.
. . . After his death I learned that he had exhibited some signs of loss of
memory. . . He was unreasonably sanguine about his tactics. He told a gentleman in San Francisco that there would be no more war after his tactics
were published; that the system was so perfect that, given two countries and
their resources, the result of a conflict between them could be calculated
with mathematical certainty.

My impression, when he first spoke to me about his troubles, was, that he
was in a state of nervous depression, partly owing to his catarrhal troubles,
but principally to overwork and hard study.

You know as well as I his ability and devotion to duty. Under all these
troubles every detail of his duty as post and regimental commander was
attended to as carefully as if he were in perfect health.[17]

Before shooting himself in the head with his service revolver, Upton wrote a letter of resignation to the adjutant general on March 14, 1881. Ever since people have wondered why. Even Upton's physicians do not pretend to know. Historians have noted that Upton lacked humor. He had grown up in the Burned-Over District of upstate New York, noted for its religious and reforming zeal. He had no amusements, which obviously contributed to his productivity.

But perhaps Upton's enormous success during the war did not prepare him for disappointment. His friend William C. Church called Upton excitable and intense.[18] But his influence endured into the twentieth century, when obvious military dangers did exist and even conscription was accepted. Henry du Pont had circulated Upton's unfinished manuscript among the army officer corps.

Upton even had an influence on the naval officer corps, having encouraged his friend Stephen B. Luce to found the Naval War College. Luce told Church, "I used to talk to my old and lamented friend Genl. Upton about it a great deal. He was very enthusiastic and urged me on to make a move in regard to it."[19] In a letter of October 16, 1877, Upton told Luce, "Your project is a worthy one. . . . Someone must start the scheme, and I sincerely hope that as you have done so, you may be able to inaugurate the course and witness its triumph."[20]

Secretary of War Elihu Root (1899–1903) relied heavily upon Upton's work for his own reforms, and Upton's *Military Policy* was published by the War Department in 1904. In 1916, Newton D. Baker became secretary of war. The chief of staff, General Hugh Scott, recalls, "I took . . . to Secretary Baker . . . the report by General Emory Upton on the military policy of the United States or rather want of policy."[21] In World War I, the army was organized basically as Upton had recommended. Elements of Upton's tactics, such as the infantry squad, remained influential into World War II. George S. Patton's heavily marked up copy of *The Military Policy of the United States* is at the United States Military Academy Library. Historians writing on military policy were heavily dependent on Upton's work—for decades there was no other—and his conclusions, and even language, dominated the debate during the first half of the twentieth century.

Leading military historians—including T. Harry Williams, Russell Weigley, and Stephen Ambrose—have analyzed Upton's work. Williams and Weigley are very critical, especially of Upton's enthusiasm for European models for reform and of his criticism of "interference" in military matters by politicians.[22] Yet it is a sign of Upton's influence that in Weigley's book with the subtitle *Military Thought from Washington to Marshall*, Grant and Sherman share a chapter, while Sherman's protégé, Upton—who was not even a general until Grant promoted him at Spotsylvania—gets a full chapter: "Emory Upton: The Major Prophet of Professionalism," and another chapter is devoted to "The Disciples of Emory Upton."[23] Even Upton's critics admire his ability to combine the careers of combat leader and theorist.

In another sign of Upton's continuing influence, a provocative paper was read in 1995 at the Army War College called "Making Do with Less, or Coping with Upton's Ghost." Its author, Eliot Cohen, is highly critical of Upton and what he calls "The Uptonian Hunker" as a reaction to demobilization, calling on soldiers to rid themselves of "the troubled and persistent ghost of Major General Emory Upton."[24] That is not likely.

Despite the many (and valid) criticisms of Upton by Williams and Weigley, one can still agree with Stephen Ambrose who called Upton the best.[25] One reason is that civil-military relations, about which Upton was obviously wrong, have never really been a problem in this country. Before his suicide, Upton was considered the model army officer, and for some he still is. In addition to zeal, he had extraordinary intelligence, *coup d'oeil de guerre*, loyalty (up and down), and a willingness to risk his own life.[26]

Upton's old friend General James Harrison Wilson always liked to have the last word. "He was," Wilson said of Upton, "the equal of Custer or Kilpatrick in dash and enterprise, and vastly the superior of either in discipline and administration. . . . He was incontestably the best tactician of either army . . . he had a real genius for war, together with all the theoretical and practical knowledge which any one could acquire in regard to it . . . up to the time when he was disabled by the disease which caused his death he was, all things considered, the most accomplished soldier in our service."[27]

Appendixes
Notes
Bibliography
Index

Appendix A:
Roll Call

"I'm going there to meet my classmates, they've gone before me one by one."
—From a song of the 1860s, "I Am a Poor Wayfaring Stranger"

Class of May 1861 (in Order of Class Standing
with Nongraduates Following in Alphabetical Order)

1. HENRY ALGERNON DU PONT (Delaware), Corps of Engineers, second lieu-
    tenant, May 6, 1861; first lieutenant, Fifth U.S. Artillery, May 14, 1861; cap-
    tain, March 24, 1864; chief of artillery, Department of West Virginia, May
    24–July 28, 1864; brevet major, September 19, 1864; brevet lieutenant
    colonel and Medal of Honor for the Battle of Cedar Creek, Virginia, Octo-
    ber 19, 1864. He resigned from the army in 1875, was president of the Wilm-
    ington & Northern Railroad (1879–1899), and was vice president of the
    family chemical firm and was instrumental in keeping it in the family in
    1902. He served in the U.S. Senate from Delaware (1906–1917), where he
    helped the Virginia Military Institute get reimbursed for being burned down
    by Federal troops in 1864. He wrote books about that campaign and about
    his family in the 1920s. He died in 1926.
2. CHARLES E. CROSS (Massachusetts), Corps of Engineers, was killed at
    Franklin's Crossing, Virginia, June 5, 1863. Adelbert Ames said, "No nobler
    youth ever wore the cadet uniform."[1]
3. ORVILLE ELIAS BABCOCK (Vermont), Corps of Engineers, served with dis-
    tinction as an engineer and as an aide to General Ulysses S. Grant. Babcock
    was brevetted brigadier general, U.S. Army, on March 13, 1865. When
    Grant became president in 1869, Babcock became his extremely influential
    private secretary and the center of controversy. Babcock was indicted with
    the Whiskey Ring on December 9, 1875. President Grant offered to tes-
    tify at a criminal trial but instead gave a deposition supporting Babcock,
    who was acquitted on February 28, 1876. After leaving the White House,

Babcock became an inspector of lighthouses, drowning in Mosquito Inlet,
Florida, on June 2, 1884.

4. HENRY WALTER KINGSBURY (born in Illinois, appointed from New York),
    colonel of the Eleventh Connecticut, was mortally wounded at Antietam
    on September 17, 1862, by the troops of his brother-in-law David R. Jones,
    and died the next day.

5. ADELBERT AMES (Maine) served in the artillery at Bull Run, where he was
    wounded and won the Medal of Honor. He became colonel of the Twenti-
    eth Maine on August 29, 1862, and brigadier general of volunteers on May
    20, 1863. His Second Division captured Fort Fisher, North Carolina, on Jan-
    uary 15, 1865. He became brevet major general, U.S. Army, on March 13,
    1865. Ames was appointed provisional governor of Mississippi on June 15,
    1868. He was elected to the U.S. Senate in 1870 and became the elected
    governor of Mississippi in 1874, where he was a defender of civil rights.
    After the Democrats won control of the legislature, Ames resigned on
    March 29, 1876. In 1898, he served as a general in Cuba during the Span-
    ish-American War. George Plimpton is his great-grandson.

6. LLEWELLYN GRIFFITH HOXTON (born in Washington, D.C., appointed at
    large) resigned from the U.S. army on May 25, 1861, and served in the Con-
    federate artillery. He taught mathematics at the Episcopal High School of
    Virginia near Alexandria and died in 1891.

7. ADELBERT RINALDO BUFFINGTON (Virginia) became chief of ordnance for
    Philip Sheridan's army near Mexico in 1865. A military inventor, Buffing-
    ton rose to chief of ordnance (1899–1901) and died in 1922.

8. EMORY UPTON (New York), second lieutenant, Fourth U.S. Artillery, May
    6, 1861; first lieutenant, Fifth U.S. Artillery, May 14, 1861; colonel, 121st
    New York Infantry, October 23, 1862. After he demonstrated his new tac-
    tics at Spotsylvania, he was promoted to brigadier general of volunteers on
    May 12, 1864. After Third Winchester, he became brevet major general,
    U.S. Volunteers (October 19, 1864). In 1865, he commanded the Fourth
    Cavalry Division and, with James Harrison Wilson, defeated Nathan Bed-
    ford Forrest at Selma, Alabama. He became brevet major general, U.S.
    Army on March 13, 1865. Upton served as commandant of cadets at West
    Point (1870–1875) and was an advocate of army reform and professional-
    ism. He was the influential author of *Infantry Tactics* (1867), *The Armies of
    Asia and Europe* (1878), and *The Military Policy of the United States* (1904).
    Upton committed suicide in 1881.

9. NATHANIEL RIVES CHAMBLISS (born in Virginia, appointed from Tennessee)
    resigned from the Third U.S. Artillery to join the Confederacy, where he com-
    manded arsenals in Selma and Charleston. After the war he edited a newspa-
    per, taught mathematics at the University of Alabama, and married Anna
    Hardee (whose father had been commandant of cadets). He died in 1897.

10. EDMUND KIRBY (born in New York, appointed at large) became a second lieutenant in the First U.S. Artillery on May 6, 1861. He became a first lieutenant eight days later. Kirby fought with the coolness of a veteran at First Bull Run. He also fought in the Peninsula campaign and declined a transfer to the Topographical Engineers in July 1862. He fought in the Maryland campaign and the battle of Fredericksburg, commanding Battery I, First U.S. Artillery. At Chancellorsville, he was mortally wounded on May 3, 1863. He was nursed in Washington by Fanny Ricketts, wife of General James Ricketts, who wanted Kirby's mother to get a decent pension and recommended Lieutenant Kirby's promotion to brigadier general. Kirby died on May 28, 1863, after receiving a deathbed promotion to general, which was delivered that day by Abraham Lincoln.

11. JOHN ISAAC RODGERS (Pennsylvania), Upton's roommate, served in the artillery and taught mathematics at West Point. He became a general and chief of artillery during the Spanish-American War, retired in 1902, and died in 1931.

12. SAMUEL NICOLL BENJAMIN (New York) joined the artillery, was brilliant in the defense of Knoxville, was wounded at Spotsylvania, and won the Medal of Honor.

13. JOHN ADAIR (born in Kentucky, appointed from Oregon Territory) served in the Union army for eight months before becoming the only deserter in the class of 1861. He went to Canada, where he worked as a gold miner in Cariboo, British Columbia. Returning to Astoria, Oregon, in 1869, he was a farmer, manager of a salmon hatchery, and land developer. He became involved with the Oregon state militia and became known as Colonel Adair. He also received a contract from the United States Army for construction of river improvements. Adair married Dr. Bethenia Owens in 1884. She is in *Notable American Women*,[2] and he is in her autobiography, *Dr. Owens-Adair: Some of Her Life Experiences*, which indicates that one of those life experiences was losing her life savings in his scheme to reclaim coastal marshland. John Adair died in 1915.

14. JOHN WHITNEY BARLOW (born in New York, appointed from Wisconsin) went into the Second U.S. Artillery, served at Bull Run and the Peninsula campaign (brevet captain, May 27, 1862, for Hanover Court House). As assistant professor at West Point (1862–1863), Barlow taught geography. He transferred to the Topographical Engineers (July 24, 1862) and the Corps of Engineers (March 3, 1863). He was promoted to brevet major for the Atlanta campaign (July 22, 1864) and brevet lieutenant colonel for Nashville. Barlow's *Report of a Reconnaissance of the Basin of the Upper Yellowstone in 1871* was published by Congress. Barlow became general and chief of engineers on May 2, 1901, and retired the next day. He died in Jerusalem in 1914 but is buried in Arlington.

15. CHARLES EDWARD HAZLETT (Ohio) became a second lieutenant, Second U.S. Cavalry (May 6, 1861) and a first lieutenant, Fifth U.S. Artillery (May 14, 1861). He drilled volunteers, fought at Bull Run, and served in the defenses of Washington. In 1862, he fought at Yorktown, Gaines's Mill, Malvern Hill, Antietam, and Fredericksburg. At Gettysburg on July 2, 1863, Hazlett appreciated the importance of Little Round Top and had the guns of his Battery D, Fifth U.S. Artillery, pulled up the hill. Hazlett's heroism would always be remembered by a young officer on General Gouverneur Warren's staff, Lieutenant Washington Roebling (who built the Brooklyn Bridge). While leaning over the dying General Stephen Weed, Hazlett was shot in the head and killed.

16. CHARLES E. PATTERSON (born in Indiana, appointed from Missouri) joined the Confederacy and died on April 8, 1862, from wounds received at Shiloh.

17. HUGH JUDSON KILPATRICK (New Jersey) joined the First U.S. Artillery and was wounded at Big Bethel, June 10, 1861. He became lieutenant colonel, Second New York Cavalry (September 25, 1861), colonel (December 6, 1862), brigadier general, U.S. Volunteers (June 13, 1863). Kilpatrick commanded the Third Cavalry Division at Gettysburg and Sherman's cavalry on the March to the Sea. Kilpatrick became major general, U.S. Volunteers on June 18, 1865. His play about West Point cadets in the Civil War, *Allatoona*, was revised by Christopher Morley. Kilpatrick was U.S. Minister to Chile from 1865 to 1868 and again in 1881, when he died there of Bright's disease. His granddaughter Lady Thelma Furness introduced the Prince of Wales to Wallis Warfield Simpson. His great-granddaughter is Gloria Vanderbilt.

18. FRANKLIN HARWOOD (born in Rhode Island, appointed at large) served in the Third United States Artillery in California and took a battery to New Mexico in the summer of 1862. He transferred to the engineers, served as an aide to General Meade, and died in 1883.

19. GEORGE WARREN DRESSER (born in Connecticut, appointed from Massachusetts), who attended Phillips Academy at Andover before West Point, served with artillery, engineers, ordnance, and the inspector general's office. After resigning in 1865, he worked on railroads as a civil engineer before becoming editor of *The American Gas Light Journal* in 1875. Dresser was also a consulting engineer with an office in the Trinity Building in New York. He died in Newport, Rhode Island, in 1883.

20. CHARLES McKNIGHT LEOSER (Pennsylvania) was acting adjutant of the Eleventh New York, Ellsworth's Zouaves, from May to July of 1861 and colonel from August 1861 to April 1862. He resigned a volunteer colonelcy and became a junior officer in the Second U.S. Cavalry, was captured at Trevilian Station (June 11, 1864), and went to Libby Prison. After the war,

Leoser became publisher of *Bonfort's Wine and Spirit Circular* and a member of the New York Yacht Club. In 1893, Leoser wrote a provocative piece entitled "The Grand Army as a Pension Agency."[3] He was also commander of a Grand Army of the Republic post that said pensions should only go to those incapacitated by wounds. The veterans organization kicked Leoser's post out. He died in 1896.

21. HENRY CORNELIUS HASBROUCK (New York) went into the artillery. From 1863 to 1865, he was assistant professor of philosophy at the Military Academy. He fought the Modoc Indians in California (1873) and was commandant of cadets (1882–1888). He became a general in the Spanish-American War and governor of Pinar del Rio, Cuba. Hasbrouck retired in 1903 and died in 1910.

22. WILLIAM ANTHONY ELDERKIN (New York) became an artillerist and a husband, marrying Fannie Gurley, daughter of Dr. Phineas Gurley, minister of the New York Avenue Presbyterian Church, where Abraham Lincoln rented a pew. Elderkin returned to West Point (1862–1864) to teach mathematics and artillery tactics. From 1867 to 1869, Elderkin was sheriff of Richmond. He retired a colonel in 1898 and died in 1900.

23. FRANCIS ASBURY DAVIES (Pennsylvania) joined the Second U.S. Artillery but returned to West Point in 1862 as instructor of infantry, and later as assistant professor of French. In 1868, he resigned and worked in insurance and the Post Office, and he died in 1889.

24. CHARLES CARROLL CAMPBELL (Missouri) joined the First U.S. Cavalry but was dismissed on June 6, 1861, for tendering his resignation in the face of the enemy. He was second in command of the First Missouri Infantry (Confederate) at Shiloh. He later commanded the arsenal at Atlanta and was chief of ordnance on the staff of General Joseph Wheeler. After the war, Campbell worked for the U.S. Corps of Engineers and died in 1912.

25. MALBONE FRANCIS WATSON (New York) served in the First U.S. Cavalry before transferring to the Fifth U.S. Artillery. He lost a leg at Gettysburg, after which he taught French at West Point. Watson retired in 1870, was assistant engineer of New York City's Department of Docks and became commissary officer of the Soldier's Home in Dayton, Ohio, in 1882. He died in 1891.

26. JOHN BENSON WILLIAMS (Michigan) went into the infantry and fought at Bull Run, Malvern Hill, Antietam, and Fredericksburg. After sick leave, he was dismissed on February 11, 1863, for what is now called post traumatic stress disorder. Williams taught at Hyatt's Military Institute in Pennsylvania. He died in Canada in 1903 at his home in Charlesbourg-Ouest, Quebec.

27. GUY VERNON HENRY (born at Fort Smith, Arkansas, appointed at large) went into the First U.S. Artillery but became colonel of the Fortieth Massachusetts in 1863. He won the Medal of Honor at Cold Harbor and was a

brevet brigadier general at the end of the war. Henry compiled a biographical dictionary, *Military Record of Civilian Appointments in the United States Army.*[4] In 1870, he transferred to the Third U.S. Cavalry. In 1876, he was with George Crook's column, which was defeated by Crazy Horse at the Rosebud, eight days before Little Bighorn. Twenty years later Henry wrote an article called "Wounded in an Indian Fight."[5] In 1897, he became colonel of the black Tenth Cavalry. During the Spanish-American War, he became major general and was military governor of Puerto Rico in 1899. He died on October 27, 1899.

28. JACOB HENRY SMYSER (Pennsylvania) went into the artillery and fought at Shiloh and Corinth. He commanded the Detroit Arsenal, resigned in 1869, and died in 1885.

29. JACOB BEEKMAN RAWLES (Michigan) joined the artillery and served in the Department of the Gulf (1863–1864). He became colonel of the Third U.S. Artillery in 1899, general on April 13, 1903, and retired the next day. He died in 1919.

30. ERSKINE GITTINGS (Maryland) served in the artillery at Pocataligo, South Carolina, where he was wounded, and at Vicksburg. He taught at West Point (1865–1867), served in Pennsylvania (during the railroad strike of 1877), and died in 1880 at Fort Hamilton, Brooklyn.

31. JACOB FORD KENT (Pennsylvania) entered the Third U.S. Infantry and was wounded and captured at Bull Run, spending a year as a prisoner before being exchanged and serving as a staff officer. He became instructor of infantry tactics at West Point (1865–1869) and eventually colonel of the Twenty-fourth Infantry (1895). His service in the Spanish-American War earned him promotion to major general of volunteers and a sketch in the *Dictionary of American Military Biography,* which calls Kent "probably the best division commander in the campaign."[6] He died in 1918.

32. EUGENE BEAUHARNAIS BEAUMONT (Pennsylvania) joined the First U.S. Cavalry. He served on the staffs of Generals Burnside, Halleck, and Sedgwick, and in the last month of the war led a charge on a Confederate battery at Selma, Alabama, winning the Medal of Honor. Beaumont retired in 1892 and died in 1916.

33. LEONARD MARTIN (Wisconsin) went into the Fifth U.S. Artillery but became colonel of the Fifty-first Wisconsin in 1864. Resigning two years later, he worked for the Northern Pacific Railroad and the Corps of Engineers, and died in 1890.

34. JOHN SCROGGS POLAND (Indiana) joined the Second U.S. Infantry, commanded the regiment at Malvern Hill, and was aide to General Sickles at Gettysburg. At the end of the war, Poland was professor of drawing at West Point. He compiled *A Digest of the Military Laws of the United States*[7] and *The*

Conventions of Geneva, noting in 1886, "one of the universalities of modern progress, viz., the mitigation of severity in carrying on war. A . . . most beneficial modification . . . has been brought about by confining the area of war to the trained and responsible agents of the governments concerned . . . thus preventing the growth of those ineradicable animosities which spring from war itself and readily lend themselves to the initiation of new wars."[8] During the Spanish-American War, Poland rose to general, caught typhoid in Chickamauga, and died in North Carolina, on August 8, 1898.

35. ROBERT LANGDON EASTMAN (born in Pennsylvania, appointed at large) was the son of Captain Seth Eastman, who had been professor of drawing at the Military Academy. Robert Eastman went into the Sixth U.S. Infantry but his health was ruined by disease during the Peninsula campaign in 1862. Sent to West Point to teach drawing, geography, and ethics, Eastman also helped the New York City police during the draft riots. After the war, Eastman went on sick leave and died in Washington on November 7, 1865.

36. HENRY BEACH NOBLE (New York) went into the Eighth U.S. Infantry and was wounded at Cedar Mountain on August 9, 1862. Noble returned to West Point to teach geography. He died in Germany in 1898 but was buried at West Point.

37. LEROY LANSING JANES (Ohio) went into the Second U.S. Artillery, second lieutenant (May 6, 1861), first lieutenant (June 10, 1861); served at Fort Pickens and Pensacola, Florida (1862); captain (June 15, 1864). At West Point, he was assistant instructor of infantry and artillery tactics (1863–1865) and assistant professor of geography, history, and ethics (1863–1864). He resigned on December 9, 1867. A Christian reformer, Janes went to Japan three years after the Meiji Restoration. From 1871 to 1876, Janes was the extremely influential headmaster of the Kumamoto School for Western Learning. According to his biographer, "As the founder of one of the major streams of modern Japanese Christianity, Janes holds an important place in the intellectual and religious history of the Meiji period."[9] Janes died in 1910.

38. CAMPBELL DALLAS EMORY (born in Pennsylvania, appointed at large) joined the Sixth U.S. Infantry. He had a heart condition and was in garrisons on the west coast until 1864, when he joined General George G. Meade's staff. After the war, Emory stayed with Meade and was later acting judge advocate of the Department of Texas (1873–1878). He died of a heart attack in San Antonio on March 11, 1878.

39. JAMES F. MCQUESTEN (New Hampshire) joined the Second U.S. Dragoons but transferred to the Second U.S. Cavalry. Captain McQuesten was shot in the head and killed at Third Winchester (Opequon), Virginia, on September 19, 1864.

40. GEORGE OSCAR SOKALSKI (New York) joined the Second U.S. Dragoons.
    He was an aide to General Frederick Steele, served in the Vicksburg cam-
    paign, and took part in the capture of Little Rock. Sokalski died at Fort
    Laramie, Wyoming Territory, in 1867.
41. OLIN F. RICE (born in Georgia, appointed from Kentucky) joined the Ninth
    U.S. Infantry but was dismissed on June 6, 1861, for tendering his resigna-
    tion in the face of the enemy. He fought as a captain in the First Missouri
    Infantry (Confederate) at Shiloh. Rice served on the staff of General Buck-
    ner and was a colonel when the war ended. Rice became a businessman in
    St. Louis and died in 1882.
42. WRIGHT L. RIVES (born in Maryland, appointed from the District of Colum-
    bia) joined the Sixth U.S. Infantry and served as an aide to General Joseph
    Mansfield. Rives took part in the sieges of Corinth (May 1862) and Vicks-
    burg. From the end of 1863 to the end of the war, Rives served as aide to
    General John A. Dix. During the administration of President Andrew John-
    son (1865–1869), Rives was the president's military secretary. Rives retired
    for disability in 1870 and died in 1916.
43. CHARLES HENRY GIBSON (Pennsylvania) joined the Second U.S. Dragoons,
    served as an aide to McClellan in the Peninsula campaign, and got swamp
    fever. Gibson resigned in 1864 (but lived until 1911). After investing in
    Pennsylvania coal mines, he traveled in Europe and went to Santiago,
    Cuba, during the Spanish-American War (1898) for the National Relief
    Commission.
44. MATHIAS WINSTON HENRY (Kentucky) began the war in the Union's
    Mounted Rifles but resigned on August 19, 1861 (after Bull Run), and
    joined the Confederate army. He would become chief of artillery for Hood's
    division. After the war, Henry went to Mexico and later became a mining
    engineer in Nevada. He died in Brooklyn in 1877.
45. SHELDON STURGEON (New York) joined the First U.S. Infantry and was cap-
    tured at Bull Run. After being exchanged, he became a recruiter and lived
    until 1892, transferring to the cavalry after the war and retiring (for dis-
    ability) a month before Little Bighorn.

Members of the May Class Who Left West Point
Before Graduation to Join the Confederacy

JAMES M. KENNARD (Mississippi), chief of ordnance, Army of Tennessee.
JOHN PELHAM (Alabama), "the Gallant Pelham," was the most popular man in
    the Corps of Cadets, according to his classmate Adelbert Ames. Pelham was
    a descendant of John Singleton Copley's stepfather, Peter Pelham. After
    Manassas, Pelham was promoted from lieutenant to captain and then to
    command of the Stuart Horse Artillery, where he improved tactics. On

raids, Pelham's guns kept up with Jeb Stuart's cavalry. Although he was in over sixty engagements, Pelham was as modest as fearless, distinguishing himself at Williamsburg, Malvern Hill, Second Manassas (promoted to major and command of battalion), Antietam, and especially Fredericksburg, where with two guns he held up the Federal advance. He was killed in a cavalry charge on March 17, 1863, defending Kelly's Ford, Virginia.

THOMAS LAFAYETTE ROSSER (born Virginia, appointed Texas) began as a lieutenant of artillery. He was promoted to captain (September 1861) and lieutenant colonel (June 10, 1862). Rosser became colonel of the Fifth Virginia Cavalry Regiment on June 24, 1862, and fought at Catlett's Station, Second Manassas, South Mountain, Fredericksburg, and Kelly's Ford, where he was wounded. He was promoted to brigadier general on October 10, 1863 (to rank from September 28). Although unsuccessful against Custer in the Shenandoah Valley, Rosser was promoted to major general on November 4, 1864 (to rank from November 1). He broke out at Appomattox, saying "THE CAVALRY Never Surrenders!"[10] He became chief engineer of the Canadian Pacific Railway in 1881. In 1898, during the Spanish-American War, Rosser became a general of U.S. Volunteers and a symbol of national reconciliation.

George A. Thornton (Virginia), captain.

SAMUEL C. WILLIAMS (Tennessee), major, Eighteenth Battalion, Alabama Cavalry.

Class of June 1861 (in Order of Class Standing with
Nongraduates Following in Alphabetical Order)

1. PATRICK HENRY O'RORKE (born in County Cavan, Ireland, appointed from
   New York) was the one his classmates thought would become their famous
   general. He began in the Corps of Engineers, second lieutenant, June 24,
   1861, and was assistant engineer in the construction of the Washington,
   D.C., defenses, July 23–August 2, 1861. He was promoted brevet captain on
   March 15, 1862, for meritorious services with the Port Royal Expeditionary
   Corps. O'Rorke became colonel of the 140th New York Volunteer Infantry
   Regiment on September 19, 1862. He was cited for gallantry at Fredericksburg and Chancellorsville. At Gettysburg, a monument marks the spot
   where he was killed on July 2, 1863, leading a bayonet charge that helped
   save Little Round Top.

2. FRANCIS ULRIC FARQUHAR (Pennsylvania) became chief engineer, Department of Virginia and North Carolina (1863–1864) and assistant professor of
   engineering at West Point (1864–1865). In 1872, he became chief astronomer
   for the survey of the forty-ninth parallel. Major Farquhar died in 1883.

3. ARTHUR HENRY DUTTON (Connecticut) became colonel of the Twenty-first
   Connecticut in 1862. He was mortally wounded at Bermuda Hundred, Virginia, on May 26, 1864. Ten days later, in Baltimore, he was a general and
   dead at twenty-five.

4. CLARENCE DERRICK (born in Washington, D.C., appointed at large)
   resigned from the Corps of Engineers to join the Confederacy, where he rose
   to lieutenant colonel of the Twenty-third Virginia. He was wounded and
   captured at Third Winchester (Opequon) on September 19, 1864. After the
   war, Derrick was a lawyer, professor of mathematics, planter, and banker. He
   died in 1907.

5. DANIEL WEBSTER FLAGLER (New York) was chief of ordnance at Gettysburg
   for the Army of the Potomac. After the war, he worked in arsenals and
   served on committees, such as the Board on Heavy Gun Carriages. Major
   Flagler wrote A History of Rock Island Arsenal under the direction of General Stephen Vincent Benét. Describing the First Infantry in the Black
   Hawk War of 1831, Flagler says, "Lieut. Col. Zachary Taylor (afterward President of the United States) . . . and Lieut. Jefferson Davis (afterward president of the so-called Confederate States of America) . . . were members of
   the regiment. . . . The volunteers were commanded by General Whiteside,
   and Abraham Lincoln (afterward President of the United States) held the
   rank of captain in this command."[11] Flagler became general and chief of ordnance in 1891 and held that position until he died in 1899.

6. THOMAS CARR BRADFORD (Rhode Island) went into ordnance and was disabled for two months by a bursting cannon at the Washington D.C. Arse-

nal on April 4, 1863, after which he taught mathematics at West Point for six months. Captain Bradford was instructor of ordnance and gunnery at West Point when he died in 1872.

7. RICHARD MASON HILL (born in Washington, D.C., appointed at large) served as assistant ordnance officer in the Department of the Gulf and was assistant constructor of ordnance at the West Point Foundry when the war ended. Hill was a member of the board on the manufacture of 15-inch guns (1872) and assistant ordnance officer at the Springfield Armory from 1875 until his death on March 25, 1876.

8. WILLIAM HAMILTON HARRIS (New York), son of Senator Harris, became chief of ordnance in the Department of the Ohio. In 1870, William Harris left the army and became manager of a rolling mill, treasurer of a railway, and president of a shovel and dredge company. From 1887 to 1890, he drained the Valley of Mexico. He died in Italy in 1895.

9. ALFRED MORDECAI (born in Pennsylvania, appointed at large) started in the Topographical Engineers but transferred to ordnance in October 1861. He became a brevet lieutenant colonel at the end of the war for service in the field as well as in the ordnance department. Mordecai served at the Military Academy as instructor of ordnance and gunnery from 1865 to 1869 and again from 1874 to 1881. Oliver Otis Howard mentions the Mordecai family in his *Autobiography*, noting in 1908, "Alfred is now a brigadier general on the retired list. He has had an honorable and useful life in the army, always on active duty in the Ordnance Department, and very successful in his profession."[12] Mordecai retired in 1904 and died in 1920. In a letter of May 17, 1918, Peter Hains mentioned Mordecai to a colonel at West Point.[13]

10. DAVID HILLHOUSE BUEL (born in Michigan, appointed from New York) joined the First U.S. Dragoons. After transferring to ordnance, Buel served at the Watervliet Arsenal (1861–1863), was chief of ordnance in the Army of the Tennessee (1864–1865), and survived the invasion of Georgia and the March to the Sea. Brevet Lieutenant Colonel Buel was murdered by a deserter at Fort Leavenworth, Kansas, on July 22, 1870.

11. STEPHEN CARR LYFORD (New Hampshire) was commander of the Cairo, Illinois, ordnance depot from February to May, 1862, and chief of ordnance in the Department of the Tennessee from July 11, 1862, to September 6, 1863. Lyford returned to West Point as assistant professor of mathematics (1865–1867) and as instructor of ordnance and gunnery (1872). In 1874, he went to Japan, where he presented the emperor with arms and books. At the 1876 International Exhibition in Philadelphia, Lyford was a judge for sporting arms, weapons, and explosives. He died at the Frankford, Pennsylvania, arsenal, which he commanded, in 1885.

12. ALONZO HEREFORD CUSHING (born in Wisconsin, appointed from New York) was the brother of naval hero William Cushing, who blew up the

Albemarle. Alonzo Cushing joined the Fourth U.S. Artillery, becoming second and first lieutenant on June 24, 1861. He fought at Bull Run, Yorktown, Fredericksburg (brevet captain), and Chancellorsville (brevet major). On July 3, 1863, during Pickett's Charge at Gettysburg, Cushing continued to fight after he was severely wounded and his battery shot to pieces. Cushing's Battery A, Fourth U.S. Artillery, was at the spot that became "the high tide of the Confederacy," and Cushing became a symbol of courage. He was shot in the mouth and killed right after ordering his gunners to fire. His tombstone at West Point says, "Faithful until Death."

13. CHARLES CARROLL PARSONS (Ohio) went into the Fourth U.S. Artillery and fought at Shiloh and Corinth. For his heroism at Perryville, Parsons became a brevet captain and a major for Stones River; at the end of the war he would be a brevet lieutenant colonel. He returned to West Point to teach (1863–1864 and 1868–1870) but left the army to become a minister.[14] Parsons became rector of St. Lazarus Episcopal Church in Memphis. He was also editor (1871–1872) of the weekly *Banner of the Church*, which he called "a religious and literary paper."[15] Elizabeth Custer has described her husband's admiration for Parsons's decision to leave the army for a mission church.[16] Parsons refused to leave Memphis during the yellow fever epidemic of 1878, organizing relief and writing, "My dear bishop, the situation is indescribable."[17] Parsons died in the epidemic on September 7, 1878.

14. JOHN RUFUS EDIE (Pennsylvania) joined the cavalry but transferred to ordnance, serving on the staff of General Meade as ordnance officer of the Army of the Potomac from August 1863 to the end of 1864. Captain Edie died in the Government Insane Asylum, Washington, D.C., on October 29, 1874. The chief of ordnance, General Stephen Vincent Benét, ordered officers of the Ordnance Department to wear mourning for thirty days.

15. LAWRENCE SPRAGUE BABBITT (born in Massachusetts, appointed from Pennsylvania) commanded the ordnance depot of the Army of the Potomac from Yorktown to White House, Virginia, during the Peninsula campaign. After the war, Babbitt commanded the Vancouver Arsenal (1865–1871), was chief of ordnance for the Department of the Columbia (1877), and fought the Nez Perces. Colonel Babbitt retired and died in 1903.

16. GEORGE AUGUSTUS WOODRUFF (Michigan) joined the First U.S. Artillery and became a first as well as a second lieutenant on the same day, June 24, 1861. Woodruff was mortally wounded at Gettysburg during Pickett's Charge. He died the next day, July 4, 1863. He was the second 1861 graduate—Edmund Kirby was the first—to die from wounds received while commanding Battery I, First U.S. Artillery. Woodruff was twenty-two.

17. JOSEPH CRAIN AUDENRIED (Pennsylvania) started in the cavalry. His long career as an aide began at Bull Run with General Daniel Tyler; he was wounded at Antietam while serving as aide to General Edwin Sumner; dur-

ing the siege of Vicksburg, he was Grant's aide. Audenried was William Tecumseh Sherman's aide from October 1, 1863, until his death in 1880. According to Sherman, "A more honorable, chivalrous, and courteous gentleman never lived than Colonel J. C. Audenried."[18] He followed Sherman around the country and around the world, writing articles for *Harper's New Monthly Magazine* with titles like "Pyramids of Ghizeh" and "Suez Canal." Audenried saw the military academy in Cairo, noting, "Much of the system adopted at West Point is being introduced."[19]

18. JULIUS WALKER ADAMS (born in Massachusetts, appointed from Kentucky) spent the first year of the war at West Point as assistant instructor of infantry tactics. At Gaines' Mill (June 27, 1862), Adams was severely wounded; he was in hospitals from July to September of the next year, after which he was well enough to mount guns in New York harbor. Captain Adams resigned for health reasons (June 29, 1864) and died on November 15, 1865.

19. PETER CONOVER HAINS (born Pennsylvania, appointed New Jersey) joined the Second U.S. Artillery on June 24, 1861, as first lieutenant. He fired the signal gun at Bull Run and fought in the Peninsula campaign. Hains transferred to the Topographical Engineers (July 24, 1862) and the Corps of Engineers (March 3, 1863). He was chief engineer of the Thirteenth Corps from March 20 to July 4, 1863, when he became brevet major for gallant services at Vicksburg. After the war, he worked on many engineering projects, including Potomac Park in Washington. In the Spanish-American War, he was brigadier general of volunteers. He served on the first Isthmian Canal Commission and wrote influential articles about Panama. In 1903, he retired, but in World War I he returned to active duty as district engineer in Norfolk, Virginia. Hains died on November 7, 1921, at Walter Reed Army Hospital and is buried in Arlington.

20. FRANCIS HENRY PARKER (New York) served in the dragoons and artillery before becoming chief of ordnance for the Department of the Tennessee (July 1863–January 1864) and the Army of the Potomac (December 1864–June 1865). Parker commanded arsenals after the war and died in 1897.

21. JOSEPH PEARSON FARLEY (born in Washington, D.C., appointed at large) went into the Second U.S. Artillery but transferred to ordnance in October 1861 and served at the Watertown Arsenal in Massachusetts until June 1863. Farley was engaged in the bombardment of Fort Wagner and was in command of the ordnance depot at Hilton Head, South Carolina (July 1863–February 1864), and at City Point, Virginia (September 1864–March 1865). Farley was assistant professor of drawing at West Point from 1865 to 1867. His publications include *Rules for the Inspection of Army Revolvers and Gatling Guns*[20] and *Over Seas in Early Days* (1828–29),[21] which contains a letter of introduction to Lafayette for his father, John Farley, class of 1823. General Joseph P. Farley retired in 1903 and died in South Carolina in 1912.

22. Joseph Boyd Campbell (born in Pennsylvania, appointed from New Hampshire) went into the Fourth U.S. Artillery and was wounded at Antietam. He was assistant professor at West Point when the war ended. He also taught at the Artillery School (1868–1871) at Fort Monroe, Virginia. Three years later, he was in the garrison at Alcatraz Island, California. Campbell later became Indian agent for Alaska and commander of Sitka. Captain Campbell died in 1891 in Canada.

23. Henry Erastus Noyes (born in Maine, appointed from Massachusetts) joined the Second Dragoons. From December 1863 to July 1864, he was at Riker's Island, New York, on draft duty. Noyes was on George Crook's expedition in 1876. In the Spanish-American War, he was governor general of Cuba's Santa Clara province. Colonel Noyes retired in 1901 and died in 1919.

24. Philip Halsey Remington (born in Connecticut, appointed from Illinois) joined the Eighth U.S. Infantry and served as a recruiter. He was in New York during the draft riots. After the war he was in Raleigh, Fayetteville, and Camp Supply, Indian Territory. He retired for disability in 1891 and died that year.

25. William Duncan Fuller (Maine), the only 1861 graduate without a class album photograph, joined the Third U.S. Artillery. He was cited for gallantry at Williamsburg and Gettysburg. In 1866, he was convicted of mutinous conduct after he threatened to shoot the regimental adjutant. Captain Fuller transferred to the Twenty-first Infantry in 1871 and was under arrest (for threatening to shoot other officers) at Camp Apache, Arizona, from March 14 to July 22, 1872, when he resigned. He farmed in Virginia and died in 1886.

26. Justin E. Dimick (born in New Hampshire, appointed at large) became second lieutenant, Sixth U.S. Infantry, and first lieutenant, First U.S. Artillery, on June 24, 1861. He drilled volunteers in Washington and fought at First Bull Run and Fredericksburg. Commanding Battery H, First U.S. Artillery, at Chancellorsville on May 3, Dimick was shot in the spine, after having earlier been shot in the foot (which he did not let his men know). He died two days later. He was twenty-three.

27. James Pierre Drouillard (Ohio) served as aide to General Irvin McDowell for the first two years of the war. In 1863, Drouillard was aide to General William S. Rosecrans in the Army of the Cumberland. Captain Drouillard resigned in February 1865 and became an iron manufacturer on the Cumberland River. He died in 1892.

28. LeRoy S. Elbert (born in Ohio, appointed from Iowa) joined the Mounted Rifles. He served at Bull Run, the Peninsula campaign, Antietam and Fredericksburg. He was on the Stoneman raid. Elbert died of fever on September 13, 1863.

29. CHARLES HENRY BRIGHTLY (Pennsylvania) entered the Fourth U.S. Infantry, which he commanded when he was mortally wounded in the Wilderness on May 6, 1864. He died in Philadelphia on June 9.

30. EUGENE CARTER (Maine) joined the Eighth U.S. Infantry, brought prisoners of war to Fort Columbus, New York, and assisted in quelling the New York draft riots. Leaving the army in 1871, Carter was a manufacturer in Haverhill, Massachusetts, where he died in 1877.

31. SAMUEL PETER FERRIS (Connecticut) was a lieutenant in the Eighth U.S. Infantry in 1861 but became colonel of the Twenty-eighth Connecticut in November 1862. He served in the Department of the Gulf (briefly commanding a brigade on the Port Hudson expedition) and in New York City during the draft riots. Ferris was on the Bighorn expedition in 1876. He commanded a squadron of the Fifth Cavalry against the Cheyennes in February 1879 and a battalion of the Fourth Infantry in the Ute expedition in October. He died in 1882 at Fort Russell, Wyoming Territory.

32. GEORGE OWEN WATTS (Kentucky) resigned from the Mounted Rifles on August 10, 1861, and joined the Confederacy. As an engineer officer on the staff of General Buckner, Watts built the works at Fort Donelson, Fort Pillow, and Nashville. After the war, Colonel Watts was superintendent of education in Alexandria Rapids Parish, Louisiana. He died in 1905.

33. FRANK A. REYNOLDS (born in Virginia, appointed from New Mexico Territory) went into the Second Dragoons but was dismissed on July 16, 1861, for submitting his resignation in the face of the enemy. Reynolds fought for the Confederacy, rising to lieutenant colonel. In 1870, Frank and his father, General Alexander Reynolds, C.S.A., went to Egypt with their wives; father and son served in the khedive's army and lived in a run-down palace in Alexandria. In 1874, Reynolds, a colonel in the Egyptian army, returned to the United States to purchase arms for the khedive. In 1875, he died in Ilion, New York. Another colonel gave this description of the older Reynolds: "He was never sober. It was so habitual with him that people did not know that he was drunk for they had never seen him sober."[22]

34. GEORGE ARMSTRONG CUSTER (Ohio) had also lived in Monroe, Michigan, and had been a schoolteacher, extremely popular with his students. He became second lieutenant, Second Cavalry, June 24, 1861; captain, staff (George McClellan's) June 5, 1862; first lieutenant, Fifth Cavalry, July 17, 1862. General Alfred Pleasonton got Custer, who was twenty-three, promoted to brigadier general, U.S. Volunteers, June 29, 1863. On July 3 Custer repulsed Jeb Stuart at Gettysburg. He became captain, Fifth U.S. Cavalry, on May 8, 1864. Custer was relentless (becoming brevet major general, U.S. Volunteers, October 19, 1864, for Third Winchester) leading the Third Cavalry Division in Sheridan's 1864 Shenandoah Valley campaign and in

the Appomattox campaign. Custer became lieutenant colonel of the new Seventh U.S. Cavalry in 1866. In the Indian Territory in 1868, Custer was victorious at the Washita River, destroying Black Kettle's village. At Little Bighorn, on June 25, 1876, Custer and Companies C, E, F, I, and L of the Seventh Cavalry were wiped out by Crazy Horse and Sitting Bull in Custer's Last Stand.

Members of the June Class Who Left West Point
Before Graduation to Join the Confederacy

CHARLES POLLARD BALL (Alabama), colonel, Eighth Alabama Cavalry. Classmate Joseph P. Farley noted that Ball had been "the first sergeant of 'A' Company, prospective first captain of the Corps of Cadets." Farley recalls Ball's parting words in the mess hall, "'Battalion, attention! Good-bye, boys! God bless you all!' His citizen's attire warned us that he was about to leave the post, and upon permission being granted, the members of his class bore him upon their shoulders to the old south dock, where the final parting scene from this man, our favorite classmate, was one never to be forgotten. This was the first instance of a Southern boy leaving for home."[23]

WILLIAM HENRY BROWNE (Virginia) resigned April 22, 1861; captain (May 29, 1861) of Company G, Fourty-fifth Virginia; colonel (May 14, 1862). He was mortally wounded on June 5, 1864, leading a brigade that included the Forty-fifth Virginia at Piedmont, Virginia. In *The Campaign of 1864 in the Valley of Virginia*, his friend Henry du Pont describes talking with Browne after he was wounded and captured and his own sorrow when he learned of Browne's death the next morning.[24]

JOSEPH KOGER DIXON (Mississippi), major and acting assistant inspector general on the staff of General Patrick Cleburne.

WILLIAM WATKINS DUNLAP (Kentucky) was dismissed in 1861 for refusing to take the Oath of Allegiance. He became a lieutenant colonel.

PAUL FLETCHER FAISON (North Carolina) became major of the Fourteenth North Carolina on May 28, 1861. He was elected colonel of the Fifty-sixth North Carolina on July 31, 1862. The regiment of ten companies was drawn from counties near Raleigh, including Orange, Chatham, and Johnston. The regiment was part of General Bushrod Johnson's Division, and, when Matt W. Ransom was wounded, Faison temporarily commanded a brigade. Faison surrendered the remnant of his regiment at Appomattox on April 9, 1865. He died on March 3, 1896.

GEORGE H. FROST (Louisiana), captain and aide de camp to Generals Martin Luther Smith, Alexander P. Stewart, and Frank Armstrong.

JOHN JAMESON GARNETT (Virginia) was a lieutenant in 1861 and major in June 1862 in David R. Jones's Division. On November 14, 1862, Garnett became inspector of ordnance and artillery in Longstreet's Corps. On April 4, 1863, he became lieutenant colonel and commander of an artillery battalion, which fought at Gettysburg in General Henry Heth's Division. Garnett was suspended by Robert E. Lee (February 18, 1864) and relieved from duty with the Army of Northern Virginia (April 1, 1864). Garnett commanded a post in 1864 at Hicksford, Virginia, and, in November of 1864, he became inspector of artillery for the Army of Tennessee. After the war, he became a successful writer and editor in New York City, publishing a *Biographical Sketch of General Robert Edward Lee* and a *Sketch of the Life of General U.S. Grant*. Garnett committed suicide in 1902.

WILLIAM R. JONES (Virginia) resigned April 22, 1861; captain.

JOHN HERBERT KELLY (Alabama) was born on March 31, 1840, and became an orphan at age six. He became major, Fourteenth Alabama, on September 23, 1861. At Shiloh, Kelly led the Ninth Arkansas Battalion; for his hero-ism he was promoted to colonel of the Eighth Arkansas in May 1862. He fought at Perryville (October 8, 1862) and Stone River, where he was wounded. On Snodgrass Hill, Chickamauga (September 20, 1863) Kelly dis-played superb leadership as a brigade commander. General Patrick Cleburne said, "I know of no better officer of his grade in the service."[25] Kelly became the youngest Confederate general on November 17, 1863. He endorsed Cle-burne's proposal that the Confederacy should use blacks as combat troops. Kelly became a cavalry division commander (May 8, 1864) and was mor-tally wounded in Tennessee on September 2, 1864, on Wheeler's raid against Sherman's supply line. Kelly's courage and leadership were con-stantly noted by his commanders and his troops, who, even if new, fought like veterans.

BENJAMIN KING (at large) served on the staffs of Daniel Ruggles and Randall L. Gibson. At Shiloh, on April 6, 1862, Lieutenant King was killed.

JOHN LANE (at large) became a captain in 1861 and a major in March 1863. Lane commanded the Sumter (Georgia) Artillery Battalion in the Army of Northern Virginia. At Gettysburg, the battalion was in General Richard Anderson's Division. Lane became lieutenant colonel in 1865. He was the son of Senator Joseph Lane of Oregon (who believed in the right of seces-sion and ran for vice president in 1860 as John C. Breckinridge's running mate but did not take part in the war). John Lane's brother Lafayette became a congressman from Oregon and his nephew Harry a member of the United States Senate.

JOHN WILLIS LEA (born South Carolina, appointed Mississippi) lived in North Carolina and on May 16, 1861, became captain of Company I, Fifth North Carolina. When he was wounded and captured at Williamsburg, he was helped by his classmate Custer, who was the best man at his wedding. After being exchanged in November 1862, Lea was wounded at Chancellorsville and at Third Winchester on September 19, 1864. During the Appomattox Campaign, Lea commanded Robert D. Johnston's Brigade.

ROBERT HENRY LOGAN (Virginia) became adjutant of the Forty-second Virginia in 1861. He served on the staff of General John B. Floyd in late 1861 and early 1862. In 1864, Logan served on the staff of General Gabriel C. Wharton and briefly commanded Wharton's Brigade. Logan became lieutenant colonel of the Forty-fifth Virginia and was wounded and captured at Waynesborough, Virginia, on March 2, 1865.

ALEXANDER DUNCAN MOORE (North Carolina) resigned on April 22, 1861, and became a lieutenant in the Wilmington (North Carolina) Light Artillery. He was promoted to captain on May 16, 1861. Moore became colonel of the Sixty-sixth North Carolina on August 3, 1863. He was mortally wounded in the neck by a sharpshooter at Cold Harbor on June 3, 1864.

WILLIAM F. NIEMEYER (Virginia) began his Confederate service as a lieutenant of artillery. He became lieutenant colonel of the Sixty-first Virginia on May 22, 1862. He was wounded at Bristoe Station and killed at Spotsylvania on May 12, 1864.

JOHN FRANCIS O'BRIEN (appointed at large) was captain and assistant adjutant general to Generals Charles S. Winder and P. G. T. Beauregard. As a major, O'Brien served as assistant adjutant general for Generals Beauregard, John B. Magruder, and Kirby Smith.

JAMES PORTER PARKER (Missouri) was Custer's roommate and lived until 1918. Parker was probably one of those Custer had in mind when he said, "The resignation and departure of the Southern cadets took away from the Academy a few individuals who, had they remained, would probably have contested with me the debatable honor of bringing up the rear of the class."[26] Parker became lieutenant colonel of the First Mississippi Artillery.

GEORGE NORTON REYNOLDS (South Carolina) resigned in December of 1860. He became major and ordnance officer to General Magruder. Reynolds died in Charleston in 1863.

FELIX HUSTON ROBERTSON (Texas) was the son of Jerome Bonaparte Robertson, who would also become a Confederate general. Felix Robertson went into the artillery and fought at Charleston (the bombardment of Fort Sumter) and Shiloh. He became a major on July 1, 1863, and lieutenant colonel (in January 1864) and chief of artillery for General Joseph Wheeler's cavalry. He was appointed brigadier general on July 26, 1864. In southwest Virginia, on October 3, 1864, his brigade killed about one hundred wounded Federal prisoners, mostly blacks, until General John C. Breckinridge arrived and stopped the Saltville Massacre. Robert E. Lee ordered the arrest and trial of Robertson, but that never took place. Robertson, the last surviving Confederate general, died on April 20, 1928.

LUCIEN DUVERGNE SANDIDGE (Louisiana) became captain and acting assistant inspector general to Generals Daniel Ruggles and Dabney Maury.

DAVID G. WHITE (Maryland), major.

ZADOCK T. WILLETT (Tennessee), captain, Company B, Nineteenth Tennessee, killed at Shiloh.

EDWARD S. WILLIS (Georgia) became adjutant of the Twelfth Georgia on July 5, 1861. He served on Stonewall Jackson's staff in 1862. Willis became lieutenant colonel of the Twelfth Georgia on December 13, 1862, and colonel on January 22, 1863. That regiment had great admiration and affection for him. He was wounded at the Wilderness and mortally wounded at Bethesda Church, dying on May 31, 1864.

PIERCE MANNING BUTLER YOUNG (born South Carolina, appointed Georgia) quickly became adjutant of Cobb's Legion and then commander of its cavalry with the rank of major. After the Antietam campaign, he became colonel on November 1, 1862. Young distinguished himself in the Gettysburg campaign, especially at Brandy Station. He was promoted to brigadier general (to rank from September 28, 1863) and major general (to rank from December 30, 1864) and fought in the Carolinas against Sherman. Young was elected to the U.S. House of Representatives in 1868, where he was a symbol of reconciliation. In 1874, he was a member of the Board of Visitors of the U.S. Military Academy but not a candidate for reelection to Congress. Young served as U.S. consul general in St. Petersburg, Russia (1885–1887), and U.S. minister to Guatemala and Honduras (1893–1896). He died in New York on July 6, 1896. His body was taken back to Georgia, where his train was met by Confederate veterans and the United Daughters of the Confederacy.

Appendix B:
Associations and Museums Honoring
Members of the Class of 1861
and Their Families

Henry Algernon du Pont

Winterthur Museum, Garden & Library
Route 52
Winterthur, Delaware 19735
(800) 448-3883 and (302) 888-4600
The home of Colonel Henry A. du Pont, whose son, Henry Francis, developed the famous gardens.

Hagley Museum and Library
298 Buck Road
Wilmington, Delaware 19807
(302) 658-2400
Contains the papers of Henry A. du Pont and other members of his family, including his uncle Admiral Samuel Francis Du Pont, and the Du Pont Company.

Adelbert Ames

Friends of Borderland
Borderland State Park
257 Massapoag Avenue
North Easton, Massachusetts 02356
(508) 238-6566
The home of General Ames's daughter Blanche Ames Ames is now a Massachusetts State Park, with extensive mansion tours, hikes, and lectures. Civil War reenactments have been held at Borderland, and books by the general's granddaughter Pauline Ames Plimpton are still available here.

Alfred Mordecai

Mordecai Historic Park
One Mimosa Street
Raleigh, North Carolina 27604
(919) 834-4844
Commemorates the Mordecai family, especially its North Carolina branch. Other historic sites have been moved to the grounds of Mordecai House, including the Andrew Johnson birthplace.

John Pelham

John Pelham Historical Association
7 Carmel Terrace
Hampton, Virginia 23666
(757) 838-1685
Website: http://members.aol.com/jpha1982
Promotes interest and research on "the Gallant Pelham," and many of his siblings' descendants are members of it. The JPHA preserves monuments to Pelham and publishes a bimonthly, *The Cannoneer*.

George Armstrong Custer

Little Big Horn Associates
105 Bartlett Place
Brooklyn, New York 11229
(718) 646-2311
Website: http://LBHA.org
Studies the life of George A. Custer; publishes *LBHA Newsletter*, *Research Review*, and a monograph series; holds annual conference and seminar; presents John M. Carroll Award and Lawrence A. Frost Award; replaces grave markers at Little Bighorn.

Notes

The following abbreviations for frequently cited sources are used in the notes:

AFP   Ames Family Papers, Sophia Smith Collection, Neilson Library, Smith College.
BP   Orville E. Babcock Papers, The Newberry Library.
DPP   Henry Algernon du Pont Papers, Winterthur Manuscripts, Hagley Museum and Library, Wilmington, Del.
HP   Oliver Otis Howard Papers, Bowdoin College Library.
O.R.   *The War of the Rebellion: A Compilation of the Official Records of the Union and Confederate Armies.* Washington: Government Printing Office, 1880–1901.
RP   Rosser Family Papers (#1171), Special Collections Department, University of Virginia Library.
USMA Special Collections and Archives, U.S. Military Academy Library, West Point, N.Y.

1. Introduction: Buglers' Assembly

1. George A. Custer, "War Memoirs: From West Point to the Battlefield," *Galaxy* (April 1876): 454.

2. G. A. Custer, "War Memoirs: From West Point," 448. In supporting the move in 1854 to add a year, Davis was also supporting West Point's superintendent, Robert E. Lee.

3. Adelbert Ames, "Journal While Abroad," no. 2, March 26, 1867, p. 75, AFP.

4. Henry Algernon du Pont to Sophie Du Pont, January 17, 1857, DPP, W8 104. Sophie Du Pont and her husband, Admiral Samuel Francis Du Pont, capitalized the particle in their last name.

175

5. H. A. du Pont to Louisa du Pont, October 3, 1858, DPP, W8 177.

6. H. A. du Pont to Henry du Pont, October 29, 1859, DPP, W8 213.

7. G. A. Custer, "War Memoirs: From West Point," 448. Custer misspells the name of his classmate John Herbert Kelly. Joseph Wheeler was nineteenth in the class of 1859.

8. H. A. du Pont to Louisa du Pont, February 25, 1860, DPP, W8 226.

9. Kenneth W. Rapp, *West Point: Whistler in Cadet Gray, and Other Stories about the United States Military Academy* (n.p.: North River Press, 1978), 101.

10. John W. Barlow, "Personal Reminiscences of the War," *War Papers,* Commandery of the State of Wisconsin, Military Order of the Loyal Legion of the United States (Milwaukee: Burdick, Armitage & Allen, 1891), 108.

11. Joseph Pearson Farley, *West Point in the Early Sixties: With Incidents of the War* (Troy, N.Y.: Pafraets Book Co., 1902), 27.

12. Stephen Vincent Benét, *John Brown's Body* (Garden City: Doubleday, 1928), 305.

13. Ulysses S. Grant, *Personal Memoirs of U.S. Grant* (New York: Charles L. Webster & Co., 1885), 1: 38–39.

14. Circulation Records, USMA.

15. Register of Cadet Delinquencies, USMA.

16. H. A. du Pont to Louisa du Pont, December 3, 1859, DPP, W8 219.

17. G. A. Custer, "War Memoirs: From West Point," 449.

18. Morris Schaff, *The Spirit of Old West Point: 1858–1862* (Boston: Houghton Mifflin, 1907), 144–47.

19. Emory Upton to Oliver Otis Howard, October 1860, HP.

20. G. A. Custer, "War Memoirs: From West Point," 449. Custer misspells Breckinridge. Hannibal Hamlin of Maine was Lincoln's first vice president.

21. Peter S. Michie, *The Life and Letters of Emory Upton, Colonel of the Fourth Regiment of Artillery, and Brevet Major-General, U.S. Army,* with an introduction by James Harrison Wilson (New York: D. Appelton, 1885), 19.

22. Michie, *Life and Letters,* 22; letter of February 5, 1860.

23. H. A. du Pont to Louisa du Pont, March 4, 1860, DPP, W8 227.

24. Charles Dickens, *American Notes and Pictures from Italy* (London: Oxford University Press, 1957), 218–19.

25. G. A. Custer, "War Memoirs: From West Point," 449.

26. Michie, *Life and Letters,* 29. South Carolina seceded on December 20, 1860. In C. Vann Woodward, ed., *Mary Chesnut's Civil War* (New Haven: Yale University Press, 1981), 144, there is a comment on the same subject, from the opposite side of course: "Certainly we undervalued ourselves," Mary Chesnut remarks on August 13, 1861, "we had no idea they would consider it such ruin to lose us. They abused us and called us so worthless—indeed, seemed to find us a disgrace they would be glad to shake off—we had every reason to think!"

27. G. A. Custer, "War Memoirs: From West Point," 452.

28. G. A. Custer, "War Memoirs: From West Point," 450–451. The Crittenden Compromise, a series of constitutional amendments proposed by Senator
John J. Crittenden to prevent war, failed, of course.

29. Oliver Otis Howard, *Autobiography of Oliver Otis Howard* (New York:
Baker & Taylor Co., 1908), 1: 99. "This excellent professor" was John W. French.

30. Michie, *Life and Letters*, 30–31. The states that had followed South Carolina in secession were Mississippi (January 9, 1861), Florida (January 10), and
Alabama (January 11).

31. Michie, *Life and Letters*, 33.

32. G. A. Custer, "War Memoirs: From West Point," 453.

33. Farley, *West Point*, 19.

34. Howard, *Autobiography*, 1: 113. Nothing seems more absurd, of course,
than the idea of Oliver Otis Howard joining the Confederacy. The admiration
that blacks have had for Howard has been noted by a linguist. According to Stuart Berg Flexner, *Listening to America: An Illustrated History of Words and Phrases
from Our Lively and Splendid Past* (New York: Simon & Schuster, 1982), 484, "So
many blacks took General Howard's name that about a third of all *Howards* in
the U.S. are black."

35. John D. Hayes, ed., *The Mission: 1860–1862*, vol. 1 of *Samuel Francis
Du Pont: A Selection from His Civil War Letters* (Ithaca: Cornell University Press,
1969), 55–56. Admiral Du Pont, unlike the other descendants of Pierre Samuel
du Pont, spelled his name with a capital "D."

36. Howard, *Autobiography*, 1: 97.

37. James A. Padgett, ed., "The Life of Alfred Mordecai as Related by Himself," *North Carolina Historical Review* 22 (January 1945): 61.

38. Joseph Pearson Farley, *Three Rivers: The James, the Potomac, the Hudson:
A Retrospect of Peace and War* (New York: Neale Publishing Co., 1910), dedication page.

2. Flames of Rebellion

1. H. A. du Pont to Sophie Du Pont, May 25, 1861, DPP, W8 293.

2. Emory Upton, *The Military Policy of the United States* (Washington: War
Department, 1912), 229. The first two times the enemy were the British, who
occupied Philadelphia (1777) and burned Washington (1814).

3. Upton, *Military Policy*, 229, 233.

4. Barlow, "Personal Reminiscences," 109 (read February 4, 1885). An account
of the class's arrest also appears in an Emory Upton letter of May 8, 1861. Upton
mentions being taken by the police "to the station-house (Independence Hall).
. . . The cause of our arrest was a telegram from the Mayor of Jersey City, stating
that forty Southern cadets were on the train, and that their baggage contained

small-arms for the South. Under the circumstances the arrest was justifiable."
Michie, *Life and Letters*, 44. Upton was probably the only member of the class
who thought their arrest justifiable.

5. Barlow, "Personal Reminiscences," 109.

6. Barlow, "Personal Reminiscences," 109–10.

7. Barlow, "Personal Reminiscences," 110.

8. H. A. du Pont to Henry du Pont, May 8, 1861, DPP, W8 286.

9. Adelbert Ames to Oliver Otis Howard, May 12, 1861, HP.

10. H. A. du Pont to Henry du Pont, May 10, 1861, DPP, W8 287.

11. A. Ames to Howard, May 12, 1861, HP.

12. H. A. du Pont to Louisa du Pont, May 12, 1861, DPP, W8 288.

13. A. Ames to Howard, May 12, 1861, HP.

14. A. Ames to Howard, May 27, 1861, HP.

15. H. A. du Pont to Henry du Pont, May 2[?] 1861, DPP, W8 290.

16. H. A. du Pont to Sophie Du Pont, May 25, 1861, DPP, W8 293.

17. H. A. du Pont to Sophie Du Pont, June 10, 1861, DPP, W8 299.

18. Upton, *Military Policy*, 239. Union College is in Schenectady, N.Y. Over a
hundred years after Upton's "noble seminaries" remark, Harvard is considering
a memorial to its Confederate dead: "Should a memorial be erected to the 64
alumni who died fighting for the Confederacy? Nearly one-third of all the graduates of Harvard who died in the Civil War were fighting for the Confederate
cause." *Harvard University Gazette* 90.37 (June 1, 1995): 6.

19. Upton, *Military Policy*, 237, note a.

20. A. Ames to Howard, May 27, 1861, HP.

21. Peter C. Hains, "The First Gun at Bull Run," *Cosmopolitan*, August 1911:
388.

22. Hains, "Bull Run," 388.

23. G. A. Custer, "War Memoirs: From West Point," 455.

24. Michie, *Life and Letters*, 52. Absalom Baird was class of 1849; Thomas
McCurdy Vincent, class of 1853; Robert Cumming Schenck commanded a
brigade at Bull Run; Alexander McDowell McCook, class of 1852, was colonel
of the First Ohio; Robert Williams, class of 1851, was a Virginian; Dennis Hart
Mahan, professor of military and civil engineering and of the science of war, had
been first in the class of 1824.

25. Hains, "Bull Run," 388–89.

26. Hains, "Bull Run," 389–390.

27. G. A. Custer, "War Memoirs: From West Point," 460. Henry Walter Kingsbury was fourth in the class of May.

28. Hains, "Bull Run," 390–92.

29. Michie, *Life and Letters*, 54–55. Congressman Lovejoy had an older
brother, who was also a brave man. Elijah P. Lovejoy, abolitionist editor of the
Alton Observer in Illinois was killed on November 7, 1837, defending his press.

30. O.R., I, 2: 394; also quoted in Blanche Ames Ames, *Adelbert Ames, 1835–1933: General, Senator, Governor* (North Easton, Mass: privately printed, 1964), 68.

31. Hains, "Bull Run," 396.

32. Hains, "Bull Run," 396.

33. G. A. Custer, "War Memoirs: Was the Battle of Bull Run a National Disaster?" *Galaxy* (May 1876): 627–28.

34. Hains, "Bull Run," 399.

35. Hains, "Bull Run," 399.

36. Hains, "Bull Run," 399. The three others alive in 1911 were Alfred Mordecai, Joseph Farley, and Henry Noyes.

37. H. A. du Pont to Louisa du Pont, August 5, 1861, DPP, W8 308. The secretary of war was Simon Cameron.

38. Upton, *Military Policy*, 246.

39. H. A. du Pont to Sophie Du Pont, August 24, 1861, DPP, W8 311.

40. Michie, *Life and Letters*, 57.

41. Alfred Mordecai to Howard, February 11, 1862, HP.

42. P. M. B. Young to Benjamin C. Yancey, October 26, 1861, from the Benjamin Cudworth Yancey Papers, Southern Historical Collection, Wilson Library, The University of North Carolina at Chapel Hill.

43. O.R., I, 5: 956. James E. Hendrickson, *Joe Lane of Oregon: Machine Politics and the Sectional Crisis, 1849–1861* (New Haven: Yale University Press, 1967), 255, says of Senator Lane, "But although he gave his blessing to John, who left West Point to enlist in the ranks of the Confederacy, he remained aloof himself and took no part in the conflict. Like many of his generation, he did not anticipate that secession would lead inexorably to war; when hostilities commenced, he was probably realistic enough to sense the futility of bloodletting."

44. Blanche Butler Ames, ed., *Chronicles from the Nineteenth Century: Family Letters of Blanche Butler and Adelbert Ames*, 2 vols. (Clinton, Mass.: privately printed, 1957), 1: 3–4. Hannibal Hamlin, vice president of the United States, had represented Hampden, near Bangor, in the Maine legislature before becoming a congressman and senator.

3. Courage and Ambition

1. Michie, *Life and Letters*, 122.

2. Gerald F. Linderman, *Embattled Courage: The Experience of Combat in the American Civil War* (New York: Free Press, 1987), 44.

3. Thomas L. Rosser, *Addresses of Gen'l T. L. Rosser, at the Seventh Annual Reunion of the Association of the Maryland Line, Academy of Music, Baltimore, Md., February 22, 1889, and on Memorial Day, Staunton, Va., June 8, 1889.* (New York: Williams Printing Co., 1889), 34.

4. Theodore Lyman, *Meade's Headquarters, 1863–1865: Letters of Colonel Theodore Lyman from the Wilderness to Appomattox*, ed. George R. Agassiz (Boston: Massachusetts Historical Society, 1922), 139. General Samuel Sprigg Carroll, class of 1856, died in 1893. General Alexander Hays, class of 1844, was killed on May 5, 1864, in the Wilderness. General Philip Kearny, a graduate of Columbia, lost his left arm in the Mexican war and his life at Chantilly, Va., on September 1, 1862.

5. W. W. Blackford, *War Years with Jeb Stuart* (New York: Charles Scribner's Sons, 1945), 49.

6. Blackford, *War Years*, 49–50.

7. Alfred Thayer Mahan, *Admiral Farragut*, 1901 edition (New York: D. Appleton, 1892), 310.

8. Mahan, *Farragut*, 223.

9. George A. Custer to Annette Humphrey, October 9, 1863, in Marguerite Merington, ed., *The Custer Story: The Life and Intimate Letters of General George A. Custer and His Wife Elizabeth* (New York: Devin-Adair, 1950; reprint, Lincoln: University of Nebraska Press, 1987), 65. Mrs. Custer's excellent biographer, Shirley A. Leckie, points out in *Elizabeth Bacon Custer and the Making of a Myth* (Norman: University of Oklahoma Press, 1993), 310, that "Scholars who have worked in the New York Public Library archives have discovered from the few surviving originals that Merington not only edited letters, but altered and expurgated many. In the process, she heightened the couple's attractiveness. But she only followed the example Elizabeth had set earlier when she had altered letters appearing in *Following the Guidon*." It was not easy to make a saint out of George Custer.

10. *O.R.*, I, 46, part 3: 653.

11. Emory Upton, "Facts in Favor of Compulsory Retirement," *United Service: A Monthly Review of Military and Naval Affairs* 2 (March 1880): 282.

12. Blackford, *War Years*, 258.

13. Mordecai to Howard, February 11, 1862, HP.

14. H. A. du Pont to Henry du Pont, March 17, 1862, DPP, W8 332.

15. Upton, *Military Policy*, 280, 324–25.

16. Upton, *Military Policy*, 316.

17. Upton, *Military Policy*, 270–71.

18. Upton, *Military Policy*, 272.

19. Upton, *Military Policy*, 272.

20. *O.R.*, I, 10, part 1: 594.

21. *O.R.*, I, 10, part 1: 602.

22. *O.R.*, I, 10, part 1: 596.

23. Upton, *Military Policy*, 273–74.

24. Upton, *Military Policy*, 274.

25. Michie, *Life and Letters*, 59.

26. Merington, *Custer*, 30.

27. Barlow, "Personal Reminiscences," 114.

28. Upton, *Military Policy*, 310.

29. Barlow, "Personal Reminiscences," 115.

30. Barlow, "Personal Reminiscences," 115.

31. H. A. du Pont to Louisa du Pont, July 12, 1862, DPP, W8 338.

32. Upton, *Military Policy*, 298. Sherman apparently made no comment on this sentence in Upton's manuscript, or, presumably, it would have been published as a footnote. The charge of insanity had been spread by journalists—Sherman's perpetual enemies—when he was head of the Department of the Cumberland in Louisville, Ky., October 8–November 9, 1861; whether or not Sherman had lost his mind, he (temporarily) lost his job.

33. Upton, *Military Policy*, 277.

34. James A. Padgett, ed., "The Life of Alfred Mordecai as Related by Himself," *North Carolina Historical Review* 22.14 (January 1945): 93.

35. James Longstreet, *From Manassas to Appomattox: Memoirs of the Civil War in America* (Philadelphia: J. B. Lippincott Co., 1896), 262–63. For more on Kingsbury's brother-in-law David Rumph Jones, see John C. Waugh, *The Class of 1846* (New York: Warner Books, 1994).

36. H. A. du Pont to Louisa du Pont, September 25, 1862. DPP, W8 342.

37. Michie, *Life and Letters*, 63.

38. H. A. du Pont to Louisa du Pont, June 26, 1862, DPP, W8 337.

39. Report of Captain William P. Anderson, Assistant Adjutant General, Thirty-third Brigade, O.R., I, 16, part 1: 1063–64.

40. Charles T. Quintard, *Doctor Quintard, Chaplain C.S.A. and Second Bishop of Tennessee*, ed. Arthur H. Noll (Sewanee, Tenn.: University Press, 1905), 57–58. Quintard's account of Parsons at Perryville receives a full paragraph in Linderman's *Embattled Courage*, 69–70.

41. Michie, *Life and Letters*, 70–71.

42. James E. B. Stuart to John R. Cooke, January 18, 1862, in Adele H. Mitchell, ed., *The Letters of Major General James E. B. Stuart* (n.p.: Stuart-Mosby Historical Society, 1990), 250. Although Stuart calls him "a graduate of May," Pelham had left West Point to go South two weeks before graduation. Stuart's brother-in-law, John R. Cooke, was a graduate of Harvard who became a Confederate general. After mentioning Pelham, Stuart talks about his father-in-law, Philip St. George Cooke, who fought for the Union: "I have felt great mortification at Colonel Cooke's course. He will regret it but once and that will be continually. . . . It is a severe trial but the responsibility of the present state of the separation in the family rests entirely with the Colonel. Let us bear our misfortune in silence."

43. O.R., I, 21: 553.

44. Heros von Borcke, Memoirs of the Confederate War of Independence (1866; reprint, New York: Peter Smith, 1938), 2: 117–19.

45. William W. Hassler, Colonel John Pelham: Lee's Boy Artillerist (Chapel Hill: University of North Carolina Press, 1960), 148.

46. B. B. Ames, Chronicles, 1: 16; the date and the first part of the letter are missing.

4. The Vicksburg Campaign

1. Peter C. Hains, "The Vicksburg Campaign," The Military Engineer: Journal of the Society of American Military Engineers 13.69 (May–June 1921): 189.

2. Hains, "Vicksburg," 190.

3. Hains, "Vicksburg," 190–91.

4. Hains, "Vicksburg," 191.

5. Hains, "Vicksburg," 191–92.

6. Hains, "Vicksburg," 192.

7. Hains, "Vicksburg," 195.

8. Hains, "Vicksburg," 194.

9. Hains, "Vicksburg," 194.

10. Hains, "Vicksburg," 195. General John S. Bowen, class of 1853, died on July 13, 1863.

11. Peter C. Hains, "An Incident of the Battle of Vicksburg," Military Order of the Loyal Legion of the United States, Commandery of the District of Columbia, War Papers 6 (1891): 4.

12. Hains, "Vicksburg," 193.

13. Hains, "Vicksburg," 195–96.

14. Hains, "Vicksburg," 270.

15. Hains, "Vicksburg," 271. The commander of the Twenty-second Iowa was William Milo Stone.

16. Hains, "Vicksburg," 271. Griffith had a repeating rifle.

17. Hains, "Vicksburg," 271–72. Grant removed General McClernand on June 18, 1863, replacing him with E. O. C. Ord.

18. Wright Rives to Andrew Johnson, June 10, 1862, in LeRoy P. Graf and Ralph W. Haskins, eds., The Papers of Andrew Johnson (Knoxville: University of Tennessee Press, 1979), 5: 463.

19. Hains, "Vicksburg," 196.

20. Hains, "Vicksburg," 196.

21. Hains, "Vicksburg," 196.

22. Hains, "Vicksburg," 191.

23. Hains, "Vicksburg," 196, 270. Bell I. Wiley ends a chapter on fraternization with a controversial observation: "This inescapable urge of blue and gray to

intermingle and to exchange niceties suggests that—grim war though it was—
the internecine struggle of the sixties was not only in some aspect a chivalric war
but that it was in many respects a crazy and a needless war as well." Bell Irvin
Wiley, *The Life of Johnny Reb: The Common Soldier of the Confederacy* (1943;
reprint, Baton Rouge: Louisiana State University Press, 1978), 321. For the
opposite view, see James M. McPherson, *What They Fought for 1861–1865* (Baton
Rouge: Louisiana State University Press, 1994).

24. Hains, "Vicksburg," 194.

25. Hains, "Vicksburg," 194–95.

26. Hains, "Vicksburg," 193.

27. Hains, "Vicksburg," 193. Hains says 260 guns of all calibers were captured.
The figure usually given is 172 cannon.

28. Hains, "Vicksburg," 193–94. The corps commanders Hains admires are
Sherman of the Fifteenth and James B. McPherson of the Seventeenth Corps.

29. Hains, "Vicksburg," 272. Hains thought the Civil War should have ended
in 1863; Emory Upton thought it should have ended in 1862; many historians
think casualties should have stopped in November 1864, after the reelection of
Lincoln ended any chance of a Confederate political victory.

30. John Y. Simon, ed., *The Papers of Ulysses S. Grant* (Carbondale: Southern Illinois University Press, 1985), 14: 478.

31. Grant, *Personal Memoirs*, 1: 466–68.

5. Gettysburg

1. Orville E. Babcock diary, February 13, 1863. The Ulysses S. Grant Association, Morris Library, Southern Illinois University, Carbondale. Babcock mentions classmates Charles E. Cross, second in the class; J. Ford Kent, thirty-first;
and George Warren Dresser, nineteenth, who was teaching artillery tactics at
West Point.

2. Adelbert Ames to Morris Schaff, March 1908, p. 7, AFP.

3. Robert D. Heinl Jr., *Dictionary of Military and Naval Quotations* (Annapolis:
U.S. Naval Institute Press, 1966), 236.

4. Rosser, *Addresses*, 34.

5. J. Ford Kent to his sisters, May 12, 1863, Kent Papers, USMA.

6. Mitchell, *Letters of Stuart*, 309.

7. O.R., I, 25, part 1: 484–85.

8. Ezra J. Warner, *Generals in Blue* (Baton Rouge: Louisiana State University
Press, 1964), 270.

9. O.R., I, 25, part 1: 310. Darius N. Couch was thirteenth in the class of 1846.

10. Edmund Kirby to Howard, October 21, 1860, HP.

11. Babcock diary, May 8, 1863.

12. Kent to his sisters, May 12, 1863, Kent Papers, USMA.

13. Thomas L. Rosser to Elizabeth Winston, May 12, 1863, RP. In a letter to Elizabeth dated October 8, 1863, Rosser will note, "Some how or other, I always date my letters one day ahead—This is the night of the 7th."

14. Rosser to Winston, May 20, 1863, RP.

15. A. Ames to Schaff, March 1908, p. 7, AFP.

16. Babcock diary, June 18, 1863. Babcock says in his entry for September 5, 1863, "Wrote to Robt. Cross about Capt. Cross."

17. Rosser, *Addresses*, 36.

18. Rosser, *Addresses*, 39.

19. *O.R.*, I, 27, part 2: 747.

20. Rosser, *Addresses*, 39.

21. Rosser, *Addresses*, 43.

22. H. A. du Pont to Louisa du Pont, June 28, 1863, DPP, W8 350.

23. Judson Kilpatrick, "Lee at Gettysburg," *Our Magazine: A Monthly Periodical of Interesting Family Reading* (May 1871): 81–82.

24. *Congressional Record*, 43d Cong., 1st sess., February 27, 1874, 1,841.

25. *O.R.*, I, 25, part 2: 617.

26. John J. Garnett, *Gettysburg: A Complete Historical Narrative of the Battle of Gettysburg, and the Campaign Preceding It* (New York: J. M. Hill, 1888), 13–14.

27. Garnett, *Gettysburg*, 15.

28. Garnett, *Gettysburg*, 17–18.

29. Garnett, *Gettysburg*, 20.

30. *O.R.*, I, 27, part 1: 712–13.

31. Garnett, *Gettysburg*, 24.

32. Garnett, *Gettysburg*, 24.

33. Kilpatrick, "Lee," 82.

34. Eugene G. Taylor, *Gouverneur Kemble Warren: The Life and Letters of An American Soldier* (Boston: Houghton-Mifflin, 1932), 129, quoted in Harry W. Pfanz, *Gettysburg: The Second Day* (Chapel Hill: University of North Carolina Press, 1987), 223.

35. Oliver Willcox Norton, *The Attack and Defense of Little Round Top, Gettysburg, July 2, 1863* (Dayton: Morningside Bookshop, 1983), 331.

36. Taylor, *Warren*, 129.

37. Garnett, *Gettysburg*, 30–31.

38. Benjamin F. Rittenhouse, "The Battle of Gettysburg as Seen from Little Round Top," Read May 4, 1887, The Military Order of the Loyal Legion of the United States, District of Columbia No. 3; reprinted in Ken Bandy and Florence Freeland, eds., *The Gettysburg Papers* (Dayton: Morningside Bookshop, 1986), 523.

39. Eugene Beaumont to Margie Beaumont, July 4, 1863, Beaumont Letterbook, Beaumont Papers, USMA.

40. Rosser, *Addresses*, 41.

41. Theodore Roosevelt, "The Charge at Gettysburg," in Henry Cabot Lodge

and Theodore Roosevelt, eds., *Hero Tales from American History or the Story of Some Americans Who Showed That They Knew How to Live and How to Die* (New York: Century, 1895, 1915), 235. The only Union infantry that might have seen the cavalry fight in East Cavalry Field would be stragglers.

42. Garnett, *Gettysburg*, 40.

43. Garnett, *Gettysburg*, 38.

44. Reports of Brig. Gen. Alexander S. Webb, U.S. Army, commanding Second Brigade, O.R., I, 27, part 1: 429.

45. Reports of Col. Norman J. Hall, Seventh Michigan Infantry, commanding Third Brigade, O.R., I, 27, part 1: 437. Cushing has been the subject of many fine tributes, including Kent Masterson Brown, *Cushing of Gettysburg: The Story of a Union Artillery Commander* (Lexington: University Press of Kentucky, 1993), which explains the spelling of Cushing's middle name (pp. 7, 270).

46. Report of Capt. John G. Hazard, First Rhode Island Light Artillery, commanding Artillery Brigade, Second Army Corps, O.R., I, 27, part 1: 480–81.

47. Michie, *Life and Letters*, 74.

48. Garnett, *Gettysburg*, 45.

49. Kilpatrick, "Lee," 84.

50. Worthington Chauncey Ford, ed., *A Cycle of Adams Letters 1861–1865* (Boston: Houghton Mifflin, 1920), 44–45.

51. H. A. du Pont to Henry du Pont, July 12, 1863, DPP, W8 353.

52. O.R., I, 27, part 1: 225.

53. H. A. du Pont to Louisa du Pont, July 18, 1863, DPP, W8 354.

54. Babcock diary, July 27, 1863.

6. The Boy Generals

1. Rosser to Elizabeth Rosser, August 31, 1863, RP.

2. H. A. du Pont to Louisa du Pont, September 13, 1863, DPP, W8 357.

3. Rosser to Elizabeth Rosser, September 16, 1863, RP.

4. Lyman, *Meade's Headquarters*, 17.

5. O.R., I, 30, part 2: 359. In addition to Kelly, Buckner was praising division commander William Preston and brigade commanders Archibald Gracie (class of 1854) and Robert C. Trigg.

6. O.R., I, 30, part 2: 418.

7. H. A. du Pont to Henry du Pont, September 28, 1863, DPP, W8 360.

8. Rosser to Elizabeth Rosser, September 24, 1863. RP.

9. Rosser to Elizabeth Rosser, September 26, 1863, RP.

10. Wright Rives to Andrew Johnson, October 18, 1863, in Graf and Haskins, *Papers of Andrew Johnson*, 6: 425, which also has a brief biographical sketch of Rives.

11. P. M. B. Young, "The West Point Boys: Another Interesting Paper about the Men at the Military School, and Something of Their Careers . . .—General Young Tells More of the Boys of '61." *Atlanta Constitution*, March 19, 1893: 9.

12. Rosser to Elizabeth Rosser, November 1, 1863, RP.

13. Michie, *Life and Letters*, 79–80.

14. Upton, *Military Policy*, 312.

15. Douglas Southall Freeman, *Lee's Lieutenants* (New York: Scribners, 1944), 3: 298, note 80; yet Freeman (p. 297) also says of Benjamin's defense of Fort Loudon: "The entire war had witnessed no repulse more complete, by a force of insignificant numbers."

16. *O.R.*, I, 31, part 1: 341, 344.

17. H. A. du Pont to Louisa du Pont, December 1, 1863, DPP, W8 365.

18. H. A. du Pont to Henry du Pont, December 18, 1863, DPP, W8 365C.

19. H. A. du Pont to Louisa du Pont, December 15, 1863, DPP, W8 365B.

20. Rosser to Elizabeth Rosser, December 30, 1863, RP.

21. Rosser to Elizabeth Rosser, January 8, 1864, RP.

7. Custer, Rosser, and du Pont

1. Woodward, *Mary Chesnut's Civil War*, 521.

2. Henry A. du Pont, *The Campaign of 1864 in the Valley of Virginia and the Expedition to Lynchburg* (New York: National Americana Society, 1925), 3.

3. Merington, *Custer*, 79.

4. William T. Sherman, *Memoirs of General William T. Sherman*, 2nd ed. (New York: D. Appleton, 1904), 2: 460.

5. Sherman, *Memoirs*, 1: 419.

6. *O.R.*, I, 33: 161.

7. *O.R.*, I, 33: 163.

8. Madeleine Vinton Dahlgren, *Memoir of John A. Dahlgren: Rear-Admiral United States Navy* (Boston: James R. Osgood, 1882), 445–46. Two recent books claim that the Dahlgren papers found during the Kilpatrick-Dahlgren raid could have given Confederate leaders motivation to retaliate against Lincoln. See William A. Tidwell, James O. Hall, and David Winfred Gaddy, *Come Retribution: The Confederate Secret Service and the Assassination of Lincoln* (Jackson: University Press of Mississippi, 1988), and William A. Tidwell, *April '65: Confederate Covert Action in the American Civil War* (Kent: Kent State University Press, 1995).

9. Lyman, *Meade's Headquarters*, 79; letter of March 5, 1864.

10. Merington, *Custer*, 87–88.

11. William Henry Jackson, *Time Exposure: The Autobiography of William Henry Jackson* (New York: G. P. Putnam, 1940), 70–71.

12. Elizabeth Bacon Custer to Daniel S. Bacon and Rhoda Pitts Bacon (stepmother), April 1864, in Merington, *Custer*, 90–91. Francis W. Kellogg was a congressman from Michigan.

13. James Harrison Wilson, *Under the Old Flag* (New York: D. Appleton, 1912), 1: 361–62. Wilson was sixth in the class of 1860; Wesley Merritt, twenty-second.

14. George A. Custer to Elizabeth B. Custer, July 1, 1864, in Merington, *Custer*, 110–11.

15. Michie, *Life and Letters*, 88–89.

16. Michie, *Life and Letters*, 90–91.

17. John J. Garnett, ed., *Sketch of the Life of General U. S. Grant with the Programme of the Ceremonies of the Dedication of the Grant Monument in New York, April 27th, 1897, Illustrated with Portraits of General Grant and Other Distinguished Generals of the U.S. Army, and Pictures of the War Ships in the Naval Parade* (New York: Garnett & Whitman, 1897), n.p. At the end of his sketch, Garnett has this note: "This sketch has been compiled for this work, from the life of U. S. Grant by Charles A. Dana and General James H. Wilson, and from E[mma] E. Brown's life of Grant."

18. Garnett, *Sketch of Grant*, n.p.

19. Grant, *Personal Memoirs*, 2: 223–25. General Horatio Wright, second in the class of 1841, commanded the Sixth Corps; Gershom Mott, a businessman before the war, became brigadier general of volunteers in 1862.

20. H. A. du Pont, *Campaign*, 14; see also Franz Sigel, "Sigel in the Shenandoah Valley in 1864," *Battles and Leaders of the Civil War*, ed. Robert U. Johnson and Clarence C. Buel (New York: Century Co., 1887; reprint, Secaucus, N.J.: Castle, n.d.), 4: 489.

21. H. A. du Pont, *Campaign*, 26.

22. H. A. du Pont, *Campaign*, 21.

23. H. A. du Pont, *Campaign*, 21–22. Julius Stahel, who was born in Hungary and served in the Austrian army, became colonel of the Eighth New York (First German Rifles), brigadier general (1861) and major general (1863).

24. H. A. du Pont, *Campaign*, 22–23.

25. H. A. du Pont, *Campaign*, 33.

26. H. A. du Pont to Henry du Pont, May 17, 1864, DPP, W8 378.

27. H. A. du Pont to Louisa du Pont, May 24, 1864, DPP, W8 379.

28. James M. Greiner, Janet L. Coryell, and James R. Smither, eds. *A Surgeon's Civil War: The Letters and Diary of Daniel M. Holt, M.D.* (Kent: Kent State University Press, 1994), 195.

29. Michie, *Life and Letters*, 109.

30. *O.R.*, I, 51: 1249.

31. H. A. du Pont, *Campaign*, 63–64. Richard H. Brewer was twelfth in the class of 1858.

32. H. A. du Pont, *Campaign*, 68.

33. Senate Committee on Claims, *Virginia Military Institute: Hearing Before the Committee on Claims*, 63d Cong., 2d sess., February 7, 1914, on S. 544, a Bill for the Relief of the Virginia Military Institute, of Lexington, Va. (Washington: Government Printing Office, 1914), 8.

34. Michie, *Life and Letters*, 122.

35. Rosser to Elizabeth Rosser, September 13, 1864, RP.

36. H. A. du Pont, *Campaign*, 107.

37. H. A. du Pont, *Campaign*, 111–12.

38. H. A. du Pont, *Campaign*, 112.

39. H. A. du Pont, *Campaign*, 113.

40. H. A. du Pont, *Campaign*, 114–16. Du Pont gives a brief biographical sketch of his friend in a footnote (p. 114): "Emory Upton, born in New York State in 1839, graduated from the Military Academy May 6, 1861. After serving in the Regular artillery he became colonel of the One hundred twenty-first New York Volunteer Infantry and, on May 12, 1864, brigadier-general of Volunteers. Was the author of the infantry tactics which bear his name (1867) and of the Military Policy of the United States (1880). He died March 14, 1881." Du Pont also has a footnote (p. 114) on his classmate Ford Kent: "Born in 1835 and died December 22, 1918, as Major-General, U.S.A. retired."

41. H. A. du Pont, *Campaign*, 121–22. In footnotes identifying Merritt and McQuesten, du Pont gives the general one line and the general's aide, a classmate, four: "James F. McQuesten, born in New Hampshire in 1835 and graduated from the Military Academy May 6, 1861, being appointed second-lieutenant of the Second Dragoons. Was later first-lieutenant and then captain of the Second Cavalry, and aide-de-camp to General Merritt at the time of his death."

42. A. Ames to Schaff, March 1908, p. 7, AFP.

43. Rosser to Elizabeth Rosser, September 15, 1864, RP.

44. Rosser to Elizabeth Rosser, December 14, 1864, RP.

45. Elizabeth B. Custer, *Boots and Saddles, or Life in Dakota with General Custer* (New York: Harper & Brothers, 1885), 275.

46. H. A. du Pont, *Campaign*, 153.

47. H. A. du Pont, *Campaign*, 154.

48. H. A. du Pont, *Campaign*, 157–58.

49. H. A. du Pont, *Campaign*, 174.

50. H. A. du Pont, *Campaign*, 174–75.

51. Rosser, *Addresses*, 48. Sheridan's tactics are similar to what Rosser's classmate Upton called for.

52. Horace Porter, *Campaigning with Grant* (New York, 1897; reprint, Secaucus, N.J.: Blue & Grey Press, n.d.), 310–11.

53. Simon, *Papers of Grant*, 12: 414, 415n.

54. Orville E. Babcock to "Dear Uncle," November 23, 1864, BP.

55. Barlow, "Personal Reminiscences," 117–18.

56. Barlow, "Personal Reminiscences," 118. General John Logan would be incensed when Sherman chose Oliver Otis Howard to be the permanent commander of the army. Christopher Spencer's inventions were repeating rifles and rifled carbines.

57. Sherman, *Memoirs*, 2: 103–4. Kenner Garrard was eighth in the class of 1851.

58. Howard, *Autobiography*, 2: 29.

59. Howard, *Autobiography*, 2: 28–29.

60. John Edward Pierce, "General Hugh Judson Kilpatrick in the American Civil War: A New Appraisal," Pennsylvania State University, Ph.D. dissertation, 1983, 273, 6. In an earlier dissertation on Kilpatrick, George Wayne King notes, "Many other members of the unusual class of 1861 distinguished themselves." "The Civil War Career of Hugh Judson Kilpatrick," University of South Carolina, Ph.D. dissertation, 1969, 9.

61. Howard, *Autobiography*, 2: 30–32.

62. Albert E. Castel, *Decision in the West: The Atlanta Campaign of 1864* (Lawrence: University Press of Kansas, 1992), 116.

63. Rosser to Elizabeth Rosser, September 13, 1864, RP.

64. Wilson, *Under the Old Flag*, 2: 13.

65. Howard, *Autobiography*, 2: 71.

66. *O.R.*, I, 44: 368.

67. Blackford, *War Years*, 281. Hood now has his defenders who understand what he did, or tried to do, around Atlanta but not in Tennessee.

68. See William C. Davis, "The Massacre at Saltville," *Civil War Times Illustrated* 9 (February 1971), 4–11, 43–48.

69. Felix H. Robertson to George K. Miller, June 10, 1895, pp. 2–5, from the George Knox Miller Papers, Southern Historical Collection, Wilson Library, The University of North Carolina at Chapel Hill.

8. Ending the War

1. Adelbert Ames, "The Capture of Fort Fisher," *Civil War Papers* (Boston: The Military Order of the Loyal Legion of the United States, Commandery of Massachusetts, 1900), 1: 295.

2. Charles Jackson Paine commanded a division of black troops. Ames's reserve brigade was commanded by Colonel Joseph C. Abbott. Comstock not only returned, he kept a useful diary. See Merlin E. Sumner, ed., *The Diary of Cyrus B. Comstock* (Dayton, Ohio: Morningside, 1987).

3. Ames's aide was Albert G. Lawrence. Ames later noted ("Fort Fisher," 294), "Brevet Brig. General N.M. Curtis, commanding First Brigade, was prominent

throughout the day for his bravery, coolness and judgment. His services cannot be overestimated. He fell a short time before dark, seriously wounded in the head by a canister shot." See also Newton Martin Curtis, "The Capture of Fort Fisher," *Personal Recollections of the War of the Rebellion* (Boston: The Military Order of the Loyal Legion of the United States, Commandery of Massachusetts, 1900).

4. Oliver P. Harding began the day in the 203rd Pennsylvania. Pennypacker, not Custer, was the youngest general in the Civil War. Pennypacker was born on June 1, 1844. He had been elected captain of the Ninety-seventh Pennsylvania in August 1861 and promoted to major in October of that year, when he was seventeen. In 1865, Pennypacker would be promoted to brigadier general of volunteers. He was twenty.

5. Louis Bell commanded the Third Brigade.

6. A. Ames, "Fort Fisher," 280–85.

7. A. Ames, "Fort Fisher," 287.

8. H. A. du Pont to Louisa du Pont, February 3, 1865, DPP, W8 399. See Gary W. Gallagher, *The Confederate War* (Cambridge: Howard University Press, 1997).

9. Michie, *Life and Letters*, xxiv.

10. Michie, *Life and Letters*, xv.

11. Wilson, *Under the Old Flag*, 2: 207. Eli Long (1837–1903), an 1855 graduate of a military school in Frankfort, Ky., commanded the Second Cavalry Division. Oscar Hugh LaGrange commanded the Second Brigade of Edward Moody McCook's First Cavalry Division.

12. Wilson, *Under the Old Flag*, 2: 207–8. John W. Noble was colonel of the Third Iowa Cavalry. Edward F. Winslow (1837–1914), Fourth Iowa Cavalry, commanded Upton's First Brigade. Winslow became a brevet brigadier general after being recommended for promotion by Upton and Wilson. Frederick William Benteen, Tenth Missouri Cavalry, later saved the Seventh U.S. Cavalry, in the opinion of many, after George A. Custer was wiped out. In an endorsement of a promotion list (O.R., I, 49, part 1: 477) submitted by Emory Upton, General J. H. Wilson wrote on June 7, 1865, "I would also request that Lieut. Col. F. W. Benteen, Tenth Missouri Cavalry, be brevetted brigadier-general for gallant and meritorious services, not only during the recent campaign in Georgia and Alabama, but for distinguished and conspicuous bravery in the pursuit of [General Sterling] Price out of Missouri."

13. Wilson, *Under the Old Flag*, 2: 208–11. Andrew Jonathan Alexander commanded Upton's Second Brigade and later became his brother-in-law. They are buried in Auburn, N.Y., in Fort Hill Cemetery. Buried near them is Myles W. Keogh, of the Seventh U.S. Cavalry.

14. Wilson, *Under the Old Flag*, 2: 218.

15. Report of Bvt. Maj. Gen. Emory Upton, commanding Fourth Division,

of operations March 19–April 21, O.R., I, 49, part 1: 475.

16. Wilson, *Under the Old Flag*, 2: 221–22.

17. Wilson, *Under the Old Flag*, 2: 223–25. Wilson is referring to Israel Garrard, Seventh Ohio Cavalry; John H. Peters, lieutenant colonel, commanding the Fourth Iowa Cavalry; J. Morris Young, Fifth Iowa Cavalry, and Beroth B. Eggleston, First Ohio Cavalry.

18. Wilson, *Under the Old Flag*, 2: 228–30. General Frank C. Armstrong, commanding Forrest's best brigade, was born at Choctaw Agency, Indian Territory, in 1835, survived Selma, and died at Bar Harbor, Me., in 1909.

19. Garnett, *Sketch of Grant*, n.p.

20. Morris Schaff, *The Sunset of the Confederacy* (Boston: John W. Luce, 1912), 19–20.

21. O.R., I, 46, part 3: 653.

22. Rosser, *Addresses*, 46.

23. Millard K. Bushong and Dean M. Bushong, *Fightin' Tom Rosser, C.S.A.* (Shippenburg, Penn.: Beidel Printing House, 1983), 184. John McCausland died in 1927, leaving Felix Robertson of the class of June as the last surviving Confederate general.

24. Rosser, *Addresses*, 49.

25. Joshua Lawrence Chamberlain, *The Passing of the Armies* (1915; reprint, Dayton: Morningside Bookshop, 1974), 27.

26. Chamberlain, *Passing*, 265.

27. H. A. du Pont to Henry du Pont, April 15, 1865, DPP, W8 404.

9. Adelbert Ames: Reconstruction Governor

1. A. Ames, "Journal While Abroad," no. 1, August 24, 1866, 3–5. Page references are to the transcript (of extracts from the journal) that Blanche Ames Ames produced. The manuscript does not have consecutively numbered pages. The best means of identification is the date.

2. A. Ames, "Journal," no. 1, August 29, 1866, 10.

3. A. Ames, "Journal," no. 1, September 3, 1866, 16.

4. A. Ames, "Journal," no. 1, September 9, 1866, 19–20. Charles Jackson Paine (August 26, 1833–August 12, 1916) was a graduate of Boston Latin School and Harvard College (class of 1853).

5. A. Ames, "Journal," no. 1, September 15, 1866, 24.

6. A. Ames, "Journal," no. 1, September 25, 1866, 27–29.

7. A. Ames, "Journal," no. 1, September 26, 1866, 29.

8. A. Ames, "Journal," no. 1, October 1, 1866, 31–32.

9. A. Ames, "Journal," no. 1, October 3, 1866, 34.

10. A. Ames, "Journal," no. 1, November 5, 1866, 51–53.

11. A. Ames, "Journal," no. 1, November 10, 1866, 60–61.
12. A. Ames, "Journal," no. 1, November 20, 1866, 70.
13. A. Ames, "Journal," no. 1, December 9, 1866, 96–98.
14. A. Ames, "Journal," no. 1, December 10, 1866, 100.
15. A. Ames, "Journal," no. 2, January 12, 1867, 19–20. General John Adams Dix, United States Minister to France, learned French at the College of Montreal and was a fourteen-year-old army officer at the Battle of Lundy's Lane in the War of 1812. In 1863, he suppressed the New York City draft riots. General Dix returned to the United States in 1869 and was elected governor of New York in 1872. Fort Dix, in New Jersey, is named for him
16. A. Ames, "Journal," no. 2, January 17, 1867, 22–24.
17. A. Ames, "Journal," no. 2, January 30, 1867, 35–36.
18. A. Ames, "Journal," no. 2, February 3, 1867, 37.
19. A. Ames, "Journal," no. 2, February 14, 1867, 43.
20. A. Ames, "Journal," no. 2, March 23, 1867, 71–72.
21. A. Ames, "Journal," no. 2, March 25, 1867, 74.
22. A. Ames, "Journal," no. 2, March 26, 1867, 75.
23. A. Ames, "Journal," no. 3, April 22, 1867, 13–14.
24. A. Ames, "Journal," no. 2, May 29, 1867, 28.
25. Pauline Ames Plimpton, interview, New York, April 11, 1991.
26. Blanche Ames Ames, *Adelbert Ames, 1835–1933: General, Senator, Governor* (North Easton, Mass.: privately printed, 1964), 303.
27. B. B. Ames, *Chronicles*, 1: 283.
28. B. B. Ames, *Chronicles*, 1: 410.
29. B. B. Ames, *Chronicles*, 1: 468.
30. B. A. Ames, *Adelbert Ames*, 371.
31. B. B. Ames, *Chronicles*, 1: 693.
32. B. B. Ames, *Chronicles*, 1: 695.
33. B. B. Ames, *Chronicles*, 2: 30.
34. B. B. Ames, *Chronicles*, 2: 52.
35. B. B. Ames, *Chronicles*, 2: 70–71.
36. B. A. Ames, *Adelbert Ames*, 419.
37. B. A. Ames, *Adelbert Ames*, 433–434.
38. B. A. Ames, *Adelbert Ames*, 442.
39. B. A. Ames, *Adelbert Ames*, 451.
40. B. A. Ames, *Adelbert Ames*, 513.
41. B. B. Ames, *Chronicles*, 2: 613.
42. *New York Times*, June 21, 1898: 3.
43. B. B. Ames, *Chronicles*, 2: 616.
44. B. B. Ames, *Chronicles*, 2: 621–22.
45. B. B. Ames, *Chronicles*, 2: 623.
46. B. B. Ames, *Chronicles*, 2: 638.

47. B. B. Ames, *Chronicles*, 2: 651.

48. B. B. Ames, *Chronicles*, 2: 651–52.

49. B. B. Ames, *Chronicles*, 2: 659.

50. B. B. Ames, *Chronicles*, 2: 662.

51. Morris Schaff to Adelbert Ames, March 12, 1908, AFP.

52. Cullum File of Adelbert Ames, USMA.

53. "Rockefeller Ends Florida Sojourn. Beats General Adelbert Ames Seven Up in Farewell Nine-Hole Golf Games. Says Good-bye, Gives Dimes," *New York Times*, April 4, 1928: 31.

54. John F. Kennedy, *Profiles in Courage* (New York: Harper, 1956), 161.

55. B. A. Ames, *Adelbert Ames*, 556.

56. B. A. Ames, *Adelbert Ames*, 556.

57. B. A. Ames, *Adelbert Ames*, 562.

58. B. A. Ames, *Adelbert Ames*, 566.

59. B. A. Ames, *Adelbert Ames*, 567.

60. Pauline Ames Plimpton, "Orchids and Artists: Celebration Dinner at Smith," September 20, 1991, AFP; see also *Orchids and Artists: Five Centuries of Botanical Illustration from Peter Schoeffer to Blanche Ames '99* (Northampton: Smith College Museum of Art, 1991).

61. "Mrs. Oakes Ames, Women's Suffrage Leader, Dies at 91," *Brockton Daily Enterprise*, March 3, 1969.

10. George Armstrong Custer: Little Bighorn

1. *New York Times*, July 7, 1876: 1.

2. Simon, *Papers of Grant*, 16: 202.

3. Elizabeth B. Custer, *Tenting on the Plains, or General Custer in Kansas and Texas* (New York: Charles L. Webster, 1887), 679.

4. George A. Custer, *My Life on the Plains or, Personal Experiences with Indians*, with an introduction by Edgar I. Stewart (Norman: University of Oklahoma Press, 1962), 22.

5. G. A. Custer, *My Life*, 23.

6. G. A. Custer, *My Life*, 17.

7. Lawrence A. Frost, *The Court-Martial of General George A. Custer* (Norman: University of Oklahoma Press, 1968), 247.

8. John M. Carroll, ed., *The Benteen-Goldin Letters on Custer and His Last Battle* (Lincoln: University of Nebraska Press, 1991), 280–81. Those who hate Custer should like Benteen's letters to Goldin, which include such lines as, "I intend giving you a few more details concerning the S.O.B." (p. 263) and "I'm only too proud to say that I despised him as a murderer, thief and a liar—all of which I can prove" (p. 272).

9. Wilson, *Under the Old Flag*, 224–25, 262.

10. Hugh Lenox Scott, *Some Memories of a Soldier* (New York: Century Co., 1928), 454. Scott, class of 1876, served as superintendent of West Point (1906–1910) and army chief of staff (November 16, 1914–September 21, 1917).

11. Accounts of the expedition appear in G. A. Custer, *My Life on the Plains* and in Samuel Johnson Crawford, *Kansas in the Sixties* (Chicago: A. C. McClurg, 1911).

12. Custer's articles have been published in *Nomad: George A. Custer in Turf, Field and Farm*, ed. Brian W. Dippie (Austin: University of Texas Press, 1980).

13. E. B. Custer, *Boots and Saddles*, 74.

14. E. B. Custer, *Boots and Saddles*, 249, 251. Although she rode with the Seventh Cavalry on the Great Plains, in the great city her husband went to dinners that were for men only. The Century Association changed its rules when Francis T. P. Plimpton, husband of Pauline Ames Plimpton—a granddaughter of General Ames—became president. Mrs. Plimpton says, "During his presidency Francis . . . managed to have women allowed in for dinner one night a week . . . which, of course, promptly escalated to every night." Pauline Ames Plimpton, *A Window on Our World: Plimpton Papers* (New York: British American, 1989), 280.

15. E. B. Custer, *Boots and Saddles*, 263.

16. Quoted in Edward M. Coffman, *The Old Army: A Portrait of the American Army in Peacetime, 1784–1898* (New York: Oxford University Press, 1986), 298.

17. Carroll, *Benteen-Goldin*, 213–14.

18. Carroll, *Benteen-Goldin*, 213.

19. *Army and Navy Journal*, July 22, 1876: 805. Stephen E. Ambrose, *Crazy Horse and Custer: The Parallel Lives of Two American Warriors* (New York: Doubleday, 1975), 444, notes, "The world hardly needs another analysis of the battle of the Little Bighorn." This is another reason for including one from 1876 that still holds up. Custer faced the Sioux when they were at their peak strength in numbers. In the Civil War it was just the opposite; Custer was fortunate to become a cavalry general during the Gettysburg campaign, just as the Confederate cavalry was beginning its decline.

20. *New York Tribune*, July 10, 1876: 5. Walt Whitman later changed the title to "From Far Dakota's Cañons." Louis Untermeyer, ed., *The Poetry and Prose of Walt Whitman* (New York: Simon & Schuster, 1949), 431–32.

21. Edmund C. Stedman, "Custer," *New York Tribune*, July 13, 1876: 5.

22. William F. Cody, *The Life of Buffalo Bill* (London: Studio Editions, 1994), 344. It is not the least of his achievements that his book was still in print in London in 1994.

23. John Hay, *The Complete Poetical Works* (Boston: Houghton Mifflin, 1917), 77–80.

24. Candace Wheeler, *Yesterdays in a Busy Life* (New York: Harper & Brothers, 1918), 422.

25. Elizabeth B. Custer to Cornelia Otis Skinner, April 18 [1919]. Letter in the possession of the author.

26. I once asked an instructor at West Point if Custer had any defenders on the faculty. The captain said, "Yes, he's usually the same person who defends MacArthur."

27. *New York Times*, December 21, 1940: 21.

28. "A Thinking General," *Raleigh News and Observer, Parade Magazine*, March 10, 1991: 21.

11. Thomas Lafayette Rosser: Custer's Rebel Friend

1. *New York Times*, May 3, 1867: 8.

2. George A. Custer, "Battling with the Sioux on the Yellowstone," *Galaxy*, July 1876: 92.

3. G. A. Custer, "Battling," 92.

4. E. B. Custer, *Boots and Saddles*, 91.

5. E. B. Custer, *Boots and Saddles*, 275.

6. *St. Paul and Minneapolis Pioneer-Press and Tribune*, July 8, 1876; reprinted in *New York Herald*, July 11, 1876: 3–4.

7. See Pierre Burton, *The Last Spike: The Great Railway, 1881–1885* (Toronto: McClelland & Stewart, 1971), 11, 13, 20, 23–28, 44, 56, 89–91, 92, 113, 116, 140, 159, 182, and 404.

8. G. A. Custer, "Battling," 92.

9. Rosser, *Addresses*, 3.

10. Rosser, *Addresses*, 32–33.

11. Rosser, *Addresses*, 13.

12. Rosser to Senator John W. Daniel, undated [1900], RP.

13. Elizabeth B. Custer to Mrs. Rosser, February 15, 1909, RP.

12. John Whitney Barlow: Explorer of Yellowstone

1. See J. W. Barlow, *Report of a Reconnaissance of the Basin of the Upper Yellowstone in 1871*, 42d Cong., 2d sess., 1872, Senate Ex. Doc. No. 66 (Washington: Government Printing Office, 1872).

2. Barlow, *Report of a Reconnaissance*, 4.

3. Barlow, *Report of a Reconnaissance*, 4.

4. See Ferdinand Vandeveer Hayden, *The Great West: Its Attractions and Resources. Containing . . . the Recent Explorations in Yellowstone Park, "The Wonderland of America"* (Philadelphia: Franklin Publishing Co., 1880).

5. Barlow, *Report of a Reconnaissance*, 6.

6. Barlow, *Report of a Reconnaissance*, 9, 10.

7. See Jackson, *Time Exposure*, 200–201. Barlow's name appears on pp. 197 and 203.

8. Barlow, *Report of a Reconnaissance*, 14.

9. Barlow, *Report of a Reconnaissance*, 15.

10. Barlow, *Report of a Reconnaissance*, 15.

11. Barlow, *Report of a Reconnaissance*, 16–17.

12. Jackson, *Time Exposure*, 187.

13. Barlow, *Report of a Reconnaissance*, 17, 37.

13. Henry Algernon du Pont: Businessman, Senator, Author

1. Joseph Frazier Wall, *Alfred I. du Pont: The Man and His Family* (New York: Oxford University Press, 1990), 188.

2. Henry A. du Pont, ed., *L'enfance et la jeunesse de Du Pont de Nemours, racontées, par lui-même: Mémoires de P.-S. Du Pont de Nemours adressés a ses enfants* (Paris: Typographie Plon-Nourrit, 1906), iv.

3. Henry A. du Pont, *Rear-Admiral Samuel Francis Du Pont, United States Navy: A Biography* (New York: National Americana Society, 1926), 6.

4. Senate Committee, *Virginia Military Institute*, 3.

5. Senate Committee, *Virginia Military Institute*, 3–4.

6. *Address made by Col. H. A. du Pont, United States Senator from Delaware, at the Commencement Exercises of the Virginia Military Institute, June 23, 1915*, copy in Hagley Museum and Library, Wilmington, Del.

7. Henry A. du Pont, *The Real Stanton*, 1925, copy in Hagley Museum and Library, Wilmington, Del.

8. *Remarks Made by Colonel du Pont at the West Point Graduates' Dinner, Washington, D.C., March 21, 1925*, copy in Hagley Museum and Library, Wilmington, Del.

14. Judson Kilpatrick: Playwright and Diplomat

1. George W. Cullum, *Biographical Register of the Officers and Graduates of the U.S. Military Academy at West Point, N.Y., from Its Establishment, in 1802, to 1890* (Boston: Houghton Mifflin, 1891), 2: 789.

2. See Judson Kilpatrick, *The Irish Soldier in the War of the Rebellion* (Deckertown, N.J.: Independent Steam Print, 1880[?]).

3. See Judson Kilpatrick and J. Owen Moore, *Allatoona: An Historical and Military Drama*, French's Standard Drama 376 (New York: Samuel French, n.d.), originally published in 1875.

4. Christopher Morley, *The Blue and The Gray or, War Is Hell*, Revised and Edified from an Old Script by Judson Kilpatrick and J. Owen Moore (Garden City, N.Y.: Doubleday, Doran, 1930), vii–viii.

5. Wilson, *Under the Old Flag*, 2: 368.

15. Orville E. Babcock: The Rise and Fall of Grant's Secretary

1. Babcock diary, The Ulysses S. Grant Association, Morris Library, Southern Illinois University, Carbondale.

2. J. Ford Kent was thirty-first in the class of May.

3. This comment on General Patrick E. Connor indicates that Babcock realized that a man's income and expenditures should not be wildly out of touch. Babcock's defenders have pointed to the fact that he did not spend money lavishly but lived modestly as a sign of his honesty.

4. Brigham Young (1801–77) is usually reported to have had from nineteen to twenty-seven wives.

5. Allan Nevins, *Hamilton Fish: The Inner History of the Grant Administration*, rev. ed. (New York: Frederick Ungar, 1957), 1: 281. Nevins agrees with and quotes William T. Sherman, who called Babcock "a kind of intermediator between the people and the President."

6. Franz Sigel to Babcock, December 22, 1872, BP.

7. Franz Sigel to Babcock, March 1, 1873, BP. General Max Weber, who lost the use of his right arm at Antietam, was appointed collector of internal revenue in New York by President Grant.

8. Daniel E. Sickles to Babcock, February 8, 1875, BP.

9. Nevins, *Hamilton Fish*, 2: 766.

10. Allan Nevins to Orville Babcock Jr., October 1, 1936, BP.

11. House Select Committee, *Testimony Before the Select Committee Concerning the Whisky Frauds*, 44th Cong., 1st sess., 1876, Misc. Doc. No. 186, 360. Alexander Gilmore Cochran, a Democrat from Pennsylvania, was a graduate of Andover and Columbia Law School, who became general solicitor of the Missouri Pacific Railway.

12. Hamlin Garland, "An Interview with General Harry Wilson," Hamlin Garland Papers, Special Collections, University of Southern California, 15. This was not the first time General Wilson, or his advice, had been rejected by a powerful man who preferred a controversial member of the May class. Sherman had chosen Kilpatrick, rather than Wilson, to command his cavalry on the March to the Sea. Perhaps there was something about Wilson (unlike Babcock) that made the powerful uncomfortable. Perhaps he was too talented and independent to be content as a subordinate and could not hide the fact that in a larger sense, moral and intellectual, he did not think he had any superiors. "He talked well," Hamlin Garland remarked (p. 1) after his two-hour interview with Wilson, "and he

talked all the time; it was not necessary for me to even ask questions." In any case, it is not surprising that in World War I the army rejected Wilson's request to return to active duty. Can anyone imagine General Wilson taking orders from a youth like John J. Pershing, who was born the year Wilson graduated from West Point?

13. Heinl, *Dictionary*, 177.
14. D. W. Flagler to Babcock, December 17 [1875], BP.
15. Charles Pelham to Babcock, August 26, 1876, BP.
16. Garland, "Interview," 15.
17. John Y. Simon, ed. *The Personal Memoirs of Julia Dent Grant* (Carbondale: Southern Illinois University Press, 1975), 186.
18. A. Ames to Schaff, March 1908, p. 7, AFP.

16. Pierce M. B. Young: Confederate General and U.S. Diplomat

1. Simon, *Papers of Grant*, 18: 586.
2. Simon, *Papers of Grant*, 18: 586.
3. *Congressional Record*, 43d Cong., 1st sess., February 27, 1874, 1841.
4. Robert Penn Warren, ed., *Selected Poems of Herman Melville* (New York: Random House, 1967), 198.
5. *Congressional Globe*, 41st Cong., 3d sess., January 24, 1871, 704.
6. Schaff, *Spirit*, 149.
7. Steven E. Ambrose, review of *Pierce M. B. Young: The Warwick of the South*, by Lynwood M. Holland, *North Carolina Historical Review* 41 (autumn 1964): 495.
8. P. M. B. Young, "The West Point Boys: Another Interesting Paper about the Men at the Military School, and Something of Their Careers . . . —General Young Tells More of the Boys of '61," *Atlanta Constitution*, March 19, 1893: 9.
9. See P. M. B. Young, "Report on Cotton Culture," in *Reports of the United States Commissioners to the Paris Universal Exposition, 1878*, vol. 3, 46th Cong., 3d sess., House of Representatives, Ex. Doc. 42, pt. 3 (Washington: Government Printing Office, 1880).
10. Young, "West Point Boys," 9.

17. John J. Garnett: Sketches of Grant and Lee

1. Robert E. Lee to Dr. William Morris, October 18, 1866, and Robert E. Lee to John J. Garnett, December 13, 1866, photocopies in the Lee Family Papers (Mss1L51c737–738), Virginia Historical Society, Richmond.
2. John J. Garnett, ed. and comp., *The Official Programme. "Special Edition"*

(*without programme*) *for Use of Visitors to Bedloe's Island Before the Inauguration. The Statue of Liberty* (New York: B. W. Dinsmore, 1886).

3. John J. Garnett, *Tribute to Gen'l Robert E. Lee, Delivered at the Banquet of the Southern Auld Lang Syne Society, of Harlem, N.Y., on the Anniversary of Gen'l Lee's Birthday, January 20th, 1890* (New York: n.p., 1890), 4.

4. Garnett, *Tribute*, 8.

5. Garnett, *Tribute*, 5.

6. See John J. Garnett, *Biographical Sketch of General Robert Edward Lee with His Reports of the Battles of Chancellorsville and Gettysburg, and the Surrender at Appomattox. . . . Programme of the Ceremonies of the Unveiling of the Equestrian Statue at Richmond, Va., May 29th, 1890* (New York: 1890), p. 104.

7. See Garnett, *Sketch of Grant*, n.p.

8. "West Point Man a Suicide. Colonel J.G. [*sic*] Garnett Ends His Life in Hotel at Sixth Ave. and Fifteenth St.," *New York Tribune*, September 13, 1902: 3.

9. "Died," *New York Herald*, September 16, 1902: 1.

18. Peter C. Hains: Bull Run to World War I

1. Peter C. Hains, trans., *Memoir upon the Illumination and Beaconage of the Coasts of France*, by M. Léonce Reynaud (Washington: Government Printing Office, 1876), 2. It is perhaps remarkable that a graduate of West Point was able to do any translating, since, as T. Harry Williams observed, "the cadets could not have read the best works on war, for these were in French, and the French taught at the school was not sufficient to provide a reading knowledge." *P. G. T. Beauregard: Napoleon in Gray* (Baton Rouge: Louisiana State University Press, 1955), 7.

2. Peter C. Hains, "An Isthmian Canal from a Military Point of View," *Annals of the American Academy of Political and Social Science* 17 (May 1901): 399.

3. Hains, "Isthmian Canal," 406.

4. *Statement of Colonel Peter C. Hains, Corps of Engineers, U.S. Army, Before the Subcommittee of the Committee on Interoceanic Canals, United States Senate,* 57th Cong., 1st sess., February 13, 1902 (Washington: Government Printing Office, 1902), 9.

5. Sketch enclosed with letter of August 12, 1918, Cullum File of Peter C. Hains, USMA.

6. Peter C. Hains to Colonel Wirt Robinson, May 17, 1918, Cullum File of Peter C. Hains, USMA.

7. Robinson to Hains, May 20, 1918, Cullum File of Peter C. Hains, USMA.

8. Hains to Robinson, June 3, 1918, Cullum File of Peter C. Hains, USMA.

9. Hains to Robinson, June 3, 1918, Cullum File of Peter C. Hains, USMA. Felix Huston Robertson, who left the June class before graduation, died on April 20, 1928, the last surviving Confederate general. For Francis Henry Parker, see appendix A, Roll Call for the June class, no. 20. For James Parker, who went south to join the rebellion against the United States, see G. A. Custer, "War Memoirs: From West Point," 456–57.

10. *Military Engineer*, 1922; reprinted in the *Annual Report of the Association of Graduates*, June 11, 1924, 65.

19. Emory Upton: "The Class Genius"

1. Russell F. Weigley, *Towards an American Army: Military Thought from Washington to Marshall* (New York: Columbia University Press, 1962), 104. Weigley also says of Upton, "He was among those West Point graduates of 1861 who plunged so swiftly into battle . . . and won meteoric fame" (101).

2. Emory Upton, *A New System of Infantry Tactics, Double and Single Rank, Adapted to American Topography and Improved Fire-arms* (New York: D. Appleton, 1868); T. Harry Williams, *Americans at War: The Development of the American Military System* (Baton Rouge: Louisiana State University Press, 1960), 91.

3. *Army and Navy Journal*, March 19, 1881: 677.

4. Emory Upton, *The Armies of Asia and Europe* (New York: D. Appleton, 1878), 30.

5. Upton, *Armies*, 77.

6. Secretary of War John C. Calhoun's report of 1820, quoted in Upton, *Military Policy*, 149.

7. Upton, *Armies*, 361–62.

8. See Carol Reardon, *Soldiers and Scholars: The U.S. Army and the Uses of Military History, 1865–1920* (Lawrence: University Press of Kansas, 1990), 14.

9. Upton, *Military Policy*, 61.

10. Upton, *Military Policy*, 67.

11. Upton, *Military Policy*, 66.

12. Emory Upton, "Civil and Military Policy of Rome," Emory Upton Papers, U.S. Army Military History Institute, Upton Hall, Carlisle Barracks, Pennsylvania, 1. Planned as chapter 33 of *Military Policy*.

13. Upton, "Rome," 58.

14. *Army and Navy Journal*, March 19, 1881: 677.

15. Michie, *Life and Letters*, 482–83.

16. Michie, *Life and Letters*, 489–90.

17. Michie, *Life and Letters*, 491–95. Upton's body was found by his servants the next morning, March 15, 1881.

18. See *Army and Navy Journal*, March 19, 1881: 677.

19. Quoted in John D. Hayes and John B. Hattendorf, eds., *The Writings of Stephen B. Luce* (Newport, RI: Naval War College, 1975), 11.

20. Albert Gleaves, *Life and Letters of Rear Admiral Stephen B. Luce, U.S. Navy, Founder of the Naval War College* (New York: Putnam's, 1925), 170.

21. Scott, *Some Memories*, 557.

22. See Williams, *Americans at War*, 95, which includes this comment: "Upton was saying, in effect, that for the purpose of modern war the American military experience was useless." Russell Weigley, "Emory Upton," *Dictionary of American Military Biography*, ed. Roger J. Spiller et al. (Westport, Conn.: Greenwood Press, 1984), 1126, concludes, "His deepest impact, however, was a tendency to alienate American soldiers from the democratic politics and society they served."

23. See Weigley, *Towards an American Army*.

24. Eliot A. Cohen, "Making Do with Less, or Coping with Upton's Ghost," 6, 25, read at the U.S. Army War College Annual Strategy Conference, Carlisle Barracks, Penn., April 27, 1995.

25. See Stephen E. Ambrose, *Upton and the Army* (Baton Rouge: Louisiana State University Press, 1964), 159.

26. *Coup d'oeil de guerre* has been translated as the ability to accurately estimate a combat situation at a glance.

27. James Harrison Wilson, introduction to Michie, *Life and Letters*, xxvii.

Appendix A: Roll Call

1. A. Ames to Schaff, March 1908, p. 7, AFP.

2. See Edward T. James, ed., *Notable American Women, 1607–1950: A Biographical Dictionary* (Cambridge: Belknap Press of Harvard University Press, 1971), 2: 657–59.

3. Charles McKnight Leoser, "The Grand Army as a Pension Agency," *Forum*, July 1893.

4. See Guy V. Henry, *Military Record of Civilian Appointments in the United States Army*, 2 vols. (New York: Carleton, 1870–73).

5. *Harper's Weekly*, July 6, 1895: 627. Henry calls "Indian campaigning—of all warfare the most dangerous, the most trying, and the most thankless: the first because your foe is behind cover; the second, because you are often on reduced rations, exposed to intense cold, fires often being forbidden; if wounded, there is no transportation or possible care; if left on the field wounded, torture of the worst kind awaits you." He describes what awaited him at the Rosebud:

> I felt a sharp sting, as of being slapped in the face, and a blinding rush of blood to my head and eyes. A rifle-bullet had struck me in the face, under my left eye, passing through the upper part of my mouth, under the nose, and out below the right eye.

One of my sergeants put a handkerchief about my face, and with his assistance I mounted my horse, and with both eyes closed, my face badly swollen and black, presenting, I have been told, a most horrible appearance, I was led to the surgeon, who put his hand in the upper part of my mouth to see how much had been shot away, and who then told me to lie down.

I was placed on the ground with other wounded . . . I retained my revolver. I was unable to talk, both jaws having been fractured, and was quite blind. I heard many in passing me remark that I must be dead.

The Indians . . . did not molest us on our march, which was due to the fact, as we learned afterwards, that they were watching Custer and his command. . . . Arriving at Fort Russell . . . in two months, having gained sufficient strength and the use of one eye, I went to California, where, I became myself again, and returned to duty at Fort Laramie in less than a year—in time for the Crazy Horse, Ute River, and other Indian campaigns.

6. Edgar F. Raines Jr. "Jacob Ford Kent," *Dictionary of American Military Biography*, ed. Roger J. Spiller et al. (Westport: Greenwood Press, 1984), 558.

7. See John S. Poland, comp., *A Digest of the Military Laws of the United States, from 1860 to the Second Session of the Fortieth Congress, 1867, Relating to the Army, Volunteers, Militia, and the Rebellion and Reconstruction of the Southern States* (Boston: Little, Brown, 1868).

8. John S. Poland, comp., *The Conventions of Geneva and the St. Petersburg Military Commission for the Amelioration of the Condition of Soldiers Wounded in the Field. Also Conventions Between the United States and Mexico, 1882–83, for the Reciprocal Crossing of the International Boundary Line and Other Official Information, Commercia Belli, etc.* (Fort Leavenworth, Kans.: School Press, 1886), iii.

9. F. G. Notehelfer, *American Samurai: Captain L. L. Janes and Japan* (Princeton: Princeton University Press, 1985), 272–73.

10. Rosser, *Addresses*, 49.

11. Daniel W. Flagler, *A History of Rock Island Arsenal from Its Establishment in 1863 to December, 1876; and of the Island of Rock Island, the Site of the Arsenal, from 1804 to 1863* (Washington: Government Printing Office, 1877), 21.

12. Howard, *Autobiography*, 1: 97.

13. Hains says, "You are mistaken, however, in supposing Noyes and myself to be the only two members of our class left on deck. There is one other and he is a pretty lively one, Mordecai. I am sure he is not dead because I saw him a few weeks ago and I hardly think he would cross the Styx without notifying some of his friends that he was about to do so." Hains to Robinson, May 17, 1918, Cullum File of Peter C. Hains, USMA.

14. According to former Confederate chaplain Charles Todd Quintard, "I preached in . . . Brooklyn, New York, on 'Repentance and the Divine Life.' This sermon made a deep impression upon Colonel Parsons, as he told me when I subsequently met him at a reception at the residence of the Hon. Hamilton Fish."

Quintard says, "I visited him twice at West Point. . . . In 1870 he resigned his commission in the army to enter the ministry. He studied theology with me at Memphis . . . and became rector of a parish of which Mr. Jefferson Davis was a member and a vestryman." Quintard, *Doctor Quintard*, 58.

15. *Banner of the Church*, September 2, 1871: 293. Parsons's coeditor was George C. Harris.

16. Elizabeth Custer says of her husband,

> There was an officer, a classmate at West Point, who, he felt with all his heart, did right in resigning. If he had lived he would have written his tribute . . . . My husband believed in what old-fashioned people term a "calling". . . . And so it happened, when it was our good fortune to be stationed with his classmate, Colonel Charles C. Parsons, at Leavenworth, that he gave a ready ear when his old West Point chum poured out his longings for a different sphere in life. He used to come to me after these sessions, when the Colonel went over and over again his reasons for resigning, and wonder how he could wish to do so, but . . . he ended by saying, "There's nothing to be done, though, for if Parsons thinks he ought to go into an uncertainty, and leave what is a surety for life, why, he ought to follow his convictions."

Elizabeth Custer says that the next time they saw Parsons he was rector of a small mission church, noting, "The General was touched by the fearless manner in which he faced poverty and obscurity." E. B. Custer, *Tenting*, 315–21.

17. From photocopies in Cullum File of Charles Carroll Parsons, USMA, of news clipping scrapbook kept by the Rev. George C. Harris, Dean of St. Mary's Cathedral, Memphis, Tenn. Original in Local History Room, Memphis Public Library.

18. Sherman, *Memoirs*, 2: 460. According to Sherman's recent biographer, Michael Fellman, *Citizen Sherman: A Life of William Tecumseh Sherman* (New York: Random House, 1995), Sherman had a romantic interest in Audenried's widow, Mary.

19. Joseph C. Audenried, "General Sherman in Europe and the East, *Harper's New Monthly Magazine*, June 1873: 237.

20. See Joseph P. Farley, *Rules for the Inspection of Army Revolvers and Gatling Guns* (Springfield, Mass.: National Armory, 1875).

21. See John Farley, *Over Seas in Early Days (1828–29)* (Kansas City: Hudson Press, 1907), 148.

22. Charles Iverson Graves on Alexander Welch Reynolds; quoted in William B. Hesseltine and Hazel C. Wolf, *The Blue and the Gray on the Nile* (Chicago: University of Chicago Press, 1961), 217–18.

23. Joseph P. Farley, *West Point in the Early Sixties*, 24–25. In *The Spirit of Old West Point*, 184, Morris Schaff, class of 1862, recalled, "Late one night, while on my way from Montgomery to Atlanta just after the war, the ramshackle train stopped at one of the lonely stations. . . . Ball, still in Confederate gray, entered.

. . . He inquired in the kindliest way, not only for those who had borne him on their shoulders, the present Brigadier-General J. P. Farley and others, but for all his classmates."

24. See H. A. du Pont, *Campaign*, 63–64.

25. Cleburne quoted in Joseph Wheeler, *Alabama*, vol. 7 of *Confederate Military History*, ed. Clement A. Evans (Atlanta: Confederate Publishing Co., 1899), 422. General Wheeler also quotes himself: "To my brave division commander, General Kelly, who gave up his life at Franklin, while gallantly fighting at the head of his division, I ask the country to award its gratitude. No honors bestowed on his memory could more than repay his devotion." Wheeler compared Kelly to another 1861 graduate, noting, "It may be said of him, as Lee said of Pelham, another son of Alabama, 'It is glorious to see such courage in one so young.'"

26. G. A. Custer, "War Memoirs: From West Point," 454.

Bibliography

Writings and Publications by Members of the Class of 1861

Ames, Adelbert. "The Capture of Fort Fisher," *Civil War Papers* 1. Boston: Commandery of Massachusetts, Military Order of the Loyal Legion of the United States, 1900.
———. "Journal While Abroad." 3 vols. Ames Family Papers. Sophia Smith Collection, Smith College.
Audenried, Joseph C. "General Sherman in Europe and the East." *Harper's New Monthly Magazine*, June 1873.
Babcock, Orville E. Diary. The Ulysses S. Grant Association, Morris Library, Southern Illinois University, Carbondale.
———. Papers. The Newberry Library, Chicago.
Barlow, John W. *Letter from the Secretary of War, Transmitting the Report of Major J. W. Barlow, Who Accompanied a Surveying Party of the Northern Pacific Railroad, in Relation to Indian Interference With That Road.* 42d Cong. 3d sess. Ex. Doc. No. 16. Washington: Government Printing Office, 1873.
———. "Personal Reminiscences of the War." *War Papers.* Commandery of the State of Wisconsin, Military Order of the Loyal Legion of the United States. Milwaukee: Burdick, Armitage & Allen, 1891.
———. *Report of a Reconnaissance of the Basin of the Upper Yellowstone in 1871.* 42d Cong. 2d sess. Senate Ex. Doc. No. 66. Washington: Government Printing Office, 1872.
Beaumont, Eugene. Letterbook. Beaumont Papers. Special Collections and Archives. U.S. Military Academy Library, West Point, N.Y.
Custer, George A. "Battling with the Sioux on the Yellowstone." *Galaxy*, July 1876.
———. *Custer in the Civil War: His Unfinished Memoirs.* Edited by John M. Carroll. San Rafael, Calif.: Presidio Press, 1977.

———. *My Life on the Plains, or Personal Experiences with Indians*. Introduction by Edgar I. Stewart. Norman: University of Oklahoma Press, 1962.

———. *Nomad: George A. Custer in Turf, Field and Farm*. Edited by Brian W. Dippie. Austin: University of Texas Press, 1980.

———. "War Memoirs: From West Point to the Battlefield." *Galaxy*, April 1876.

———. "War Memoirs: Was the Battle of Bull Run a National Disaster?" *Galaxy*, May 1876.

Dresser, George Warren, ed. *The American Gas Light Journal*. New York, 1875–83. Biweekly publication.

du Pont, Henry A. *Address by Colonel du Pont upon the Unveiling of Major General Ramseur's Monument*, 1920, copy in Hagley Museum and Library, Wilmington, Del.

———. *Address made by Col. H. A. du Pont, United States Senator from Delaware, at the Commencement Exercises of the Virginia Military Institute, June 23, 1915*, copy in Hagley Museum and Library, Wilmington, Del.

———. *The Campaign of 1864 in the Valley of Virginia and the Expedition to Lynchburg*. New York: National Americana Society, 1925.

———. "A Crisis of Conscience: West Point Letters of Henry A. du Pont, October 1860–June 1861." Edited by Virginia T. Lake. *Civil War History*, March 1979.

———. *Early Generations of the Du Pont and Allied Families*. 2 vols. New York: National Americana Society, 1923.

———, ed. *L'enfance et la jeunesse de Du Pont de Nemours, racontées, par lui-même: Mémoires de P.-S. Du Pont de Nemours adressés a ses enfants*. Paris: Typographie Plon-Nourrit, 1906.

———. *Papers*. Winterthur Manuscripts. Hagley Museum and Library, Wilmington, Del.

———. *The Real Stanton*, 1925, copy in Hagley Museum and Library, Wilmington, Del.

———. *Rear-Admiral Samuel Francis Du Pont, United States Navy: A Biography*. New York: National Americana Society, 1926.

———. *Remarks Made by Colonel du Pont at the West Point Graduates' Dinner, Washington, D.C., March 21, 1925*, copy in Hagley Museum and Library, Wilmington, Del.

———. "West Point in the Fifties: The Letters of Henry A. du Pont." Edited by Stephen E. Ambrose. *Civil War History* 10 (September 1964).

[du Pont, Henry A., and Emory Upton]. *Artillery Tactics*. New York: D. Appleton, 1875.

Farley, Joseph P. *Rules for the Inspection of Army Revolvers and Gatling Guns*. Springfield, Mass: National Armory, 1875.

———. *Three Rivers: The James, the Potomac, the Hudson: A Retrospect of Peace and War*. New York: Neale Publishing Co., 1910.

————. *West Point in the Early Sixties: With Incidents of the War.* Troy, N.Y.: Pafraets Book Co., 1902.

Flagler, Daniel W. *A History of Rock Island Arsenal from Its Establishment in 1863 to December, 1876; and of the Island of Rock Island, the Site of the Arsenal, from 1804 to 1863.* Washington: Government Printing Office, 1877.

Garnett, John J. *Biographical Sketch of General Robert Edward Lee with His Reports of the Battles of Chancellorsville and Gettysburg, and the Surrender at Appomattox . . . Programme of the Ceremonies of the Unveiling of the Equestrian Statue at Richmond, Va., May 29th, 1890.* New York: 1890.

————. *Gettysburg: A Complete Historical Narrative of the Battle of Gettysburg, and the Campaign Preceding It.* New York: J. M. Hill, 1888.

————. *Sketch of the Life of General U. S. Grant, with the Programme of the Ceremonies of the Dedication of the Grant Monument in New York, April 27th, 1897, Illustrated with Portraits of General Grant and Other Distinguished Generals of the U.S. Army, and Pictures of the War Ships in the Naval Parade.* New York: Garnett & Whiteman, 1897.

————. *Tribute to Gen'l Robert E. Lee, Delivered at the Banquet of the Southern Auld Lang Syne Society, of Harlem, N.Y., on the Anniversary of Gen'l Lee's Birthday, January 20th, 1890.* New York, 1890.

————, ed. and comp. *The Official Programme. "Special Edition" (without programme) for Use of Visitors to Bedloe's Island Before the Inauguration. The Statue of Liberty.* New York: B. W. Dinsmore & Co., 1886.

Hains, Peter C. "The First Gun at Bull Run." *Cosmopolitan,* August 1911.

————. "An Incident of the Battle of Vicksburg." Military Order of the Loyal Legion of the United States, Commandery of the District of Columbia, *War Papers* 6, read at the meeting of February 4, 1891.

————. "An Isthmian Canal from a Military Point of View." *Annals of the American Academy of Political and Social Science* 17 (May 1901).

————. "The Labor Problem on the Panama Canal." *North American Review,* July 1904.

————. "The Panama Canal—Some Objections to a Sea-Level Project." *North American Review,* March 1905.

————. *Statement of Colonel Peter C. Hains, Corps of Engineers, U.S. Army, Before the Subcommittee of the Committee on Interoceanic Canals, United States Senate.* 57th Cong., 1st sess., February 13, 1902. Washington: Government Printing Office, 1902.

————. "The Vicksburg Campaign." *The Military Engineer: Journal of the Society of American Military Engineers* 13.69 (May–June 1921).

————, trans. *Memoir upon the Illumination and Beaconage of the Coasts of France,* by M. Léonce Reynaud. Washington: Government Printing Office, 1876.

Henry, Guy V. *Military Record of Civilian Appointments in the United States Army.* 2 vols. New York: Carleton, 1870–73.

————. "Wounded in an Indian Fight." *Harper's Weekly*, July 6, 1895.

Janes, Leroy Lansing. *Kumamoto: An Episode in Japan's Break from Feudalism.* Kyoto, Japan: Doshisha University Shashi Shiryo Henshu Sho, 1970.

————. Papers. Princeton University Library.

Kent, Jacob Ford. Papers. Special Collections and Archives. U.S. Military Academy Library, West Point, N.Y.

Kilpatrick, Judson. *The Irish Soldier in the War of the Rebellion.* Deckertown, N.J.: Independent Steam Print, n.d. [1880?].

————. "Lee at Gettysburg." *Our Magazine: A Monthly Periodical of Interesting Family Reading*, May 1871.

————, ed. *Our Magazine: A Monthly Periodical of Interesting Family Reading.* Newton, N.J.: Kilpatrick & Mattison, October 1870–November 1871.

Kilpatrick, Judson, and J. Owen Moore. *Allatoona: An Historical and Military Drama.* French's Standard Drama 376. New York: Samuel French, n.d. Originally published 1875.

Leoser, Charles McKnight. "The Grand Army as a Pension Agency." *Forum*, July 1893.

————, publisher. *Bonfort's Wine and Spirit Circular; A Semi-Monthly Journal and Price Current for the United States.* New York, n.d.

Parsons, Rev. Charles Carroll, and Rev. George C. Harris, eds. *Banner of the Church.* Memphis, Tenn., 1871. Published weekly.

Poland, John S., comp. *The Conventions of Geneva and the St. Petersburg Military Commission for the Amelioration of the Condition of Soldiers Wounded in the Field. Also Conventions Between the United States and Mexico, 1882–83, for the Reciprocal Crossing of the International Boundary Line and Other Official Information, Commercia Belli, etc.* Fort Leavenworth, Kans.: School Press, 1886.

————, comp. *A Digest of the Military Laws of the United States, from 1860 to the Second Session of the Fortieth Congress, 1867, Relating to the Army, Volunteers, Militia, and the Rebellion and Reconstruction of the Southern States.* Boston: Little, Brown, 1868.

Rosser, Thomas Lafayette. *Addresses of Gen'l T. L. Rosser, at the Seventh Annual Reunion of the Association of the Maryland Line, Academy of Music, Baltimore, Md., February 22, 1889, and on Memorial Day, Staunton, Va., June 8, 1889.* New York: L. A. Williams Printing Co., 1889.

————. Rosser Family Papers (#1171). Special Collections Department. University of Virginia Library.

Upton, Emory. *The Armies of Asia and Europe.* New York: D. Appleton, 1878.

————. "Civil and Military Policy of Rome." Emory Upton Papers. U.S. Army Military History Institute. Upton Hall. Carlisle Barracks, Penn.

————. "Facts in Favor of Compulsory Retirement." *The United Service: A Monthly Review of Military and Naval Affairs* 2 (March 1880).

————. *The Military Policy of the United States.* 4th printing. Washington: War Department, 1912. Originally published 1904.

————. A New System of Infantry Tactics, Double and Single Rank, Adapted to American Topography and Improved Fire-arms. New York: D. Appleton, 1868.

Young, Pierce M. B. "Gen. P. M. B. Young Tells the Story of West Point's Part in the War—He Was in the Graduating Class." Atlanta Constitution, March 12, 1893: 5.

————. "Report on Cotton Culture." Reports of the United States Commissioners to the Paris Universal Exposition, 1878. Vol. 3, 46th Cong. 3d sess., House of Representatives. Ex. Doc. 42, pt. 3. Washington: Government Printing Office, 1880.

————. "The West Point Boys: Another Interesting Paper about the Men at the Military School, and Something of Their Careers . . . — General Young Tells More of the Boys of '61." Atlanta Constitution, March 19, 1893: 9.

Other Sources

Ambrose, Stephen E. Crazy Horse and Custer: The Parallel Lives of Two American Warriors. New York: Doubleday, 1975.

————. Duty, Honor, Country: A History of West Point. Foreword by Dwight D. Eisenhower. Baltimore: Johns Hopkins Press, 1966.

————. Review of Pierce M. B. Young: The Warwick of the South, by Lynwood M. Holland. North Carolina Historical Review 41 (autumn 1964): 495–96.

————. Upton and the Army. Baton Rouge: Louisiana State University Press, 1964.

Ames, Blanche Ames. Adelbert Ames, 1835–1933: General, Senator, Governor. North Easton, Mass.: privately printed, 1964.

Ames, Blanche Butler, comp. Chronicles from the Nineteenth Century: Family Letters of Blanche Butler and Adelbert Ames. 2 vols. Clinton, Mass.: privately printed, 1957.

Benét, Stephen Vincent. John Brown's Body. Garden City, N.Y.: Doubleday, Doran, 1928.

Blackford, W. W. War Years with Jeb Stuart. New York: Charles Scribner's Sons, 1945.

Borcke, Heros von. Memoirs of the Confederate War of Independence. 2 vols. 1866. Reprint, New York: Peter Smith, 1938.

Brown, Kent Masterson. Cushing of Gettysburg: The Story of a Union Artillery Commander. Lexington: University Press of Kentucky, 1993.

Burton, Pierre. The Last Spike: The Great Railway, 1881–1885. Toronto: McClelland & Stewart, 1971.

Bushong, Millard K., and Dean M. Bushong. Fightin' Tom Rosser, C.S.A. Shippenburg, Penn.: Beidel Printing House, 1983.

Carroll, John M., ed. The Benteen-Goldin Letters on Custer and His Last Battle. Lincoln: University of Nebraska Press, 1991.

Castel, Albert E. *Decision in the West: The Atlanta Campaign of 1864*. Lawrence: University Press of Kansas, 1992.

Chamberlain, Joshua Lawrence. *The Passing of the Armies*. 1915; reprint, Dayton, Ohio: Morningside Bookshop, 1974.

Circulation Records. Special Collections and Archives. U.S. Military Academy Library, West Point, N.Y.

Cody, William F. *The Life of Buffalo Bill*. London: Studio Editions, 1994.

Coffman, Edward M. *The Old Army: A Portrait of the American Army in Peacetime, 1784–1898*. New York: Oxford University Press, 1986.

Cohen, Eliot A. "Making Do with Less, or Coping with Upton's Ghost." Paper read at the U.S. Army War College Annual Strategy Conference, Carlisle Barracks, Penn., April 27, 1995.

Crawford, Samuel Johnson. *Kansas in the Sixties*. Chicago: A. C. McClurg, 1911.

Cullum, George W. *Biographical Register of the Officers and Graduates of the United States Military Academy*. 3 vols. Boston: Houghton Mifflin, 1891.

Cullum Files. Special Collections and Archives. U.S. Military Academy Library, West Point, N.Y.

Current, Richard Nelson. *Those Terrible Carpetbaggers*. New York: Oxford University Press, 1988.

Curtis, Newton Martin. "The Capture of Fort Fisher," *Personal Recollections of the War of the Rebellion*. Boston: The Military Order of the Loyal Legion of the United States, Commandery of Massachusetts, 1900.

Custer, Elizabeth B. *Boots and Saddles, or Life in Dakota with General Custer*. New York: Harper & Brothers, 1885.

———. *Following the Guidon*. New York: Harper & Brothers, 1890.

———. *Tenting on the Plains, or General Custer in Kansas and Texas*. New York: Charles L. Webster, 1887.

Dahlgren, Madeleine Vinton. *Memoir of John A. Dahlgren: Rear-Admiral United States Navy*. Boston: James R. Osgood, 1882.

Davis, William C. "The Massacre at Saltville." *Civil War Times* Illustrated 9 (February 1971).

Dickens, Charles. *American Notes and Pictures from Italy*. London: Oxford University Press, 1957.

Farley, John. *Over Seas in Early Days (1828–29)*. Kansas City: Hudson Press, 1907.

Fellman, Michael. *Citizen Sherman: A Life of William Tecumseh Sherman*. New York: Random House, 1995.

Flexner, Stuart B. *Listening to America: An Illustrated History of Words and Phrases from Our Lively and Splendid Past*. New York: Simon & Schuster, 1982.

Ford, Worthington Chauncey, ed. *A Cycle of Adams Letters: 1861–1865*. 2 vols. Boston: Houghton Mifflin, 1920.

Freeman, Douglas Southall. *Lee's Lieutenants: A Study in Command*. 3 vols. New York: Scribners, 1942–44.

Frost, Lawrence A. *The Court-Martial of General George A. Custer*. Norman: University of Oklahoma Press, 1968.

Gallagher, Gary W. *The Confederate War*. Cambridge: Harvard University Press, 1997.

Garland, Hamlin. "An Interview with General Harry Wilson." Typescript in the Hamlin Garland Papers. Special Collections. University of Southern California.

Gleaves, Albert. *Life and Letters of Rear Admiral Stephen B. Luce, U.S. Navy, Founder of the Naval War College*. New York: Putnam's, 1925.

Graf, LeRoy P., and Ralph W. Haskins, eds. *The Papers of Andrew Johnson*. Vols. 5 and 6. Knoxville: University of Tennessee Press, 1979, 1983.

Grant, Ulysses S. *Personal Memoirs of U. S. Grant*. 2 vols. New York: Charles L. Webster, 1885.

Gray, John S. *Custer's Last Campaign: Mitch Boyer and the Little Bighorn Reconstructed*. Lincoln: University of Nebraska Press, 1991.

Greiner, James M., Janet L. Coryell, and James R. Smither, eds. *A Surgeon's Civil War: The Letters and Diary of Daniel M. Holt, M.D.* Kent, Ohio: Kent State University Press, 1994.

Hassler, William W. *Colonel John Pelham: Lee's Boy Artillerist*. Chapel Hill: University of North Carolina Press, 1960.

Hay, John. *The Complete Poetical Works*. Boston: Houghton Mifflin, 1917.

Hayden, Ferdinand Vandeveer. *The Great West: Its Attractions and Resources. Containing . . . the Recent Explorations in Yellowstone Park, "The Wonderland of America."* Philadelphia: Franklin Publishing, 1880.

Hayes, John D., ed. *Samuel Francis Du Pont: A Selection from His Civil War Letters*. 3 vols. Ithaca, N.Y.: Cornell University Press for the Eleutherian Mills Historical Library, 1969.

Hayes, John D., and John B. Hattendorf, eds. *The Writings of Stephen B. Luce*. Newport, R.I.: Naval War College, 1975.

Heinl, Robert D., Jr. *Dictionary of Military and Naval Quotations*. Annapolis: United States Naval Institute Press, 1966.

Hendrickson, James E. *Joe Lane of Oregon: Machine Politics and the Sectional Crisis, 1849–1861*. New Haven: Yale University Press, 1967.

Hesseltine, William B., and Hazel C. Wolf. *The Blue and the Gray on the Nile*. Chicago: University of Chicago Press, 1961.

Holland, Lynwood M. *Pierce M. B. Young: The Warwick of the South*. Athens: University of Georgia Press, 1964.

Howard, Oliver Otis. *Autobiography of Oliver Otis Howard*. New York: Baker & Taylor, 1908.

———. Papers. Bowdoin College Library.

Jackson, William H. *Time Exposure: The Autobiography of William Henry Jackson*. New York: G. P. Putnam's, 1940.

James, Edward T., ed. *Notable American Women, 1607–1950: A Biographical Dic-*

tionary. Cambridge: Belknap Press of Harvard University Press, 1971.

Kennedy, John F. *Profiles in Courage*. New York: Harper, 1956.

King, George W. "The Civil War Career of Hugh Judson Kilpatrick." University of South Carolina, Ph.D. dissertation, 1969.

Kirshner, Ralph. "Bell Irvin Wiley." *Dictionary of American Biography*. Edited by Kenneth T. Jackson, Karen E. Markoe, and Arnold Markoe. Supplement Ten. New York: Charles Scribner's Sons, 1995.

———. "Emory Upton." *American National Biography*. Edited by John A. Garraty and Mark C. Carnes. New York: Oxford University Press, 1999.

———. "Hugh Judson Kilpatrick." *American National Biography*. Edited by John A. Garraty and Mark C. Carnes. New York: Oxford University Press, 1999.

———. "Pierce Manning Butler Young." *American National Biography*. Edited by John A. Garraty and Mark C. Carnes. New York: Oxford University Press, 1999.

———. "Thomas Harry Williams." *Dictionary of American Biography*. Edited by Kenneth T. Jackson, Karen E. Markoe, and Arnold Markoe. Supplement Ten. New York: Charles Scribner's Sons, 1995.

———. "Thomas Lafayette Rosser." *American National Biography*. Edited by John A. Garraty and Mark C. Carnes. New York: Oxford University Press, 1999.

Krick, Robert K. *Lee's Colonels: A Biographical Register of the Field Officers of the Army of Northern Virginia*. 4th ed. Dayton, Ohio: Morningside, 1992.

Leckie, Shirley A. *Elizabeth Bacon Custer and the Making of a Myth*. Norman: University of Oklahoma Press, 1993.

Lee, Robert E. Letters. Photocopy of letterbook in the Lee Family Papers Mss 1L51c737-738. Virginia Historical Society, Richmond.

Linderman, Gerald F. *Embattled Courage: The Experience of Combat in the American Civil War*. New York: Free Press, 1987.

Longacre, Edward G. *The Cavalry at Gettysburg: A Tactical Study of Mounted Operations During the Civil War's Pivotal Campaign, 9 June–14 July 1863*. Rutherford, N.J.: Fairleigh Dickinson University Press, 1986.

Longstreet, James. *From Manassas to Appomattox: Memoirs of the Civil War in America*. Philadelphia: J. B. Lippincott Co., 1896.

Lord, Ruth. *Henry F. du Pont and Winterthur: A Daughter's Portrait*. New Haven: Yale University Press, 1999.

Lyman, Theodore. *Meade's Headquarters, 1863–1865: Letters of Colonel Theodore Lyman from the Wilderness to Appomattox*. Edited by George R. Agassiz. Boston: Massachusetts Historical Society, 1922.

Mahan, Alfred Thayer. *Admiral Farragut*. New York: D. Appleton, 1892.

Martin, Samuel J. *"Kill-Cavalry" Sherman's Merchant of Terror: The Life of Union General Hugh Judson Kilpatrick*. Teaneck, N.J.: Fairleigh Dickinson University Press, 1996.

McPherson, James M. *What They Fought for 1861–1865*. Baton Rouge: Louisiana State University Press, 1994.

Merington, Marguerite, ed. *The Custer Story: The Life and Intimate Letters of General George A. Custer and His Wife Elizabeth*. New York: Devin-Adair, 1950. Reprint, Lincoln: University of Nebraska Press, 1987.

Michie, Peter S. *The Life and Letters of Emory Upton, Colonel of the Fourth Regiment of Artillery, and Brevet Major-General, U.S. Army*. Introduction by James Harrison Wilson. New York: D. Appelton, 1885.

Milham, Charles G. *Gallant Pelham: American Extraordinary*. Introduction by Major General U. S. Grant, 3rd. Washington, D.C.: Public Affairs Press, 1959. Reprint, Gaithersburg, Md.: Old Soldier Books, 1987.

Miller, George Knox. Papers. Southern Historical Collection. Wilson Library. University of North Carolina at Chapel Hill.

Mitchell, Adele H., ed. *The Letters of Major General James E. B. Stuart*. N.p.: The Stuart-Mosby Historical Society, 1990.

Morley, Christopher. *The Blue and The Gray or, War Is Hell*. Revised and Edified from an Old Script by Judson Kilpatrick and J. Owen Moore. Garden City, N.Y.: Doubleday, Doran, 1930.

Morrison, James L. *"The Best School in the World": West Point, the Pre-Civil War Years, 1833–1866*. Kent, Ohio: Kent State University Press, 1986.

Nevins, Allan. *Hamilton Fish: The Inner History of the Grant Administration*. Rev. ed. 2 vols. New York: Frederick Ungar, 1957.

Norton, Oliver Willcox. *The Attack and Defense of Little Round Top, Gettysburg, July 2, 1863*. Dayton, Ohio: Morningside Bookshop, 1983.

Notehelfer, F. G. *American Samurai: Captain L. L. Janes and Japan*. Princeton, N.J.: Princeton University Press, 1985.

———. "L. L. Janes in Japan: Carrier of American Culture and Christianity." *Journal of Presbyterian History* 53.4 (winter 1975).

Orchids and Artists: Five Centuries of Botanical Illustration from Peter Schoeffer to Blanche Ames '99. Northampton: Smith College Museum of Art, 1991.

Padgett, James A., ed. "The Life of Alfred Mordecai [class of 1823] as Related by Himself." *North Carolina Historical Review* 22.14 (January 1945).

Pfanz, Harry W. *Gettysburg: The Second Day*. Chapel Hill: University of North Carolina Press, 1987.

Pierce, John E. "General Hugh Judson Kilpatrick in the American Civil War: A New Appraisal." Pennsylvania State University, Ph.D. dissertation, 1983.

Plimpton, Pauline Ames. *The Ancestry of Blanche Butler Ames and Adelbert Ames*. New York: Wizard Graphics, 1977.

———. "Orchids and Artists: Celebration Dinner at Smith." September 20, 1991. Typescript in Ames Family Papers, Sophia Smith Collection, Smith College.

———. *A Window on Our World: Plimpton Papers*. New York: British American, 1989.

Porter, Horace. *Campaigning with Grant*. New York: Century, 1897. Reprint, Secaucus, N.J.: The Blue & Grey Press, n.d.

Pullen, John J. *The Twentieth Maine, A Volunteer Regiment in the Civil War*. Philadelphia: J. B. Lippincott, 1957.

Quintard, Charles T. *Doctor Quintard, Chaplain C.S.A. and Second Bishop of Tennessee*. Edited by Arthur H. Noll. Sewanee, Tenn.: University Press, 1905.

Raines, Edgar F., Jr. "Jacob Ford Kent." *Dictionary of American Military Biography*. Edited by Roger J. Spiller, Joseph G. Dawson III, and T. Harry Williams. Westport, Conn.: Greenwood Press, 1984.

Rapp, Kenneth W. *West Point: Whistler in Cadet Gray, and Other Stories about the United States Military Academy*. N.p.: North River Press, 1978.

Reardon, Carol. *Soldiers and Scholars: The U.S. Army and the Uses of Military History, 1865–1920*. Lawrence: University Press of Kansas, 1990.

Register of Cadet Delinquencies. Special Collections and Archives. U.S. Military Academy Library, West Point, N.Y.

Rittenhouse, Benjamin F. "The Battle of Gettysburg as Seen from Little Round Top." The Military Order of the Loyal Legion of the United States, District of Columbia, No. 3. Reprinted in *The Gettysburg Papers*, edited by Ken Bandy and Florence Freeland. Dayton: Morningside Bookshop, 1986.

Roosevelt, Theodore. "The Charge at Gettysburg." *Hero Tales from American History or the Story of Some Americans Who Showed That They Knew How to Live and How to Die*. Edited by Henry Cabot Lodge and Theodore Roosevelt. New York: Century, 1895. Reprinted, 1915.

Schaff, Morris. *The Spirit of Old West Point. 1858–1862*. Boston: Houghton Mifflin, 1907.

———. *The Sunset of the Confederacy*. Boston: John W. Luce, 1912.

Scott, Hugh Lenox. *Some Memories of a Soldier*. New York: Century, 1928.

Sergent, Mary Elizabeth. *They Lie Forgotten: The United States Military Academy 1856–1861, Together with a Class Album for the Class of May, 1861*. Middletown, N.Y.: Prior King Press, 1986.

———. *An Unremaining Glory (Being A Supplement to They Lie Forgotten): A Class Album for the Class of June, 1861 (Custer's Class) United States Military Academy West Point, New York, Together with Additional Material on the Class of May, 1861*. Middletown, N.Y.: Prior King Press, 1997.

Service Records. National Archives, Washington, D.C.

Sherman, William T. *Memoirs of General William T. Sherman*. 2 vols. New York: D. Appleton, 1904.

Sigel, Franz. "Sigel in the Shenandoah Valley in 1864." *Battles and Leaders of the Civil War*. Edited by Robert U. Johnson and Clarence C. Buel. New York: Century, 1887. Reprint, Secaucus, N.J.: Castle, n.d.

Simon, John Y., ed. *The Papers of Ulysses S. Grant*. 22 vols. Carbondale: Southern Illinois University Press, 1967–98.

———, ed. *The Personal Memoirs of Julia Dent Grant*. Carbondale: Southern Illinois University Press, 1975.

Spiller, Roger J., Joseph G. Dawson, and T. Harry Williams, eds. *Dictionary of American Military Biography*. Westport: Greenwood Press, 1984.

Starr, Stephen Z. *The Union Cavalry in the Civil War*. 3 vols. Baton Rouge: Louisiana State University Press, 1979–85.

Sumner, Merlin E., ed. *The Diary of Cyrus B. Comstock*. Dayton, Ohio: Morningside, 1987.

Taylor, Eugene G. *Gouverneur Kemble Warren: The Life and Letters of An American Soldier*. Boston: Houghton-Mifflin, 1932.

Tidwell, William A., James O. Hall, and David Winfred Gaddy. *April '65: Confederate Covert Action in the American Civil War*. Kent, Ohio: Kent State University Press, 1995.

———. *Come Retribution: The Confederate Secret Service and the Assassination of Lincoln*. Jackson: University Press of Mississippi, 1988.

Untermeyer, Louis, ed. *The Poetry and Prose of Walt Whitman*. New York: Simon & Schuster, 1949.

Urwin, Gregory J. W. *Custer Victorious: The Civil War Battles of General George Armstrong Custer*. Rutherford, N.J.: Fairleigh Dickinson University Press, 1983.

U.S. Congress. House Select Committee. *Testimony Before the Select Committee Concerning the Whisky Frauds*. 44th Cong., 1st sess., 1876. Misc. Doc. No. 186. Washington: Government Printing Office, 1876.

———. Senate. *Report of the Commission Appointed Under the Eighth Section of the Act of Congress of June 21, 1860, to Examine into the Organization, System of Discipline and Course of Instruction of the United States Military Academy at West Point*. 36th Cong., 2d sess., 1860. Misc. Doc. No. 3. Washington: Government Printing Office, 1860.

———. Senate Committee on Claims. *Virginia Military Institute: Hearing Before the Committee on Claims*, 63d Cong., 2d sess., February 7, 1914, on S. 544, a Bill for the Relief of the Virginia Military Institute, of Lexington, Va. Washington: Government Printing Office, 1914.

U.S. Military Academy. *Annual Reunion of the Association of the Graduates of the United States Military Academy at West Point*. 1872–1918.

Utley, Robert M. *Cavalier in Buckskin: George Armstrong Custer and the Western Military Frontier*. Norman: University of Oklahoma Press, 1988.

Vanderbilt, Gloria. *Black Knight, White Knight*. New York: Knopf, 1987.

Wall, Joseph Frazier. *Alfred I. du Pont: The Man and His Family*. New York: Oxford University Press, 1990.

Warner, Ezra J. *Generals in Blue: Lives of the Union Commanders*. Baton Rouge: Louisiana State University Press, 1964.

The War of the Rebellion: A Compilation of the Official Records of the Union and Confederate Armies. Washington: Government Printing Office, 1880–1901.

Warren, Robert Penn, ed. *Selected Poems of Herman Melville*. New York: Random House, 1967.

Waugh, John C. *The Class of 1846: From West Point to Appomattox: Stonewall Jackson, George McClellan and Their Brothers*. New York: Warner Books, 1994.

Weigley, Russell F. "Emory Upton." *Dictionary of American Military Biography*. Edited by Roger J. Spiller, Joseph G. Dawson III, and T. Harry Williams. Westport, Conn.: Greenwood Press, 1984.

———. *History of the United States Army*. New York: Macmillan, 1967.

———. *Towards an American Army: Military Thought from Washington to Marshall*. New York: Columbia University Press, 1962.

Wert, Jeffry D. *Custer: The Controversial Life of George Armstrong Custer*. New York: Simon & Schuster, 1996.

Wheeler, Candace. *Yesterdays in a Busy Life*. New York: Harper & Brothers, 1918.

Wheeler, Joseph. *Alabama*. Vol. 7 of *Confederate Military History*. Edited by Clement A. Evans. Atlanta: Confederate Publishing, 1899.

Wiley, Bell Irvin. *The Life of Johnny Reb: The Common Soldier of the Confederacy*. Indianapolis: Bobbs-Merrill, 1943. Reprint, Baton Rouge: Louisiana State University Press, 1978.

Williams, T. Harry. *Americans at War: The Development of the American Military System*. Baton Rouge: Louisiana State University Press, 1960.

———. *P. G. T. Beauregard: Napoleon in Gray*. Baton Rouge: Louisiana State University Press, 1955.

Wilson, James Harrison. *Under the Old Flag: Recollections of Military Operations in the War for the Union, the Spanish War, the Boxer Rebellion, etc.* 2 vols. New York: D. Appleton, 1912.

Woodward, C. Vann, ed. *Mary Chesnut's Civil War*. New Haven: Yale University Press, 1981.

Index

Publisher's Note

Ralph Kirshner, a graduate of McGill University, lives in Chapel Hill, North Carolina. He has lectured at Gettysburg College and the Royal Military College of Canada and has written articles on members of the class of 1861 and other Civil War and historical figures for the *Dictionary of American Biography* and the *American National Biography*. He serves as the program chair of the Civil War Round Table of North Carolina and is on the Barondess/Lincoln Book Award Committee of the Civil War Round Table of New York.